What Is the Good Life?

To Mom - whose love of the good life
is as infectious as it is
generous!

Merry Christmas!
Love,
Drew
12/24/23

What Is the Good Life?

Perspectives from Religion, Philosophy, and Psychology

Drew Collins
Matthew Croasmun
Editors

BAYLOR UNIVERSITY PRESS

Cover Design by *the*BookDesigners
Book Design by Baylor University Press

The preparation of the chapters in this volume were supported by a grant from the John Templeton Foundation (#57579). The opinions expressed in this publication are those of the authors and do not necessarily reflect the views of the John Templeton Foundation.

Library of Congress Cataloging-in-Publication Data

Names: Collins, Drew, 1984- editor. | Croasmun, Matthew, 1979- editor.
Title: What is the good life? : perspectives from religion, philosophy, and
  psychology / Drew Collins, Matthew Croasmun, editors.
Description: Waco : Baylor University Press, 2023. | Includes
  bibliographical references and index. | Summary: "Presents perspectives
  on human flourishing and the life worth living from eight different
  traditions, religious and secular"-- Provided by publisher.
Identifiers: LCCN 2023026706 (print) | LCCN 2023026707 (ebook) | ISBN
  9781481318013 (paperback) | ISBN 9781481318037 (adobe pdf) | ISBN
  9781481318020 (epub)
Subjects: LCSH: Quality of life. | Quality of life--Religious aspects. |
  Human beings--Philosophy.
Classification: LCC HN25 .W485 2023 (print) | LCC HN25 (ebook) | DDC
  301--dc23/eng/20230731
LC record available at https://lccn.loc.gov/2023026706
LC ebook record available at https://lccn.loc.gov/2023026707

Contents

Introduction

Drew Collins and Matthew Croasmun

"Is this enough? At the time, it didn't seem like enough."

So asks David Foster Wallace on page 2 of his long essay, "A Supposedly Fun Thing I'll Never Do Again," as he recounts his time aboard a seven-night luxury cruise (a "7NC") on assignment from *Harper's*. Asked to provide the magazine with "a sort of really big experiential postcard," Wallace takes the opportunity to reflect not on how different life aboard the ship is, but how *similar* it is to normal life—or more accurately, how the way passengers live on board the ship reflects back to them their hopes, dreams, and expectations for what life *off* the boat should be like.

For nearly one hundred pages, Wallace recounts the variety of "pampering" possibilities on the 7NC with incredible detail—"The food was superb, the service impeccable, the shore excursions and the shipboard activities organized for maximal stimulation down to the tiniest detail"—and, more often than not, to great comedic effect: "The ship was so clean and so white it looked boiled . . . Temperatures were uterine. The very sun itself seemed present for our comfort." But the ridiculousness of what he observes—"I have heard upscale adult U.S. citizens ask the Guest Relations Desk whether snorkeling necessitates getting wet, whether the skeetshooting will be held outside, whether the crew sleeps on board, and what time the Midnight Buffet is"—is matched by an unrelenting bleakness that colors his entire experience. "On board," he writes, "especially at night, when all the ship's structured fun and reassurances and gaiety-noise ceased—I felt despair."

As Wallace describes it, this despair is a feeling that emerges not *despite* the ship's myriad distractions and delights, but *in light* of them. For Wallace, the fact that most aboard the ship are "age 50+ people, for whom their own mortality is something more than an abstraction," combined with the inescapable assault of the ocean's corrosion and decay on everything it touches, raises the subject of mortality and death in a way that cannot be avoided. "On a 7NC Luxury Cruise," he writes, "we are skillfully enabled in the construction of various fantasies of triumph over just this death and decay."

This triumph is offered under two possible pursuits: "One way to 'triumph' is via the rigors of self-improvement . . . diet, exercise, megavitamin supplements, cosmetic surgery . . . time-management seminars, etc." This approach is to transcend "death-dread" through a series of activities designed to provide us with a sense that we are bringing death under our control. The other approach, equally popular aboard the boat, is "not hard work but hard play . . . not a transcendence of death-dread so much as just drowning it out."

"Is this enough?"

Wallace's question at the start of the essay looms over its entirety, occasionally glinting in the light of his paratactical presentation of the luxuries that characterize life on the ship. And it asks us to consider two different but interlocking responses. On the one hand, the answer could only be "YES!" There is more food, more fun, more opportunity for personal growth than a person could possibly need. It's not just enough. It's more than enough. But at the same time, the answer to Wallace's question is necessarily "No." This is not a denial of the aforementioned abundance but a reflection on it. For in the question "Is this enough?" Wallace isn't so much asking us to do some math, to tally up the resources at our disposal to see if it meets some standard of existential sufficiency, as he is pushing us to consider whether we're not asking the wrong questions.

On the 7NC, we live our lives in the light of questions like "how do I get what I want?" or even "what do I really want?" But when Wallace asks, "Is this enough?" he's asking a question further upstream from these. Not "what do I want?" but "what is *worth* wanting?" And, in light of this account of *worth*: How are we to live? *What is the life worth living?*

This is the question around which each chapter in this volume orbits. Of course, one might respond: "What else would a collection of essays summarizing religious and philosophical traditions be about?" But it is not so simple as that. For it often appears as if religious and philosophical traditions are today treated similarly to the options described in the 7NC brochure—activities that divert our attention from the dread of death or provide us with means of improving ourselves without every inquiring into "who" we are, what the world around us is, and what "improvement" might mean therein. Even the most conservative and committed adherent of a tradition like these might find it easy to confuse the difference between their tradition *fulfilling* their desires (i.e., how to get what I want), helping them *get in touch* with their desires (i.e., what do I want) and their tradition *shaping* the desires themselves (i.e., what is worth wanting).

Have we come to view even the world's great religious and philosophical traditions from within a fantasy constructed on the luxury cruise? Have we excused ourselves from doing the work of identifying our own view of the world and our place in it? And what would an alternative approach look like?

In the chapters that follow, leading scholar-practitioners from nine different traditions—religious and secular—each offer an account of the good life, as construed from within their respective traditions. While our inheritance of various traditions can be distorted in the ways we just described (and many more besides!), when we ask the fundamental question of the shape of the good life, we do so in the midst of multiple colliding, collaborating, and contending traditions. Some of these are instantly recognizable: religious traditions like the Abrahamic faiths and the Hindu and Buddhist traditions offer accounts of matters of ultimate concern and cast visions of flourishing life—here and now, and, in some cases, in some sort of world beyond this one. Of course, these days, we choose not merely among religions, but we also choose between being "in or out" of religion entirely. Diverse secular humanist authors and communities offer their own accounts of the good life; these, too, are *traditioned* ways of thinking about the good life. Philosophical traditions like utilitarianism and Confucianism (or Ruism, as it is known to many insiders to the tradition)—and many others beside—articulate visions of flourishing life and commend particular ways of living. But the contemporary "good life" marketplace is not reserved only for these august, "classic" philosophical and religious traditions and those self-consciously reasoning outside of them. Psychology is at least as pervasive in many corners, not simply as a tool to investigate and describe the well-being of lives lived within or at the overlap of many of these traditions, but as a purveyor of a particular vision of the good life itself and a contender for our allegiance. This, too, it seems to us, needs to be reckoned among the traditions within and at the overlap of which we do our discernment of the shape of lives worthy of our humanity.

In their concern for this issue, the visions articulated here are united. But from this unified concern comes a rich diversity of distinct responses. In hopes of clarifying this distinctiveness, the authors have employed a common threefold heuristic schema of *agency*, *circumstance*, and *affect*:

(1) The agential aspect concerns human beings as actors in the world. It encompasses questions of deeds, character or virtue, and projects, and it deals with these not only in terms of obligation, but also of desirability. In treating the agential as just one aspect of human flourishing, we assume that visions of human flourishing do not reduce to accounts of what it is right or good to do.

(2) The circumstantial aspect concerns the character of the various contexts (social, ecological, etc.) in which human beings are situated. An articulation of this aspect responds to the question "In what kind of world is it good (or best) to live?"

(3) The affective aspect concerns how human flourishing feels, broadly understood. It encompasses assessments of various feelings (e.g., pain or pleasure) and emotions (e.g., joy or sorrow). While supposed by most traditions to be intimately tied to both agency and circumstance, affect is in principle distinguishable from them. For instance, a person's affective response to a good circumstance might be negative, and different visions of flourishing might evaluate that disjunction contrarily.

Any particular account of human flourishing, we propose, can be seen as offering answers to the questions of what constitutes flourishing under each aspect and the relative significance of these aspects. At the extreme, a vision might claim that one aspect is of no importance for flourishing. Perhaps, for instance, a person's flourishing might be entirely independent of how they feel. In such a case, the question of the content of the affective aspect of flourishing becomes incoherent. For the most part, the visions outlined below avoid such extremes and instead present a rich and complex account of how they interweave and shape one another. In any case, this proposal is intended to be formal, facilitating our hearing of the distinctive claims of each vision on its own terms.[1]

As such, we hope that this common framework facilitates a fresh engagement with normative traditions for those who have little previous experience with them *and* for those who have been immersed in one or more of them through their respective histories, doctrines, rituals, and so forth. Our hope is that this framework serves to reorient and recast the traditions such that their existential horizons are more clearly discerned while underscoring both the distinctness and normativity that characterizes each vision of the good life.

At the same time, it is precisely in delineating the distinctness of each tradition in these existential terms, in terms of the vision of the life worth living, that this approach allows for new and often surprising perspectives on how these traditions compare with one another. The comparative approach to traditions is a necessity in today's world—but not all comparative approaches are created equal. In presenting these distinct articulations of visions of the good life from within this formal and existentially oriented framework, this book offers its own vision for the comparative analysis of world religions and traditions, wherein the very significance of the comparison itself, and the inevitability of both similitude and divergence, becomes a matter not of abstract interest, or even of ethical duty, but of one's own existence and vision of life. It is our hope that you will encounter here a new lens through which to understand traditions, secular or religious, not simply as distinct constellations of truth claims but as visions of human existence. In so doing, we hope that you will come to see why embracing our own existential subjectivity needn't entail that we embrace relativism.

Two additional aspects of the accounts collected here are worth underscoring. First, they are focused not on describing what is good in isolated, discrete dimensions of life—actions, circumstances, emotions—but what the good life is comprehensively: the actions, circumstances, and emotions that characterize the good life, and how they interrelate with one another. Second, the descriptions are presented as universal. Without denigrating or denying the salience of other traditions and their visions of the good life, each chapter here is offered as a possible account of the good life *for everyone*, albeit with particular caveats that arise within certain traditions (e.g., the distinction in Buddhism between the lay and monastic life, or the covenantal distinction in Judaism between Jews and gentiles).

This second aspect points to another distinctive feature of this collection. Each chapter, at its heart, is a work of *advocacy* for a particular vision, rather than merely a description of the tradition's range of potential visions (though the latter may help clarify and sharpen the former). In other words, this volume should not be mistaken for an introductory textbook to world religions and philosophical traditions. It is, rather, an invitation to discern the shape of flourishing life in dialogue with the visions each chapter commends.

Our hope is that you feel addressed directly by each vision of the good life while at the same time being acknowledged, respected, and affirmed (and not supplanted) in your own agency. For although these traditions provide distinct accounts of what a good life consists in, they are united in making claims about the world and our place in it—normative claims, with ineradicable existential force. We must grapple with these claims if we're given the opportunity. And extending an invitation to first-person grappling is, in a nutshell, what this book is about.

Anantanand Rambachan presents Hinduism's vision of flourishing life as determined by the pillars of *artha* (wealth), *kama* (pleasure), *dharma* (social obligations), and *moksha* (liberation). Acknowledging the diversity of the tradition and the difficulties of presenting generalizations, while at the same time focusing on the Advaita tradition of Hinduism, Rambachan discerns a similar reluctance towards generalizations in Hinduism itself, perhaps most notably in its emphasis on different visions that correlate to different "stages of life." "The good life" looks very different—in fact, may *be* something very different—at each of these life stages. Rambachan emphasizes the way in which this vision draws on a constellation of strong and apparently competing claims to provide a balanced vision of life, one that embraces universal normative claims while construing their import in dialogue with "the wider context, economic, political, and social, within which this life is sought."

Yoni Brafman and Alan Mittleman's chapter on Judaism explores the idea of flourishing as a function of service to God, "fidelity to God's covenant and its commandments (*mitzvot*)." While the normativity of different accounts of flourishing is embraced and explored in different ways by each chapter in this volume, here the notion of *command* itself is inextricable from the Jewish vision, something that becomes abundantly clear in the Bible's commandment to *rejoice*. "How is that possible? Can joy be *commanded*?" Brafman and Mittleman ask. The question, they find, comes into focus when Judaism's account of the individual is brought into line with its concern for the collective community, leading to the conclusion that human affect and emotion are no less social and public realities than human actions and circumstances. Jewish joy, therefore, "cannot be focused solely on the self but must be extended to include one's family and the poor. Proper joy must overflow; it must cause others to rejoice."

In Robert Emmons and Roxanne Rashedi's account, positive psychology (PP) is oriented around a vision of the good life that is measurable and quantifiable. Positive psychology advocates for an empirically supported, scientific framework for answering the questions of what makes a life worth living, how such a life can be achieved, and how it can be sustained. On this empirical basis, PP seeks to revitalize the Aristotelian "teleological idea that human life and human well-being consist in nature-fulfillment" and the notion that a particular set of virtues are intrinsic to the common core of human nature and human flourishing. Focusing on the virtue of gratitude as a "touchstone of the good life," Emmons and Rashedi depict PP as upholding a vision of the good life that, on the one hand, is compatible with those advocated by religious and philosophical traditions, but on the other hand, looks less like a set of amorphous aspects of life than a specific, repeatable, demonstrably positive set of decisions (agential) and experiences (circumstantial) which can be measured by their subjective or emotional responses (affective).

Miroslav Volf, Matthew Croasmun, and Ryan McAnnally-Linz summarize Saint Paul's account of the good life as the unity of agential, circumstantial, and affective flourishing in his definition of the kingdom of God as "righteousness, peace, and joy in the Holy Spirit" (Rom 14:17). They draw our attention to the Christian tradition's need to distinguish between a "penultimate" vision of flourishing life achievable in this life and an "ultimate" vision of flourishing life that awaits us in the next. Part of wisdom in this life, then, becomes managing the tension between living *toward* the ultimate vision of flourishing as a norm, on the one hand, while also navigating the limits imposed by the "unfitting" conditions of a world broken by sin and awaiting its final form in the world to come.

Bin Song and Stephen Angle focus on joy, the "existential primer of all proper human affections," to explain the interlocking relationship between metaphysical, ontological, and ethical claims of Confucianism (Ruism). "For a Ruist," they write, "to live a joyful good human life is to know the original state of the world, to make efforts of cultivating oneself, and to reach one's due state of being." Here, joy is both the inspiration and fruit of the good life, a reflection of and response to the reality of human existence.

While Utilitarianism aims to increase the well-being of all beings, Peter Singer and Katarzyna de Lazari-Radek begin by distinguishing between "the good life"—the life with the most intrinsic good, that is, pleasure—and "the morally good life." On the one hand, this renders the goodness of agency and circumstance as instrumentally good insofar as they contribute affec- tively—in other words, insofar as they yield pleasure or *happiness*. On the other hand, the connection Singer and Lazari-Radek point out between this vision and the twenty-first-century movement known as "effective altruism" suggests that such instrumentalization might heighten, rather than dimin- ish, the agential and circumstantial obligations of the morally good life.

Paul Jeffrey Hopkins and Jongbok Yi's chapter offers a Buddhist vision of the good life structured around three levels of agential being developed across the centuries in India and Tibet. In this form of Buddhism, human flourishing arises out of thorough analysis of the circumstantial aspect of human entrapment in a round of pain called cyclic existence. Therefore, human flourishing depends upon an initial agential aspect of realistic assessment of the condition of ordinary life impelled by ignorance, which leads to afflictive desire and hatred. This analytic precursor leads to a wish for oneself to leave the state of cyclic existence.

HRH Prince Ghazi and Ismail Alatas explore the Islamic vision of the good life in close dialogue with the Qur'an and the *ahadith*, drawing upon their depictions of agency, circumstance, and affect, while framing these within the additional categories of "existence" and "anthropology." Delv- ing into these Islamic texts through a series of basic existential questions— "What is life?" "Why is life?" "When is life?" "Where is life?" etcetera—the structure of the chapter sheds light on the nature of the Islamic vision it portrays, connecting convictions about the nature of God (existence) to convictions about the nature of God's creatures (anthropology) and the kind of life appropriate to such creatures (agency, affect, circumstance).

Is this enough? Certainly not. But if we truly want to find the answer to that question, we ought to heed Wallace's warning, put down the cruise brochure, and, perhaps in dialogue with these traditions (and the myriad of others embraced by people around the world), ask ourselves: What sort of life is worthy of our shared humanity?

Note

1   See the introductory remark distinguishing between the "good life" and the "morally good life" in ch. 7, by de Lazari-Radek and Singer, for a possible exception to this.

1

A Hindu Vision

Anantanand Rambachan

INTRODUCTION: THE HINDU TRADITION

What is spoken of today as Hinduism is an astonishingly diverse phenomenon, as suggested by the word "Hindu" itself. This term has been used at different times, and even at the same time, to signify geographical, religious, cultural, and in more recent times, national realities. "Hindu" is the Iranian variation for the name of a river that the Indo-Europeans referred to as the Sindhu, Greeks as the Indos, and the British as the Indus. Those who inhabited the regions drained by the Indus river system were derivatively called Hindus. They did not share a homogenous religious culture. Brian K. Pennington has traced in fine detail the complex process of interaction between colonial Christian missionaries and Hindu subjects that resulted in the discourse about a homogenized Hinduism. Missionaries, according to Pennington, were initially bewildered by the diversity of Hindu ritual practices and the variety of doctrines and deities that they encountered. In order to challenge the Hindu tradition, missionaries had to identify and confer uniformity upon it. In this way, missionaries could think of Hinduism in ways akin to Judaism, Christianity, and Islam. In a similar way, those who defended the tradition, like Ram Mohan Roy, presented it also as having a certain coherent uniformity.[1] The reality is that the religious life of India has always been richly diverse, reflecting the variation of its geography, cultures, and languages.

It is helpful to think of "Hinduism" like the name of a family recogniz-able through shared features. Though generalizations are hazardous, various scholars have identified some common features and themes.[2] These include the following: (1) recognition of the significance of the four Vedas as sources of authoritative teaching; the four Vedas (*Rg*, *Sama*, *Yajur*, and *Atharva*) are widely acknowledged by Hindus to contain revealed teachings, and acceptance of the authority of the Vedas is commonly regarded as necessary for Hindu orthodoxy, even though such acceptance may be merely formal and nominal; (2) the belief in a moral order and rebirth (*karma* and *samsara*), emphasizing human responsibility and the short- and long-term consequences of actions; (3) the affirmation of an ultimate reality, spoken of as *brahman*, that is regarded as both transcendent and immanent; (4) the view that ignorance (*avidya*) of the nature of this reality is the fundamental human problem and the primary cause of suffering; and (5) an optimistic outlook flowing from the belief in the possi-bility of liberation (*moksha*). These common orientations provide the fabric, as it were, out of which a rich theological diversity has been woven.

The boundaries between the various Hindu traditions are permeable, and membership in a subtradition is not formal. On the whole, Hindu traditions are decentralized and without the governing institutions, prescribing right belief and practice, that may be present in other religions. The traditions comprising this ancient extended family continue to intermingle, influenc-ing and being influenced by each other. If we keep this fact of diversity in mind, our generalizations will not mislead.

Advaita Vedanta

My discussion in this essay draws from a variety of Hindu traditions, but most specifically from the tradition of Advaita. Advaita is one of several Hindu theological traditions that look to the four Vedas as sources of authoritative teachings. More specifically, these traditions look to the dialogues in the last sections of the Vedas, the Upanishads, as the repository of the highest teach-ings in the scripture. For this reason, the name Vedanta (literally "end of the Veda") is usually appended to Advaita. Advaita is an exegetical tradition that derives its teachings from a reading of the meaning of the Upanishads. "Advaita" literally means "not-two" and identifies the tradition's distinctive mode of characterizing the relationship between the infinite brahman, the world, and human beings. Describing this relationship as "one" or "two" is not, according to Advaita, appropriate. It is not "one," because the relationship between brahman as cause and world as effect is asymmetrical. The world, as an effect, originates from brahman and is dependent upon brahman for its existence. The existence of brahman, on the other hand, is independent, and brahman is not limited by the finitude of the world. Brahman is immanent in the world while also transcending it. The relationship between brahman and the world is not "two," since brahman constitutes the ultimate ontological ground of the world and human beings.

Advaita looks to a line of distinguished teachers for the interpretation of its authoritative texts and for the transmission of its teachings. The most distinguished among these is Shankara (ca. eighth century CE), who wrote extensive commentaries on the Upanishads and who is credited with the legacy of the finest systematic exposition of Advaita.[3]

My discussion of the good life in the perspective of the Hindu tradition will be structured broadly under the categories employed by several entries in this volume: *life going well, life being led well,* and *life feeling as it should.*[4] I will explore these components by analyzing the traditional Hindu *purusharthas.* These are the four human goals of wealth (*artha*), pleasure (*kama*), ethics (*dharma*) and liberation (moksha), considered necessary for a flourishing life.[5] While it is necessary to discuss these goals in some order or sequence, one should not expect that their fulfillment also proceeds in a similar order. The ideal is a simultaneous pursuit and realization of all four ends and the achievement of balance among them. I begin with the component of life going well.

LIFE GOING WELL: WEALTH (ARTHA) AND PLEASURE (KAMA)

Contrary to popular impressions, the Hindu tradition is neither life-denying nor narrowly otherworldly. The Hindu goals of wealth (artha) and pleasure (kama) indicate that, broadly speaking, this tradition's account of life going well includes having and enjoying good health, possessions, and family. Though equated generally with wealth, artha includes also power, social prestige, and success. Hinduism has never given its blessings to involuntary poverty and material deprivation. The tradition recognizes the need of every human being for access to those necessities (food, clothing, shelter, money) that make life possible and comfortable and that enable one to fulfill social obligations.

A key ingredient of artha is good health, and the Hindu daily prayer is for all to be free from disease (*sarvesantu niramayah*). The pursuit of the four goals of Hindu life requires good health, and Kalidasa (fourth to fifth centuries CE), one of the most famous among the writers of ancient India, spoke of a healthy physical body as a primary instrument for ethical pursuits.[6] Although the classical Yoga system of Patañjali aims ultimately for liberation, physical well-being is not neglected.[7] It is integrated with mental, emotional, and spiritual health for a holistic and comprehensive understanding of human well-being. India developed a thriving indigenous system, Ayurveda, (lit. knowledge of life) for diagnosing and treating disease. In a beautiful poetic invocation of the Atharva Veda (19.67.1–8), worshippers pray for a life of a hundred autumns:

> For a hundred autumns, may we see,
> For a hundred autumns, may we live,
> For a hundred autumns, may we know,
> For a hundred autumns, may we rise,
> For a hundred autumns, may we thrive,
> For a hundred autumns, may we be,
> For a hundred autumns, may we become,
> Aye, and even more than a hundred autumns.[8]

The hope here is not just for a long life, but for one that is full of physical and mental vitality. In the Vedas, a flourishing human community is one that is free from poverty, illiteracy, and disease.

Kama (pleasure) further expands the Hindu conception of life going well. The goal of kama reminds us that Hinduism is not life-negating or otherworldly. Hindus are not so spiritually minded that they despise the gain and enjoyment of material things. Kama includes sensual as well as aesthetic enjoyment. Sculpture, music, and dance have flourished with the blessing of the Hindu tradition, and Hindus love to celebrate life through these forms. The good life is more than just having the ascetic minimum for survival.

Kama must not be equated narrowly with sexual pleasure, but a fulfilling sexual life is certainly an important part of its meaning.[9] After noting the impact of colonial Victorian values on Hindu attitudes to sexuality,

John M. Koller correctly notes that "sexual activity was considered not only legitimate but an important and valuable activity and aim in life, treated with frankness and respect in popular literature. Without a general acceptance of the value and importance of human sexual activity, the great erotic poems, songs, and sculpture of India would not have been accepted and certainly would not have become important vehicles and expressions of religious devotion."[10]

In the broadest sense, kama includes all those activities in the good life that are not goal- or outcome-oriented. In the Hindu tradition, such actions are described as *lila* (play), exemplified in a special way in our play with children, walking with a loved one, or enjoying a meal in the company of family and friends. These are activities that celebrate life. The Hindu Vaishnava tradition, centered on the worship of God as Vishnu, and in a special way on God's incarnation as Krishna, speaks of Krishna's activities as lila and gives the highest value to his childhood play with his friends and parents, reminding us that play is a divine attribute. In the Bhagavadgita 7:11, Krishna gives his approval to pleasure that is not opposed to virtue.[11] Materialistic and consumer-driven cultures that value only goal-oriented activities need to be reminded of the meaning and significance of lila.

LIFE LED WELL: DHARMA

The goal of dharma speaks to the moral dimension and the relational context of human life and gives content to the ideal of life being led well. Dharma is a rich and multifaceted concept and, therefore, difficult to translate. The word is derived from the Sanskrit root (*dhr*) meaning to support or sustain and, while including moral values, dharma is concerned in a special way with human obligations and duties. In relation to the goals of artha and kama, dharma emphasizes the social context in which we pursue these. Through dharma, we are reminded that the selfish and uncontrolled pursuit of wealth and pleasure lead to social chaos and disharmony. Dharma asks that we broaden our perspective to incorporate the good and well-being of the community. It reminds us that our rights are only possible and meaningful in a context where equal, if not greater, recognition is given to our duties and obligations. The personal attainment of wealth and pleasure by inflicting pain and suffering on others, or by denying them the opportunity to freely seek these two ends, is opposed to dharma. The Mahabharata emphasizes that one should seek artha in ways that avoid harm, deception, and cheating. One's gain must not be unlawful or result in another's loss; such gains, ignoring dharma and driven by greed, are self-destructive.[12]

The fundamental ethical principles underlying dharma are listed in various sources. One well-known and widely cited list occurs in the Yoga Sutras of Patañjali and include noninjury, truthfulness, refraining from stealing, self-control, and freedom from coveting.[13] These are general ethical values that are regarded as applicable to all human beings. Patañjali himself states that "these *yamas* [virtues] are considered the great vow. They are not exempted by one's class, place, time, or circumstance. They are universal" (II.31). If there is consensus across Hindu traditions about the significance of these five virtues, there is also agreement that noninjury (*ahimsa*) is the paramount virtue. According to the Mahabharata (XIII:125:25), "Ahimsa is the dharma. It is the highest purification. It is also the highest truth from which all dharma proceeds." In conflicts between the various yamas, ahimsa is the normative value. The Mahabharata tells a story of villagers who were pursued by robbers and sought shelter in a forest. Kaushika, a sage, lived in the forest and had made a vow to tell the truth. When questioned by the robbers about the villagers, Kaushika told the truth. The villagers were discovered, robbed, and killed. The sage was sent to hell, because the consequence of his truth-telling was harm (*himsa*). While ahimsa (noninjury) is a negative word, Mahatma Gandhi, its best-known exponent in recent times, emphasized that it should be understood not only as avoiding injury to others but positively as love that expresses itself in compassion and caring for others. In fact, all Hindu traditions consider faithfulness to ethical values that include compassion and care for others as essential to the meaning of a good and worthy life. Bhagavadgita (12:13) describes as dear to God the person who hates no one, who is friendly and compassionate toward all, who is not possessive and self-centered, and who is forgiving and balanced in joy and sorrow.

The fact that Patañjali specifies these virtues to be universal reminds us that not all of the obligations of dharma are universal. Obligations also depend, for example, on the life-stage of a person and whether one is an unmarried student, a married person, a retiree, or a renunciant. Traditionally, dharma is also dependent on one's location in the *varna* system of priests, military and political leaders, merchants and farmers, laborers, and outcastes or untouchables. When dharma is interpreted narrowly within this rigid hierarchical order, the emphasis is placed on the faithful performance of birth-derived duties, social order, and stability. The good life is then understood within the limits of a conservative social order that is represented as divinely ordained. Though acknowledging that dharma has been explicated with reference to caste duties, I want to emphasize the universal ethical values discussed above as constituting the core of its meaning. I have argued elsewhere for greater focus on these universal norms and "a rejection of dharma as implying the unequal rights and privileges of caste."[14]

In the Bhagavadgita, one of the important components of the good life is good work. The term used in the text is *svadharma*. Dharma, as noted above, emphasizes the complex web of relationships from which we are inseparable and by which we are nourished. We have a moral obligation to contribute to the sustenance of the whole of which we are a part and which makes our existence and flourishing possible. The Bhagavadgita (3:12) speaks of a thief as one who enjoys what is received from creation without giving back anything. Situating work in the context of dharma gives it a moral and cosmic significance. Our work becomes a significant way in which we contribute to the flourishing of the whole. One whose work does not contribute to the common good lives in vain (3:16).[15]

The Limits of Wealth, Pleasure, and Duty

Though giving approval to the pursuit of wealth and pleasure within the ethical framework of a regard for the common good, Hindu traditions call attention to the limits of these ends. A life circumscribed by these ends is ultimately unsatisfactory and inadequate and leaves us wanting and restless. The reasons are many. The gains of wealth and pleasure are transient, leaving us hopelessly addicted to their momentary gratification and always wanting more. Since gains such as wealth, power, and fame are never evenly distributed, their value is derived from the fact that some possess more. When we link our own self-worth inextricably with such gains, we condemn ourselves to a competitive anxiety that demands always having more than others. There is never contentment.

The necessary and valuable obligations of dharma are also not without their limits. Huston Smith described well why even dharma leaves us
wanting . . .

> Faithful performance of duty brings respect and gratitude from one's
> peers. More important, however, is the self-respect that comes from
> doing one's part. But in the end, even these rewards prove insuffi-
> cient. For even when time turns community into history, history,
> standing alone, is finite and hence ultimately tragic. It is tragic not
> only because it must end—eventually history, too, will die—but in its
> refusal to be perfected. Hope and history are always light years apart.
> The final human good must lie elsewhere.[16]

In the Katha Upanishad (2:14), the student asks to be instructed about the
reality that is different from dharma and its opposite, *adharma*.[17] The implication here is that, though important, dharma is not the highest good.

DISSATISFACTION WITH THE FINITE: NACHIKETAS AND YAMA

A life going well is desirable but will not, by itself, constitute the good life in
the Hindu tradition. There are numerous examples in the Upanishads of dis-
satisfaction with life even when it seems to be going well. The "quarrel with
life," as Miroslav Volf puts it, is very much present in these texts.[18]

One of the best-known of these accounts is the encounter between
Nachiketas and Death (Yama) in the Katha Upanishad. Like many dialogues
in the Upanishads, this one also begins with a story. Nachiketas' father, Usan,
is performing a grand religious ceremony in which he is required to give
away his possessions. Nachiketas notices that his father is being miserly by
giving away only those cows that are old and incapable of producing young.
To call his father's attention to his miserliness, Nachiketas stood up in the
gathering and asked three times, "Father, to whom will you give me?" In a fit
of anger and embarrassment, Usan shouted, "To Death I give you."

Nachiketas arrived at the abode of Death and waited patiently for three
days. Upon his return, Death apologized for his absence and offered Nachiketas three gifts as a reward for his patience. First, Nachiketas asked that his
father be free from anger toward him. Second, he asked for instruction
about a special religious ritual. His third request surprised Death: "There is
this doubt about a man who is dead. 'He exists,' say some; others, 'He exists

not.' I want to know this so please teach me." Death pleads with Nachiketas not to ask for this teaching; it is subtle and difficult to understand: "Do not press me; release me from this."

To distract and dissuade Nachiketas from inquiring about life's meaning beyond finite gains, Death offers him all that we associate with life going well: family, wealth, health, longevity, and power: "Choose sons and grandsons who'd live a hundred years! Plenty of livestock and elephants, horses, and gold! Choose as your domain a wide expanse of earth! And you yourself live as many autumns as you wish!" (1.23).

Nachiketas' response is a classic statement of the religious concern. Without negating the importance of wealth and pleasure, it points to a gain beyond the transient:

> Since the passing days of a mortal, O Death
> sap here the energy of all the senses;
> And even a full life is but a trifle;
> so keep your horses, your song and dances!
>
> With wealth you cannot make a man content;
> Will we get to keep wealth, when we have seen you?
> And we get to live only as long as you will allow!
> So this alone is the wish that I'd like to choose. (1.26)

Nachiketas' declaration to Death, "With wealth you cannot make man content," is at the heart of the Hindu indictment of materialism. Beyond the destructive social consequences of greed, materialism lures us with a false promise of delivering contentment. The purpose of Death's dazzling offers to Nachiketas is to ensure that Nachiketas has not come to his religious quest hoping to find more ephemeral forms of pleasure. Death instructs Nachiketas about the deathless reality, but only after Death is certain that Nachiketas' quest is mature and properly motivated and that he appreciates the limitations of worldly attainments. A religious tradition that promises nothing beyond worldly goods is a case of the blind leading the blind:

> Wallowing in ignorance, but calling themselves wise,
> Thinking themselves learned, the fools go around,
> staggering like a group of blind men
> led by a man who is himself blind. (2.5)

LIBERATION (*MOKSHA*): THE ULTIMATE GOOD

The Mundaka Upanishad (1.1.3–5) classifies knowledge into two categories: lower and higher.[19] Interestingly the text includes in the category of lower knowledge religious rituals and allied disciplines (phonetics, grammar, etymology, metrics, astronomy) meant for the gain of wealth and pleasure in this or another world. In the Upanishads and the Bhagavadgita, heavenly worlds are not denied, but the gain of these worlds is not equated with liberation or knowledge of the imperishable brahman. These worlds are gained as a consequence of meritorious actions (ritual and ethical) but have a temporary character.[20] Generally speaking, Hindu traditions do not forbid or condemn such forms of religious practice; the limits of these gains, however, are emphasized. The Bhagavadgita (7:16–18) acknowledges the diversity of ends people seek from their religious traditions and identifies four types of religious worshippers: (1) the distressed, (2) the one who seeks material security and pleasure, (3) the seeker of God, and (4) the wise one who knows and is devoted to God. The text describes them all as virtuous but reserves its highest praise for the knower of God, who is constantly united with God in love. Not all religious practices are oriented toward the highest purpose of religion.

Religions cannot be indifferent to human suffering caused by the lack of those necessities that contribute to life going well, especially to structures of injustice and oppression, whether economic, political, or sociocultural. At the same time, Hindu traditions teach that the highest purpose of religion is to remove ignorance about the ultimate reality, enabling us to live joyful lives in harmony with its nature.

With the Mundaka Upanishad, we may say that the primary concern of religion is a higher wisdom (*apara vidya*) through which, in the words of the text, "one gains the imperishable."[21] The text describes the imperishable as that:

> What cannot be seen, what cannot be grasped,
> without color, without sight or hearing,
> without hands or feet;
> What is eternal and all-pervading,
> [extremely subtle, all-pervasive,]
> That is the immutable,
> Which the wise see everywhere. (1.1.6; translation modified)

Similar to the distinction in the Mundaka Upanishad between a lower and higher knowledge is the Katha Upanishad's (2.1–3) distinction between the ultimate good (*sreyas*) and the proximate good (*preyas*). The terms here are more difficult to translate precisely. *Sreyas* is the highest human good (liberation or moksha) and includes both the goal and the path. *Preyas*, on the other hand, translated often as the "pleasurable" or "gratifying," includes all the objects of transitory enjoyment offered by Death and rejected by Nachiketas, such as wealth, pleasure, and power. These two choices are described in the Upanishad (2.2) as always presenting themselves before us: "The wise assess them, note their difference; and choose the good over the gratifying; but the fool chooses the gratifying rather than what is beneficial." The wise person is not choosing *sreyas* over *preyas* from disgust or fear of the latter. The choice is a conviction born from the understanding that while there are many legitimate worldly achievements and forms of enjoyment, there is a human need for fullness that these leave unsatisfied, hence Nachiketas' conclusion that wealth will never satisfy.

It is clear that, for the Hindu tradition, true human flourishing is impossible without choosing *sreyas*, a goal that is not in conflict with, but which points to, an end beyond worldly prosperity. The Svetasvatara Upanishad (6:20) could not be clearer on this point: "Only when people will be able to roll up the sky like a piece of leather will suffering come to an end without first knowing God." The term translated here as "God" is *devam*, literally "the shining one." Earlier (6:12), the same Upanishad speaks of unending joy (*sasvatam sukham*) as belonging only to those who know this one being as existing in themselves.

The Chandogya Upanishad (7) tells the story of the great scholar Narada, who was the most learned person of his time. He had mastered the Vedas, grammar, rituals, mathematics, logic, ethics, philology, warfare, science, astronomy, and the fine arts! In spite of his encyclopedic knowledge, Narada seeks out a teacher with a confession and a request: "I am in sorrow; free me from this sorrow."[22]

For the person who experiences suffering in the midst of pleasure and plenty, the advice given in the Mundaka Upanishad (1.2.12) is to approach a teacher who is wise in the teachings of the sacred texts and who is centered in the infinite (brahman). The Mundaka Upanishad also reminds the teacher of her obligations to the student:

> To that student who approaches in the proper manner, whose mind is calm and who is endowed with self-control, the wise teacher should fully impart the knowledge of brahman through which one knows the true and imperishable person. (1.2.13; my translation)

LIBERATION: THE OVERCOMING OF IGNORANCE (AVIDYA)

In the Advaita tradition, which is the special focus of our discussion here, the root cause of the sorrow experienced by Narada and others in the Upanishads is ignorance (*avidya*) of the relationship between the human self (*atma*) and the limitless brahman. In the condition of ignorance, we regard the human self as different and separate from all other selves and the world of nature. As such, it is taken to be incomplete and inadequate, with the consequence that one experiences a continuous sense of anxiety. The sense of inadequacy and incompleteness that results from ignorance causes the multiplication of desires in an effort to overcome this condition of lack. We exert ourselves beyond reasonable needs for ends such as wealth, fame, and power, hoping that the gain of these will free us from self-inadequacy. We discover, however, in the course of time and through analysis of our experiences that every finite gain provides only a short-lived sense of fullness, and we are left wanting. As Shankara writes in his commentary on Chandogya Upanishad (7.23.1), "the finite or the *small* always gives rise to longing for what is more than that."[23]

The problem, from the perspective of Advaita, is not one of an intrinsic lack in the self, but one of knowing. The tradition teaches that the self that is falsely regarded as separate and incomplete is, in fact, ontologically identical in nature with brahman. The solution to this problem of ignorance does not involve the creation or bringing into existence of a previously nonexistent entity or bridging a spatial or temporal distance between oneself and brahman. There is no separation between the human being and brahman, spatially or temporally; the bridge to be crossed is one of ignorance, and this is crossed in a disciple-teacher relationship where one receives teaching about the nature of the self that transforms one's self-understanding and relationship with others. Liberation is not a change in the state or nature of the self. The change implied in the attainment of liberation is the removal of ignorance. "Really," states Shankara in his commentary on Brhadaranyaka Upanishad (4.4.6), "there is no such distinction as liberation and bondage in the self, for it is eternally the same; but the ignorance regarding it is removed by the knowledge arising from the teachings of the scripture, and prior to the receiving of these teachings, the effort to attain liberation is perfectly reasonable."[24]

Ignorance of the self has serious consequences, but the nature of the self is not altered by ignorance. Thinking that the self is separate and different in nature from brahman does not make it so. Freedom (moksha) is the direct consequence of right knowledge of the nature of the self and its relationship with brahman. This freedom from ignorance, the Advaita tradition teaches, is attainable here and now. It is spoken of as living liberation, since it is not contingent on the death of the physical body. In the Chandogya Upanishad (6.14.2), the human condition under ignorance is likened to that of someone forcibly taken away from his beloved home, blindfolded, and left in the wilderness. A kind person answers his plea for help, removes his blindfold, and shows him the way home. In a similar manner, a compassionate person liberates the *avidya*-bound individual by pointing out her identity with the limitless brahman. Advaita soteriology finds its culmination in this life and world, here and now.

LIBERATION AND JOY: *ANANDAM*

The implications of liberation in life are profound for our relationships with others, and I have emphasized identity and empathy with all beings, compassion, and generosity as among the foremost of these.[25] Here, I want to discuss the meaning of liberation in relation to the third formal component of the good life, life feeling good. The Sanskrit terms closest in meaning to this component are *sukham* and *anandam*. These terms are usually translated as "happiness" or "joy," and while these translations are not misleading, they will require some qualification and clarification.

Liberation is consistently described as a state of freedom from *duhkham* (sorrow) and as the attainment of joy (*sukham*). The Bhagavadgita (5:23) describes the liberated individual as "a happy person" (*sa sukhi narah*). She rests happily in the body, knowing a joy that is imperishable (5:13; 5:21). This joy is the greatest of gains and endures even in the midst of the heaviest sorrow (6:22). We may say that the characterization of joy in the Bhagavadgita suggests that it endures even when life may not be going well.

The discussion of anandam, the term used more often in the Upanishads, needs careful interpretation. Anandam is used to describe the nature of brahman. Brhadaranyaka Upanishad (4.3.32) describes brahman as the highest joy (*param anandah*) and creatures as living on a fraction of this joy. Taittiriya Upanishad (3.6) identifies brahman with anandam and speaks of all beings as originating from, sustained by, and returning to anandam. If anandam is the very nature of brahman, then it cannot be a transient phenomenon or experience subject to time and displaced by its opposite. There is nothing in the nature of brahman that is noneternal. Anandam describes the very nature of the ever-present brahman as full, complete, and without lack. A liberated person is one who understands herself to have the nature of brahman, in a manner similar to a clay pot understanding itself to have the nature of clay, or waves in the ocean having the nature of water. This understanding liberates from feelings of inadequacy and incompleteness. Anandam, therefore, describes both the nature of brahman and the positive affective state of one who knows her relationship with brahman. Anandam is associated also with peace (*shanti*). In the Bhagavadgita (4:39), the consequence of wisdom is supreme peace. Words like "joy" and "peace," in Advaita, are attempts to describe the intrinsic nature of this self.

Is there a joy that is experienced in the gain of wealth, or a sense of pleasure that is different from the joy that is the nature of brahman? One certainly "feels good" when desires are fulfilled and goals accomplished. From the Advaita perspective, it is a misunderstanding to think that there is a joy that is distinct from the nature of brahman. The Advaita claim is that in the fulfillment of a desire for an object or end, the mind of the desirer, hitherto made restless by want, becomes free of agitation, and the joy that is intrinsic manifests. A helpful analogy is the dispelling of clouds to reveal an ever-existing sun. The sun is always present but often obscured by thick clouds. The winds that move the clouds away do not produce the sun but remove the obstacle that blocked its light from shining through. In a similar way, the fulfillment of a desire temporarily removes the condition of inadequacy that stands in the way of the innate fullness of the self. When the intrinsic nature of joy is not understood, it is attributed to the gain of an external object or to the object itself. Such joy, however, becomes transient, since its nature is misunderstood and new gains are sought. Even though brahman as intrinsic joy is unchanging, joy seems to vary with the condition of one's mind. One who understands the fullness of brahman and its identity with the self can claim this joy without depending on external gains. As Shankara puts it in his commentary on Taittiriya Upanishad (2.7.1), "In as much as those who have realized brahman are seen to be as happy as one is from obtaining an external source of joy—though, in fact, they do not take the help of any external means of happiness, make no effort, and cherish no desire—it follows, as a matter of course, that brahman is, indeed, the source of their joy. Hence, there does exist that brahman which is full of joy and is the spring of their happiness."[26] The joy of the liberated is not self-centered, since it is the nature of the self that is the self of all. It is meaningful, therefore, that the Bhagavadgita twice (5:25 and 12:4) describes the liberated as rejoicing in the flourishing of all beings.

The joy spoken of in the Hindu tradition as the fruit of liberation is identical, as noted above, with peace (*shanti*). Peace is associated in the Bhagavadgita (2:70–71) with overcoming greed. The text, in fact, teaches that there can be no joy without peace (2:66). Supreme joy flows in the mind of one who is peaceful (6:27). Katha Upanishad (1.3.13) describes the self that is identical with brahman as peace; those who understand the nature of the self enjoy eternal peace (2.2.13). The state of joy and peace described in these texts is also a condition of balance or equilibrium, described especially in relation to experiences of gain and loss, success, and failure.[27] The gain of the eternal changes one's perspective on finite gains and losses, enabling one to negotiate more wisely the inevitable dualities of life. The Bhagavadgita (14:24; 12:19) includes the dualities of praise and censure in the midst of which one retains emotional balance. There is a greater and abiding gain in relation to which lesser gains and losses do not overwhelm.

Joy and peace are essential ingredients of the good life in the Hindu tradition, but these are not enduring without an awakening to the transcendent and immanent eternal source and ground of the universe.

TENSION BETWEEN *DHARMA* AND *MOKSHA*: CHOICES IN THE BHAGAVADGITA

But do the concerns and obligations of dharma ever come into conflict with moksha? If so, how do we choose? The relationship between dharma and moksha highlights important tensions in the Hindu tradition about the nature of the good life and the significance of the eternal for our life in the world. To highlight this tension, I turn to the narrative of the Bhagavadgita. First, however, a word about the four stages of Hindu life.

For the progressive attainment of the four goals of life, Hinduism recommends that the human life be organized into four stages; each of these has its own objectives (as well as duties and responsibilities). The first is the student stage, devoted to study and acquiring the skills and virtues necessary for a successful professional life. The second stage is that of the householder, where the focus is on the goals of wealth, pleasure (through marriage and family satisfaction), and duty (dharma) through community involvement. The third is the stage of the forest-dweller, conceived as a semiretired stage devoted to contemplation, religious inquiry, and social service. Finally, the fourth stage—renunciation (*samnyasa*)—is devoted to the pursuit of liberation (moksha). Generally speaking, one enters the fourth stage only after completing the first three. However, the option of entering the fourth stage from any of the first three is also a possibility.

The responsibilities of dharma, both ritual worship and the fulfillment of obligations to family and community, are necessary and binding. The exception is the renouncer, who entered the fourth stage. The renouncer is freed from the obligations to perform daily offerings into the sacred fire and also from the responsibilities of professional, community, and family duties. The renouncer enters a state of existence comparable to one who has died.[28] His identity is no longer connected with family or community, and this is signified by the assumption of a new name. Renunciation results in the dissolution of marriage, freedom from contractual debts, and the distribution of property among heirs. Renouncers typically moved away from family and community, walking from village to village except during the rainy season when they were at liberty to have a fixed abode. The renouncer represents the otherworldly and even world-denying expression of Hindu religious life. Liberation is conceived of as requiring turning away from society and from those relationships and obligations that follow from life in family and community.

This understanding of the religious life is the context for the dialogue between Krishna and Arjuna in the Bhagavadgita. Briefly, the text tells of the rivalry between two sets of cousins (Pandavas and Kauravas) for a kingdom in North India. The Kaurava leader, Duryodhana, is power-hungry and unwilling to do justice to his cousins. All efforts to make peace prove futile, and war is inevitable. Arjuna instructs Krishna, who has volunteered to be his charioteer, to drive his chariot between the two armies so that he could look at the opposing forces. Arjuna is overwhelmed by what he sees. Friends, family, and revered teachers stand ready to fight against him in support of the Kauravas. This throws him into a moral crisis.

Arjuna knows well that the only choice that will free him from his obligations as a soldier is entry into the fourth stage of Hindu life, the life of the renouncer. Faced with the moral dilemma of having to engage family and friends in battle, he expresses a preference for renunciation and entry into the life of the monk to pursue the fourth and highest goal of Hindu life, liberation: "Indeed, instead of slaying these noble gurus it would be preferable to live on alms here on earth" (2:5).

Krishna, Arjuna's teacher and charioteer on the battlefield, the one Arjuna asks for guidance in the midst of his dilemma, does not discourage Arjuna's desire for liberation. This is, after all, the acknowledged highest goal of life across Hindu traditions. What he does beautifully, however, is question the necessity for world-renunciation in the pursuit of liberation and living out its meaning. Everyone, teaches Krishna, renouncer and non-renouncer, performs actions: "Indeed, no one, even in the twinkling of an eye, ever exists without performing action" (3:5). Since a literal renunciation of action is impossible, Krishna makes the case for the necessity of a transformed motivation in action. Actions that are motivated by greed hinder and are opposed to liberation. He commends nonattached action (*asaktah karma*) as an alternative and better way of being in the world.

Unlike attached action (*saktah karma*), which is promoted by greed, nonattached action originates from a desire for the flourishing of the interrelated whole. It is the enlarging of the field of one's concern to include all beings. Krishna equates the renunciation of attachment with having a regard for all life, the universal common good. Arjuna thought that he needed to renounce his life in the world, and the goals of wealth, pleasure, and social obligations, for the sake of the religious life; Krishna asked him not to turn away from the world, but to free himself from greed. He must always consider the universal common good in all that he does.[29] Krishna's teaching on nonattached action does not mean the absence of consideration for one's well-being. Admittedly, the search for harmony between self-interest and the common good is not always a matter of easy discernment. A regard for one's own well-being does not inherently exclude the concern for the flourishing of all.

The Bhagavadgita does not exempt us from renunciation. The renunciation that it commends is not a traditional turning away from the world and from engagement in the life of family, community, and profession. Krishna defines renunciation and the renunciant in a manner that shifts the emphasis from the outward to the inward. The true renouncer is one without greed and hate; the one who fulfills commitments in the world without craving for the results of action. One ought to engage in actions that promote the universal common good, not because of the certainty of outcomes, but because consideration for the well-being of others is the proper way of acting. One must not be attached to inaction because of uncertainty about generating a particular result (2:47). Nonattached actions (karma) constitute a yoga, a way of being in the world that is conducive to liberation and expresses the meaning of liberation. In this way, a possible conflict between the fulfillment of obligations in the world (dharma) and the commitment to liberation (moksha) is overcome.

Different from the otherworldliness of traditional renunciation, which leans toward a negative attitude to the world, perceiving it as obstructive in nature, the spirituality of the Bhagavadgita is world-embracing. It invites a seeing of the world that is infused with the awe, reverence, and mystery flowing from the awareness of the divine in all and all in the divine. The world is not separate from God, but is seen to exist within and to be sustained in every moment by God. "One who sees Me everywhere and sees everything in Me," says Krishna, "is not lost to Me and I am not lost to her" (6:30). The Bhagavadgita describes Arjuna as experiencing the world "glowing with the radiance of God." This mode of encountering the world is spoken of in the Hindu tradition as *darshan*, or sacred seeing.

In a series of poetic verses, the Bhagavadgita articulates the meaning of this sacred seeing that is *darshan*, where the world is experienced as divine outpouring and celebration. We are asked to see the radiance of God in the light of the sun, moon, and fire and to experience the divine in the taste of water (7:8), in the fragrance of the earth (7:9), and in the gift of reason (7:10).

> I am the strength of those who are strong and free from lust and greed. I am desire in beings which is in accord with virtue. (7:11)

The Bhagavadgita's invitation to see the universe as a sacred reality, the many infused with the One, is also presented as having a worshipful dimension. This dimension is also a feature of the text's explication of renunciation. Renunciation is not the abandonment of actions but the performance of action as a loving offering to God.

> A human being attains life's highest purpose by worshipping with his own work the One from whom all beings originate and who exists in all. (18:46)

> "Whatever you do, whatever you eat, whatever you offer in worship, whatever you give, do it as an offering to me." (9:27; my translations)

In the vision of the Bhagavadgita, therefore, the good life is one in which the love of God, who exists equally in all beings, becomes the most fundamental motivation for action in the world, which is focused on the universal common good. The emphasis on divine immanence is significant and cannot be missed in the text:

> God exists in the heart of all beings. (18:61)

> The Supreme Lord exists equally in all beings; the Imperishable in the perishing. One who sees this, sees truly. (13:27)

The implication of this teaching is that the love of God must include the love and service of human beings. We cannot value God and devalue human beings. It is also the source of the inherent dignity and equal worth of every human being, and our antidote to any effort to deny the personhood, worth, and dignity of another. Divine immanence requires that we not give assent or support to any social or cultural system that is founded on human inequality and indignity. To see women as inferior to men, to prefer a boy over a girl, to mistreat the elderly, to ascribe unequal worth and to demean persons on the basis of birth, and to discriminate and practice violence against gay people are all in fundamental contradiction to divine immanence. Today, it calls us with urgency to reverence for our common home, the earth; to united efforts to halt its degradation; and to promote ecological responsibility in our nations, communities, and corporations. In this way, the wisdom of Hinduism's fourth goal enriches the meaning of "life being led well."

Isa Upanishad 1

Central dimensions of the Hindu understanding of joy and the good life are succinctly articulated in the first verse of the Isa Upanishad: "This entire universe, moving and unmoving, is enfolded in God. Renounce and enjoy. Do not covet the wealth of others."[30] I turn to this verse in some detail.

The opening sentence affirms the existence of a transcendent reality, named here as *isa* (lit. ruler) and describes the universe as enfolded by God. Nothing and no one is outside of God; nothing exists separately from God. The description of the universe as enfolded in God points to the primacy of God and the asymmetrical relationship between God and the world. It points also to the precious worth of the universe that is enfolded in God, as a child in the hands of a mother or father. The text invites us to see the universe as a sacred reality that exists within God and as God's gift to us. A gift of God is referred to in Sanskrit as *prasada*, and no Hindu worship, in temple or home, is complete without receiving something, generally edible, that represents God's gift. *Prasada* is a mode of experiencing the world as divine gift.

The seeing of creation in its connectedness to God, and as God's, is presented here as a mode of renunciation that liberates us from the urge to possess, to claim, to dominate, and to see the universe as existing solely to serve our needs. These are anxiety- and fear-inducing attitudes that instrumentalize the significance of the world as only in relation to human needs. We evaluate ourselves only by how much of it we are able to own and possess in relation to those who have less. We close our eyes to its sacred value. The renunciation that flows from seeing the world in God enhances our enjoyment of the world as divine expression. We can delight and enjoy the world as divine gift (*prasada*). This includes the air we breathe, the food we eat, and the clothing and jewelry that we wear. Our enjoyment of the world is sanctified when we see it as divine gift in which the gift-giver is always present. The renunciation commended in this verse is not a rejection or turning away from the world, but our own loving embrace of, caring for, and enjoyment of all that exists.

The final line of the Isa Upanishad text, "Do not covet the wealth of others," speaks to us of our human relationships and the need to cultivate relationships, at all levels, that are not motivated by greed, but which reflect the joy of generosity and sharing. It is the call to value other human beings intrinsically and not on the basis of whether they are useful or not to our own desires. Greed, in relationships with other human beings or the natural world, does not express the vision of the world enfolded in God. Greed desacralizes the universe and is also the outcome of its desacralization. It is the antithesis of the beauty and the joy in creation that the Isa Upanishad offers us by speaking of all as enfolded in God.

CONCLUSION

The pillars of the good life in the Hindu tradition are wealth, pleasure, ethical and social obligations, and liberation (artha, kama, dharma, and moksha). In a broad sense, artha and kama correspond to the circumstantial dimension of the good life, and dharma to the agential. I hesitate to equate moksha with the affective dimension since, especially in the Advaita tradition, it includes right knowledge of the nature of the self and its relationship with brahman. At the same time, the outcome of this knowledge is an affective state described by the word anandam. Anandam signifies freedom from self-lack and inadequacy and the embrace of oneself as full and complete. Positively, it is a state of joy or delight.

The Hindu tradition is not antimaterialistic and has never glorified involuntary poverty. The satisfaction of basic human needs for nutrition, shelter, healthcare, and so on is vital for a good life. In fact, the tradition goes further and stipulates that the good life will be incomplete without the joys that we derive from music, song, dance, art, sports, good food, friends, and family. This good life is not one that is lived in ascetic minimum. These two goals are appropriately described as circumstantial, since their realization is contingent on factors that are not entirely within one's control. One's ability, for example, to attain economic prosperity may depend on the existing system of resource control and distribution, job opportunities, and fair wages. The enjoyment of life that kama assumes requires certain material assets. These are important reasons why it is improper to discuss the good life as an individual pursuit, without attentiveness to the wider context, economic, political, and social, within which this life is sought.

The goals of wealth and pleasure are not considered as unique to human beings, but dharma is so regarded. The capacity for dharma is one that is unique to us as a species. Within the limits of circumstances, fidelity to dharma requires that we concern ourselves not only with our own well-being, but the well-being of others. In Hindu mythology, the symbol of dharma is a bull, whose four feet are truth, purity, compassion, and generosity. These are some of the important values associated with the practice of dharma. The pursuit of wealth and pleasure, which is indifferent to the common good and inflicts suffering on others, violates the commitment to dharma. In this sense, dharma has priority over artha and kama.

Dharma, as we have seen, is not the highest good. This is reserved, across Hindu tradition, for liberation (moksha). Although there are ascetic traditions and interpretations that teach the necessity for giving up the pursuits of artha and kama for the sake of liberation, the Bhagavadgita is a prominent sacred text that teaches an attractive way of harmonizing all four pursuits. The essence of this teaching, as already discussed, is that the goals of wealth and pleasure are not instrinsically flawed. These become problematic when we are not cognizant of their limits, when we are consumed by greed, and when we ignore considerations for the universal common good. Moksha, in Advaita, is the fruit of knowledge of brahman and its relationship with the human self. Through moksha, one comes to recognize brahman as the self of all beings; many texts speak of seeing oneself as the self of all. Understanding brahman's indivisibility is the deepest identity one can have with another. The consequence of right knowledge is learning to identify with others in joy, suffering, compassion, and generosity. It is the truth of brahman that provides the ultimate justification and rationale for the values that are associated with dharma. At the same time, a life that honors the obligations of dharma is necessary for liberation; liberation is not possible for one who does not give up violence toward other beings. As the Katha Upanishad states it, "One who has not abstained from evil conduct, whose senses are not controlled and whose mind is not concentrated and calm cannot gain the self through knowledge" (2.24). The gain of moksha does not negate the other goals, but gives new meaning and perspective to these in a balanced life. Returning to the opening verse of the Isa Upanishad, it is the seeing of the world existing in and wrapped in the divine that makes possible the embrace and enjoyment of the good life.

Notes

1   See Brian K. Pennington, *Was Hinduism Invented?* (New York: Oxford University Press, 2005).

2   See Ramakrishna Puligandla, *Fundamentals of Indian Philosophy* (Nashville, Tenn.: Abingdon, 1975), 25–26; and Troy Wilson Organ, *Hinduism* (Woodbury, N.Y.: Barron's Educational Series, 1974), 28–34.

3   For an overview of Advaita Vedanta, see Anantanand Rambachan, *The Advaita Worldview: God, World and Humanity* (Albany: State University of New York Press, 2006).

4   See Miroslav Volf, *Flourishing: Why We Need Religion in a Globalized World* (New Haven, Conn.: Yale University Press, 2015), 74–75.

5   There are elaborate discussions of these four ends in various textbooks of dharma (Dharma Shastras) and in the epics (Mahabharata and Ramayana).

6   *Shariramadyam khalu dharma sadhanam.*

7   Patañjali (ca. second century BCE) is the author of the Yoga Sutras, the earliest systematic exposition of Yoga. Yoga is regarded as an orthodox system since it accepts the authority of the Vedas.

8   See Abinash Chandra Bose, *Hymns from the Vedas* (Bombay: Asia Publishing House, 1966).

9   The *Kamasutra* of Vatsyayana (fourth century CE) has kama, and particularly sexual pleasure, as its subject matter.

10 John M. Koller, *The Indian Way* (New York: Macmillan, 1982), 66.

11 Shri Bhagavadgita, trans. Winthrop Sargeant (Albany: State University of New York Press, 1993). The text is dated around 150 BCE–250 CE. All quotations cited hereafter are from this translation.

12 See Y. Krishan, "The Meaning of the Purusarthas in the Mahabharata," in *Moral Dilemmas in the Mahabharata*, ed. Bimal Krishna Matilal, 57–58 (Shimla: Indian Institute of Advanced Studies, 1989). The Mahabharata (400 BCE–100 CE), is traditionally attributed to the author Vyasa, but the name just means "compiler." It is considered to be the longest work in Indian literary history and consists of one hundred thousand verses. The content is diverse but, at its core, it is the story of the rivalry between two sets of cousins, culminating in a climactic battle that sets the scene for the Bhagavadgita dialogue.

13 See Yoga Sutras of Patañjali, trans. Edwin F. Bryant (New York: North Point Press, 2009), II.30.

14 See Anantanand Rambachan, *A Hindu Theology of Liberation* (Albany: State University of New York Press, 2015), 185.

15 I have developed these arguments in more detail in a recent essay, "Worship, the Public Good and Self-Fulfillment," in *Calling in Today's World: Voices from Eight Faith Perspectives*, ed. Kathleen A. Cahalan and Douglas J. Schuurman, 107–32 (Grand Rapids: Eerdmans, 2016).

16 Huston Smith, *The World's Religions* (New York: HarperCollins, 1991), 19.

17 See *Upanishads*, trans. Patrick Olivelle (Oxford: Oxford University Press, 1996). All quotations cited hereafter are from this translation unless otherwise indicated.

18 See Volf, *Flourishing*, 71.

19 Though "lower" (*apara*) and "higher" (*para*) are the most common translations, I think the text is distinguishing between knowledge of the non-transcendent and knowledge of the transcendent, or of the perishable and imperishable. It speaks of higher knowledge as that by which the imperishable is known.

20 See Bhagavadgita 9:20–21: "Having enjoyed the vast world of heaven, they enter the world or mortals when their merit is exhausted. Thus conforming to the law of the three Vedas, desiring enjoyments, they obtain the state of going and returning."

21 *tadaksaramadhigamyate*. My translation.

22 Translation modified.

23 See *Chāndogya Upaniṣad with the Commentary of Śaṅkara*, trans. Ganganatha Jha (Poona: Oriental Book Agency, 1942).

24 See *Bṛhadāraṇyaka Upaniṣad with the Commentary of Śaṅkarācārya*, trans. Swami Madhavananda (Calcutta: Advaita Ashama, 1975).

25 See Rambachan, *Hindu Theology*, ch. 4, and *Advaita Worldview*, ch. 7.

26 Translation modified. See *Eight Upaniṣads with the Commentary of Śaṅkarācārya*, trans. Swami Gambhirananda, 2 vols. (Calcutta: Advaita Ashrama, 1665–1966).

27 See Bhagavadgita 2:38, 2:48.

28 See Patrick Olivelle, *Saṃnyasa Upanishads: Hindu Scriptures on Asceticism and Renunciation* (New York: Oxford University Press, 2006), 75. This is an excellent study of the tradition of renunciation in Hinduism.

29 For an elaboration of these ideas, see Anantanand Rambachan, "Renunciation *of* Vocation and Renunciation *within* Vocation," in *Hearing Vocation Differently*, ed. David Cunningham (Oxford: Oxford University Press, forthcoming).

30 *Isavasyam idam sarvam yat kim ca jagatyam jagat, tena tyaktena bhunjitha, ma gridhah kasyasvid dhanam* (my translation). Of this opening verse, Gandhi is reported to have said, "If all the Upanishads and all the other scriptures happened all of a sudden to be reduced to ashes, and if only the first verse in the Isa Upanishad were left in the memory of the Hindus, Hinduism would live forever.

2

A Buddhist Vision

Paul Jeffrey Hopkins and Jongbok Yi

In Buddhism, the genuine good life is deeply connected to a profound understanding of the interconnectedness of all phenomena, including all sentient
beings. All phenomena are *dependently arisen* through causes and effects; no
one in the world, from fellow human beings to animals, plants, trees, and so
on, exists independently or apart from one's environment. In the *Flower Gar-
land Sutra*, the idea of "dependent-arising" is often explained with the analogy
of Indra's net. The nodes of this net are wish-fulfilling jewels that reflect each
of the other jewels' nodes without obstruction. As these jewel nodes are dependently linked to one another, when one jewel is lifted, the entire net is lifted
along with it.[1] Indra's net, therefore, "symbolizes a cosmos in which there is an
infinitely repeated interrelationship among all the members of the cosmos."[2]
Furthermore, a jewel node reflecting the images of the remaining nodes in the
net signifies that the intricately intertwined network of causality—the whole
world—is founded upon the principle of interdependence. If we consider human flourishing from this perspective, since each sentient being is a node in
the net, neither one's genuine good life nor human flourishing can be attained
without securing the welfare of fellow sentient beings and their supporting
environment, that is, the earth itself.

About the cosmological setting:

> Our own world, in a system of one billion worlds, was formed when
> a great and powerful blue wind began blowing and circulating in the

shape of a half moon. Great rains of seven types of precious sub-
stances fell and formed a vast white round ocean, supported by the
dense winds. From the turbulence of the ocean were formed a yellow
square of gold and then earth. From the dependent-arising of the
combination of these three, a red triangle of fire formed, at which
time the basis of the great Mount Meru and its surrounding moun-
tains, four continents, and eight sub-continents was complete.

At first the land surface was a marvelous substance that someone, through previous conditioning, was led into eating. Until that
time, their spontaneously produced bodies had no anus or genitals;
for the sake of excretion these now appeared. Gradually, the marvelous radiance of the beings degenerated, and the earth became hard
with a corn-like plant growing in abundance. Some, however, were
not satisfied with merely taking their portion day by day and began
hoarding. Some began stealing; some killed; houses were built to hide
the sexual act. Gradually the sins were committed, and the causes of
birth in the bad migrations were made. The twenty eons of formation were finished with the formation of the birth-places for animals,
hungry ghosts and hell-beings.

The pattern was produced a billion times simultaneously, providing
lands for gods, demi-gods, humans, animals, hungry ghosts, and hell-
beings in accordance with their nature as determined by previous deeds.[3]

This whole network of living beings and the manifold world systems issues
from all of our actions, or karma. The causes and effects of all beings' actions
in the past as well as the present moment are responsible for the creation
of the world we are experiencing. His Holiness the Fourteenth Dalai Lama
explains that our actions are the creators of our world:

> The outside world appears as a result of the acts of sentient beings who
> use this world. These acts, or karmas, in turn originate in the intentions
> and motivations of those beings who have not yet taken control of their
> minds. The "creator of the world," basically, is the mind.[4]

The Dalai Lama explains that the actions of beings are responsible for the current state of the world as well as for one's capacity for genuine happiness, and
then further elaborates that our mind is ultimately responsible for human

flourishing. Our intentions and the verbal and physical activities flowing from our intentions are the causes of the world we experience and will become the fundamental source of our human flourishing.

In the same vein, Shāntideva, an eighth-century Indian scholastic monk who taught at Nālanda Monastery, elucidates the importance of mind from a slightly different angle:

> Where could I possibly find enough leather
> To cover the whole surface of the earth?
> Leather just on the soles of my shoes
> Is equal to covering the entire earth's surface.
> Likewise, although it's impossible for me
> To completely avert external events;
> I should avert my mind.
> [Then] what need to ward off anything else?[5]

No one can ever escape the experience of suffering if the antidote for it is sought externally. Buddha Shākyamuni explains the endless and countless hardships of this life in four statements summarizing the doctrine:

(1) Existence in any world is unstable, it is swept away.

(2) Existence in any world has no shelter and no protector.

(3) Existence in any world has nothing of its own; one has to leave everything behind and pass on.

(4) Existence in any world is incomplete, dissatisfactory, and caused to be enslaved by craving.

Buddha further explains that our life is unstable, as we grow weaker and weaker because of aging; our life has no shelter or protector, as nobody can relieve our pain by sharing it; our life has nothing of its own, as we cannot endlessly enjoy sensual pleasure, nor bequeath our personal possessions to the next life; our life is dissatisfactory, as beings are enslaved by craving as desires know no end.[6] Seeking a cure for suffering from outside of oneself is like attempting the impossible mission of covering the surface of the earth with leather. Just as wearing a pair of leather shoes is easier and more practical,

seeking a cure for suffering within oneself is the only way to subdue misery
and achieve a good life. Thus, Buddha says:

> All experiences are preceded by mind,
> Led by mind, and made by mind.
> Speak or act with a corrupted mind,
> And suffering follows
> As the wagon wheel follows the hoof of the ox.
> All experience is preceded by mind,
> Led by mind,
> Made by mind.
> Speak or act with a peaceful mind,
> And happiness follows
> Like an ever-present shadow.[7]

To summarize, human flourishing, one's genuine good life, can be achieved
when the supporting environment attains happiness through one's own and
others' actions, and these actions originate from one's mind or mental attitude.

THREE LEVELS OF BUDDHIST FLOURISHING

Let us look at a Buddhist view of the good life popular in Tibet that is based
on a typology of religious persons offered by the Bengali scholar Atisha
(982–1054) in his *Lamp for the Path to Enlightenment*.[8] In the third through
fifth stanzas of his highly influential poem, Atisha speaks of persons as being
of three types:

> [3] Persons who seek for their own sake
> The mere pleasures of cyclic existence
> By whatsoever techniques
> Are to be known as low.

> [4] Persons who seek merely their own peace—
> Having turned their backs on the pleasures of cyclic existence
> And having a turning away from sinful deeds—
> Are to be called "middling."

> [5] Persons who thoroughly wish
> To extinguish thoroughly all sufferings of others
> [Through inference of such] by way of the suffering
> Included in their own continuum are supreme.

These three levels of beings—those of small, middling, and great agential capacity—have served as the framework that has influenced the perspective out of which texts were written and the world was viewed, through to the present day. Definitions were formulated for the three types of agential beings based on Atisha's stanzas but drawing on a wide range of Indian texts.

Beings of Small Agential Capacity

Utilizing the first stanza cited above (stanza 3), the definition of a being of small capacity is: a person who seeks mere high status in cyclic existence.[9] Atisha's word "mere" in the phrase "The mere pleasures of cyclic existence" means that persons on this level do not seek anything beyond the pleasures of this or future lifetimes as a human, demi-god, or god within the round of birth, aging, sickness, and death—and "for their own sake" means that such persons do not seek to bring about others' welfare.

This first class of beings—those of small capacity—is divided into three sublevels: low of the small, middling of the small, and supreme of the small:

Beings of Three Capacities

(1) Beings of small capacity

  (a) low small capacity

  (b) middling small capacity

  (c) supreme small capacity

(2) Beings of middling capacity

(3) Beings of great capacity

The definition of a being of the low level of small capacity is: a person who seeks the mere happiness of this lifetime through nonreligious means. The lowest level of those of small capacity are said to be "the lowest beings" and "rash," or lacking consideration of their own circumstantial situation.

The definition of a being of the middling agential level of small capacity is: a person who achieves the mere happiness of this lifetime through religious and nonreligious means. The distinctiveness of persons on this level is that they also use religious means to bring about happiness in this lifetime, and in this sense are said to be both "rash" and "nonrash." However, though those in the "middling of the small" category use religious means in their pursuit of pleasure in this lifetime, Ngag-wang-leg-dan (1900–1971), Abbot

Emeritus of the Tantric College of Lower Lhasa just before the escape from the Chinese Communist invasion in 1959, spoke of them as not religious enough to count as religious practitioners, due to their short-term motivation. On one occasion he told of a question put to Atisha about the effects of using religious means with an agential motivation limited in circumstantial outlook to improvement in the present lifetime. He reported that Atisha's answer was that the effect was rebirth in a hell, because good karma was being consumed through directing its effects to the superficial affairs of this lifetime, thereby leaving bad karmas to manifest in the next lifetime. The story provides a boundary between experience and nonexperience of religious flourishing in this tradition. The crucial issue is motivation: the scope of the nonreligious is limited to the affairs of this lifetime, whereas the circumstantial scope of the religious is more long-term, taking into account other lifetimes.

This circumstantial perspective is seen in the definition of a being of the supreme level of small capacity: a person who seeks the mere happiness of a future lifetime by only religious means, not emphasizing this lifetime. This third level is "supreme" within the low category and makes use of desire without rashness, since it solely employs religious means. The agential shift to a longer-range circumstantial perspective—from concentrating on the pleasures of this lifetime to those of future lifetimes—constitutes the first step in becoming a religious person.

From this description, we can identify that in this tradition the initial experience of religious flourishing is a change of motivation, in the sense not of turning away from happiness but of recognizing that happiness needs to be achieved beyond the present lifetime and thus appropriate means must be implemented in order to gain it. This requires turning away from sole involvement with the temporary pleasures of the present, in order to ensure pleasure in the future. Instead of seeking pleasure through the direct activities of accumulating wealth, power, and friends, one views the ten virtues (abstaining from killing, stealing, sexual misconduct, lying, divisive talk, harsh speech, senseless chatter, covetousness, harmful intent, and wrong views) as a better means for gaining a high position in the long run. Those same virtues, if not impelled by the motivation to improve future lives, are not included within the practice of religion and cannot constitute the initial experience of religious flourishing, but even without such motivation, the virtues hold one back from the frights of lower future lives as hell-beings, hungry ghosts, and animals. The religious have agentially extended their circumstantial horizon to recognize the process of causes and conditions that construct the round of the pain in cyclic existence and at this level of flourishing are seeking to mold their futures more intelligently. The affective feeling of this extension is one of relaxed relief from the pressured perspective limited to overemphasis on the fleeting present.

Beings of Middling Agentive Capacity

Just as persons become of supreme agentive small capacity by extending the perspective that is the foundation of their behavior to focus on seeking relief from suffering in future lifetimes, persons advance to middling capacity by extending their concern for the plight of suffering to the entirety of cyclic existence. Thus, the definition of a being of middling agentive capacity is: a person who is posited from the viewpoint of mainly seeking liberation for his or her own sake by way of turning the mind away from the marvels of cyclic existence.

The definition is drawn from Atisha's *Lamp for the Path to Enlightenment* (stanza 4):

Persons who seek merely their own peace—
Having turned their backs on the pleasures of cyclic existence
And having a nature of turning away from sinful deeds—
Are to be called "middling."

The phrase "merely their own peace" indicates that persons on this level mainly seek only their own welfare; the mention of their "having turned their backs on the pleasures of cyclic existence" indicates that they have overcome their attachment to all of the marvels of cyclic existence; and "having a nature of turning away from sinful deeds" indicates a nature of avoiding sinful activities at all times.

Still, such a strict description does not hold true for all persons of middling capacity, since some beings on this level sometimes engage in sinful deeds through the force of afflictive emotions or bad friends, despite mainly having an intention to leave cyclic existence like a blazing fire. There are even beings of great capacity who slip into such waywardness.

As the future Buddha, Maitreya, says in his *Ornament for the Great Vehicle Sutras*, "Through the afflictive emotions oneself is destroyed, sentient beings are destroyed, and ethics are destroyed," and the *Nirvana Sutra* says, "Bodhisattvas are not as concerned with crazy elephants and so forth as they are with bad friends."

The shift in circumstantial perspective on this second level of the experience of religious flourishing is more long range in that it takes account not just of the next lifetime (or a few future lifetimes) but of the whole series of lifetimes and the precariousness of one's situation in it. Through practice of the path, one is seeking to be prevented from the entire uncontrolled circumstantial round of birth, aging, sickness, and death in all of its forms.

The difference in the scope of the religious perspective—the range of that from which oneself as an agent is seeking to be held back—comes from more accurately penetrating the nature of appearances. This is done by understanding the pervasiveness of the suffering of being under the uncontrolled influence of karma and afflictive emotions and by understanding that any state within cyclic existence, no matter how pleasurable, will eventually lead to lower states, given the undeniable presence of negative karma.

If human flourishing depends upon how we use our mind, how should we use our mind in order to be happy? In the *Simile of the Snake Sutta*, Buddha says that letting go of what does not belong to "me" or "I" is a way to attain a good life. He explains that any of the five components that make up a human being—physical form, feeling, perception, mental formations, and consciousness—have no "owner" and are therefore not "mine":[10]

> "If people carried off the grass, sticks, branches, and leaves in this Jeta Grove, or burned them, or did what they liked with them, would you think: 'People are carrying us off or burning us or doing what they like with us'?" "No, venerable sir." "Why not?" "Because that is neither our self nor what belongs to our self." So too, bhikkhus, whatever is not yours, abandon it; when you have abandoned it, that will lead to your welfare and happiness for a long time.
>
> Just like being disinterested in someone else's diamond in a shop window, one should cultivate a way of letting go of what does not belong to oneself. It seems that the emphasis should be on clearly

seeing how the mind generates desire for objects, instead of focusing on the objects of attachment since it is the mind that foreruns everything.[11]

Releasing what is not mine might not be easy for beings of lesser or beginning capacity, since they seek for happiness only in this lifetime without considering the possibility of countless lives in cyclic existence. In the *Buddha's Parable Sutra*, Buddha taught King Prasenajit using a parable on the taste of life and death and the faults and mistakes that issue from clinging to cyclic existence:

> A person was running away from a mad elephant in the wilderness, but could not find any place to hide. When he found a tree root dangling down into an empty well, he grabbed it and went down the root into the well. There were black and white rats gnawing the root above him, and four poisonous snakes on its side were about to bite him. On the bottom of the well, a poisonous serpent was aiming at him. Terrified by the snakes and the serpent, he was very worried about the thinning tree root. At that time, five drops of honey fell into his mouth from a beehive hanging on the tree. As the tree was shaken, angry bees swarmed down to sting him. And more, a wildfire was burning the tree down.[12]

When the king asked, how dare he taste the honey while being surrounded by immediate dangers? the Buddha told him that all sentient beings are caught in the same situation in their lives but are blinded by chasing after the five "drops of honey," which represent money, sex, reputation, food and drink, and sleep. Although we are threatened by time—the impermanence of all phenomena (elephant), day and night (black and white rats), endless confusion (decayed root), false thinking (bees), the suffering of death (the poisonous serpent), and so on in the realm of cyclic existence (an empty well) caused by ignorance (wilderness), we ordinary human beings are oblivious to imminent dangers while indulging ourselves in transient pleasures. However, the more we seek these pleasures, the worse the consequences will be. Shāntideva (VII.65) says:

> If I am not satisfied with desirable objects,
> Which are like honey smeared on a razor's edge,

Why am I satisfied with meritorious conduct,
Whose fruition is happiness and thence peace?[13]

In this way, realizing that we are endangered due to being ignorant of our existential situation is an important step toward leading a good life in Buddhism. Here, to beings of low and middling small capacities, a flourishing life means this life, whereas it means this and future lives to the highest of the small capacity beings and above. In this context, in the *Three Principal Aspects of the Path*, Tsongkhapa (1357–1419) says:

Whoever are not attached to the pleasures of transient existence,
Whoever strive to make leisure and fortune worthwhile,
Whoever are inclined to the path pleasing the Conqueror Buddha,
Those fortunate ones should listen with a clear mind.[14]

Seeking only fleeting or temporary pleasures never brings lasting satisfaction, for inner contentment is the genuine foundation of human flourishing. Then how can we let go of what we usually cannot release at this time? Regarding this, Lama Thubten Yeshe explains that it does not mean that we are to entirely renounce all desire from the outset, but that we must work to reduce our cravings.[15]

Therefore, renunciation means less craving; it means being more reasonable, instead of putting too much psychological pressure on oneself and acting crazy. The important point for us to know, then, is that we should have less grasping at sensory pleasures, because most of the time our grasping at, our craving desire for, worldly pleasure does not give us satisfaction.

All individuals, regardless of level, can practice lessening their attachment to sensory pleasure. As Buddha said above, letting go of whatever is not mine is a good practice. In the same vein, Shāntideva (V.62–63) suggests that one should analyze one's body to reduce craving for sensual pleasure by understanding that the body is not one's own:

First, with your intellect,
Separate the layer of skin [from the flesh],
[And then,] with the blade of wisdom,
Separate the flesh apart from the skeleton.
And having split open even the bones,

Look inside, down to the marrow,
And examine by yourself,
"Is there any essence?"[16]

When we examine our bodies to find the self that we claim is "mine," we will not be able to find any parts or organs that belong to "me," so, there is nothing we really need to cling to. Also, since our bodies are actually parts from and of our parents' bodies, they are never our own.

By reducing the intentional action of craving, one can open a way to live a flourishing life. Shāntideva (V.70) suggests that we regard our bodies as a boat carrying us to the destination:

Consider the body as a boat,
Which is merely the support of going and coming;
Turn it into a wish-fulfilling body
In order to benefit sentient beings.[17]

By renouncing faulty mental habits such as clinging to sense objects, instead of literally giving up one's body and desire, one can lead a flourishing life.

On this level, the experience of religious flourishing is comprised predominantly by the affective feeling of generating disgust for the entire round of uncontrolled rebirth. This experience lays the groundwork for realization of emptiness, selflessness. As before, the agential advance comes not from turning away from happiness but from recognizing a greater happiness and the means to achieve it, disgust for the process of entrapment in a round of pain called cyclic existence. Therefore, flourishing at this level depends upon the agential aspect of realistic assessment of the condition of ordinary life impelled by ignorance that provides the basis for afflictive desire and hatred. This greater perspective impels meditation on the selflessness of persons and other phenomena in order to undermine the afflictive emotions that are built on misperception. Such meditation, in turn, leads to direct cognition of the true status of persons such that, gradually, various levels of afflictive emotions can be removed from the mental continuum forever. Thus, the affective aspects are various—disgust and terror for the power of karma (actions) and hopefulness based on insight into the fundamental weakness of ignorance despite its having driven a beginningless round of suffering.

Beings of Great Capacity

Just as persons become of middling agential capacity by extending their motivational outlook to include seeking relief from all of cyclic existence, persons advance to great agential capacity by extending understanding of their own circumstantial plight in cyclic existence to a more profound level—realization that others are in a similar circumstantial plight. The definition of a being of great capacity is: a person who is posited from the viewpoint of seeking the omniscience of Buddhahood by way of having come under the influence of great compassion in order that Buddhahood might be attained in the continuums of other sentient beings.

The definition is from Atisha's *Lamp for the Path to Enlightenment* (stanza 5):

> Persons who thoroughly wish
> To extinguish thoroughly all sufferings of others
> [Through inference of such] by way of the suffering
> Included in their own continuum are supreme.

The phrase "by way of the suffering included in their own continuum" indicates how these persons infer others' suffering based on their own experience of suffering. They have become intent on others' welfare, wanting to extinguish thoroughly all of their sufferings, that is to say, all levels of their suffering in cyclic existence, both gross and subtle. "Extinguish thoroughly" means to remove obstructions together with their predispositions through a variety of techniques, training in the many stages of the paths, and implementing them in helping others.

On this level, practitioners are concerned about four defective conditions that are salient circumstances opposing flourishing in all sentient beings:

(1) cyclic existence;

(2) seeking a solitary peace, which is mere liberation for their own sake;

(3) obstructions to liberation; and

(4) obstructions to omniscience.

The shift in perspective on the circumstances of life without full enlightenment that takes place with this third and highest level of the experience of religious flourishing is of far wider scope in that others' suffering has become the primary concern.

The change in outlook is often compared to an ordinary attitude of filial concern made extraordinary by extending its scope beyond its usual range to all beings. Just as on the level of the practices of a being of low and middling agential capacity, the quest for happiness is not forsaken but is reaffirmed with a higher goal, so here ordinary concern and compassion are not replaced by otherworldly attitudes but are extended far beyond their usual scope and are thereby transformed.

In the earlier phase, the scope of a practitioner's religious concern (and hence of their spiritual flourishing) advanced from concern with suffering in a future life to concern with one's own cyclic existence in general; now it advances to concern with the plight of all sentient beings. All beings are to be held back from all levels of suffering.

In terms of how such progress in an ever-widening perspective is made, one passes from the level of ordinary low capacity to that of special low capacity by reversing the emphasis on the appearances of the present lifetime; this is done by agentially realizing, through exertion at study and meditation, that:

- the present situation as a human endowed with pleasurable features is valuable;
- one will not stay long in this life; and
- lifetimes as animals, hungry ghosts, and hell-beings are bereft of such fortunate circumstances.

Then one passes from this level of flourishing to that of a being of middling agential capacity by reversing the emphasis on the appearances of future lives, thereby developing a definite intention to leave cyclic existence. This level of flourishing is accomplished by reflecting on the inevitable effects of karma and the many varieties of suffering certain to be induced by one's own bad karma. It is necessary agentially to meditate on:

- suffering, so that a wish to separate from cyclic existence will be generated;
- impermanence, so that attachment to the mental and physical aggregates of this life will be eliminated; and

- the final nature of phenomena, selflessness, so that attachment
  to what belongs to oneself (including one's own body) will be
  overcome.

Through this process, an attitude seeking liberation can be generated in full form such that it can serve as a platform to advance to the level of a being of great agential capacity by developing the unusual compassion of being willing oneself to take on the burden of freeing other beings from suffering and joining them with happiness.

This level of flourishing is accomplished by agentially cultivating in meditation a sense of closeness with all beings, thereby becoming aware of their suffering, as inferred from one's own situation, which was realized earlier on the paths of beings of small and middling capacity. Compassion itself has the affective aspect of feeling that one has come under the control, the influence, of others in the sense that one must respond to their afflictive circumstantial situation with empathy and commitment to acting to relieve their plight. The feeling of empathy is compared even to feeling fire on the skin and striking through to flesh.

The highest level of genuine human flourishing is accomplished when the well-being of all other beings is fostered as a central practice, even though the virtue of nonviolence, refraining from aggression, is common to all levels of Buddhist flourishing; the difference here is that compassion has become the central motivating factor. The idea of nonviolence in Buddhism starts from a speculation on one's natural love of oneself. In the *Mallikā Sutta*, Buddha expounds on the importance of seeing others as being equal in status with oneself. On the upper terrace of the palace, King Prasenajit asks his queen Mallikā: who is more dear to her than herself? The queen answers, "There is no one, great king, more dear to me than myself. But is there anyone, great king, dearer to you than yourself?" The king agrees that he himself is dearest to himself in the world. When the couple reported their conversation, the Buddha stated:

Having traversed all quarters with the mind,
One finds none anywhere dearer than oneself.
Likewise, each person holds oneself most dear;
Hence, one who loves himself should not harm others.[18]

Buddha proposes quite simple but helpful reasoning to develop the idea of refraining from aggression: I should cherish others because others cherish themselves just as I cherish myself. In the *Dhammapada* (129 and 131) Buddha again emphasizes that loving oneself and understanding that others also cherish their lives is the source for developing an attitude of nonviolence:

> All tremble at violence;
> All fear death.
> Seeing others as being like yourself,
> Do not kill or cause others to kill.
> . . .
> If, desiring happiness,
> You use violence
> To harm living beings who desire happiness,
> You will not find happiness after death.[19]

If we renounce our attachment to "I" and "mine," and if we deeply understand that others too want happiness and not suffering, by dismantling the delusive wall built around an "I," we will naturally practice refraining from violence or aggressive behavior in daily life. We are all interconnected, and our flourishing depends deeply on others' welfare. Therefore, Shāntideva (VIII.173) says:

> Also, if [you] want to make yourself happy,
> Do not isolate your own [happiness] by yourself.
> Also, if [you] want to protect yourself,
> Always protect others.

Through this heartfelt understanding of the direct relationship between my own and others' good life, one can develop loving-kindness and compassion for one's own sake as well as that of others.

It needs to be noted that Chandrakīrti (fl. eighth century CE; I.10–11) explains that selfishly motivated charity brings benefits to oneself over the course of lifetimes, and thus we would have to call this a form of human flourishing:

> All these beings want happiness, but human
> Happiness does not occur without resources.
> Knowing that resources arise from giving,

The Sage first discoursed on that.
Even for beings with little compassion,
Brutal and intent on their own aims,
Desired resources arise from giving,
Causing extinction of suffering.[20]

Since a genuine good life depends on one's mind as well as others' welfare, giving is an essential practice for those who want to live well in order to be able to engage in practice. Thus, even though Buddha says in the *Dhammapada* that there is no limit to craving, "Not even with a shower of gold coins, would we find satisfaction in sensual craving,"[21] resources are needed in order to survive, and thus Chandrakīrti calls on those looking to promote their own welfare to engage in giving, to be generous. This does not contradict his saying in the same text that due to clinging to the delusive concept of an inherently existent "I," ordinary beings have endless attachment such that they circulate in the various levels of cyclic existence powerlessly "like a bucket traveling in a well."[22]

Compassion, the focus of flourishing on this high level, is often included in the discussion of patience, the third of six perfections to be cultivated in Great Vehicle Buddhism. As was quoted above, the "I" looking into what is claimed to be itself, the "I," cannot be located in any part of the body or mind; through this investigation, one can strengthen the foundation of patience. To deal with myriad challenges and sufferings, and with those who wish to harm us, the Dalai Lama offers a compelling point. First, he quotes Shāntideva (VI.47), who says that bullying by someone hostile to us is actually a field for growing the positive power of merit, because that person provides us with an opportunity to practice patience:

Having been incited by my actions,
Those who harm me emerge.
And if these sentient beings fall to a hell,
Is it not I who destroyed them?

The Dalai Lama, commenting on Shāntideva's stanza, says that if we apply the understanding of karma—cause and effect—the reason that perceived enemies harm us is that we caused harm at some previous time. Furthermore, those who are hostile toward us will definitely face the consequences of their harmful intentions and actions. He says, "From this point of view, it is we who are harming our opponents, for in the future they will suffer because of the harmful act we ourselves have instigated."[23]

The Dalai Lama then presents a more fundamental perspective on patience. That is, since mind is not matter, it cannot be harmed. Even if someone speaks triggering things, it cannot harm one physically.[24] Therefore, if we think that we can be hurt by somebody's nasty words, those are our mere imagination. We need to ask ourselves which part of us is harmed by harsh words. To those who might worry that enemies look down on us due to our not responding to them, he says:

> However much fame and praise we get, we can only enjoy it for this
> life. On the other hand, if we get angry with others, thinking they are
> damaging our reputation and success in this life, the negative actions
> we thus accumulate will follow us in our future lives.[25]

However much we strive to tightly grasp what we have or want, all of it will sooner or later disappear. Therefore, instead of trying to protect ourselves by intensely reacting to perceived enemies, if we turn these situations into opportunities to practice patience, instead of creating bad karma, we will accumulate merit, which, at minimum, will eventually yield circumstances such as good friends, good reputation, health, prosperity, and so on.

An Integrated Gradation of Practices

The paths of the three levels can be seen to serve as an integrated gradation of practices; they are not mutually contradictory. By not cultivating the merely self-centered aspects of the paths of the lower levels, the paths of the three levels come to form a coherent, integrated whole. The higher levels do not cancel the lower ones but are built on the lower and continue to be reinforced by them. The great compassion that is so central to the motivation of a being of great capacity is founded on realistic appraisal of one's own plight in cyclic existence, as is understood through the practices of a being of small and middling capacity. Even more so, realization of emptiness (the final nature in terms of the selflessness of persons)—detailed on the level of practice for a being of middling capacity for gaining liberation from cyclic existence—is preliminary to realizing the final nature in terms of the selflessness of phenomena, through concentration on which one is liberated from the obstructions to omniscience, the primary intent of a being of great capacity. In addition, beings of middling and great agential capacity need a continuum of favorable lives in order to complete their respective paths and thus still need the practices of a being of small agential capacity in order to ensure good rebirths.[26]

Thus, for a being of great capacity, the practices of all three beings are intertwined; the lower ones both form the foundation for the higher and remain important aspects of continual practice. It can be seen that the lower levels of religious flourishing cannot be dismissed as merely preliminary, in favor of more ultimate concerns; they remain an important aspect of a practitioner's intentionality throughout the entire scope of practice. The picture that emerges from considering such a broad range of practices is far richer than what is gained from considering only ultimate concerns.[27]

To summarize: The process is a withdrawal from lower involvements— first from seeking pleasures only within the scope of the present lifetime, then from seeking the pleasures of cyclic existence in general, and then from self-centeredness. At the same time, it requires an extension to higher involvements—first to concern with future lifetimes, then to liberation from all of cyclic existence, and then to others' welfare.

CONFLICT WITH OUR OWN NATURE

The descriptions of the paths of persons of the three capacities is a perspective indicating that beings are not familiar with their own nature and that training is required to overcome obstacles preventing greater levels of flourishing from being manifested. These three levels of agential engagement hold practitioners back from a series of increasingly subtle, counterproductive attitudes to a series of more salutary concerns. The stages progress from short-term self-orientation to long-term self-orientation and then to other-orientation—each stage requiring a profoundly ethical transformation. Even the self-oriented stages are built on practices that are aimed at not harming others (compassion) and culminate eventually, as a being of great capacity, in a commitment to helping others (great compassion).

Each of these phases of withdrawal is from a mental perspective characterized by multiplicity and a fracturing of attention—being sunk in attachment to the manifold appearances and purposes (1) of the presently appearing world, (2) of future lifetimes, and (3) of being sunken in the inequality of self-cherishing.

Even though the logical presentation of the threefold typology of practices may make it seem as if the progression from one circumstantial level to another is a smooth process of gradually acquiring a new outlook, the very structure of three tiers suggests that the experience of religious flourishings in each succeeding level is inaccessible and even foreign when we are on a lower level. The upper levels are outside the experience of those on lower levels—they are dramatically other. One may study about the upper levels, but being a person of a higher level is outside of one's experience.

A realistic appraisal of one's own motivation, in the face of carefully considering this typology, tends to yield a self-identification as very low on the scale; the typology gives practitioners both a means to assess accurately their present condition and goals to strive toward. The typology itself thereby exerts an influence on practitioners, beckoning toward the development of a more profound flourishing but also making it clear that those levels are foreign.

On the other hand, the usage of common concerns—first with one's own suffering and then with familial responsibility—as means to deepen and then broaden one's perspective indicates that the seeds of the higher levels are common to all. Seen in this light, the higher attitudes are present in a shared seed-form which, through repeated training, can be extended in a process of development, even if they are profoundly other in the sense that they are outside present agential manifestation, their experiential implications being unbearable to the present personality structure.

In the practices of the beings of three capacities, energies are withdrawn and elements common to the ordinary mind are emphasized and expanded, but the experience of such withdrawal and expansion can be fraught with uneasiness. Attempts to expand common concern for one's own and one's friends' welfare to larger perspectives can be characterized with a sense of alienness because of the attachments that must be overcome in order to open the way for such new perspectives, and similarly the manifestation of the mind of clear light—the inner nature of all conscious experience—can evoke such a great sense of alienness that it is feared as a force annihilating oneself, because of self-identification with mental and physical factors that are contrary to one's own deeper nature.

Thus, the experience of religious flourishing on many levels may evoke a sense of dread—of the loss of directionality that pursuit of temporary pleasures affords, of the loss of permanence, of the loss of a solidly existent sense of self, and of the loss of one's very being—facing what is awesomely other than one's present, limited perspective. Nevertheless, after acculturation by means of paths of practice, the very same insights are perceived as like finding a lost treasure. As the Fifth Dalai Lama says about the experience of realizing emptiness:

> This initial generation of the Middle Way view is not actual special insight; however, like a moon on the second day of the month, it is a slight finding of the view. At that time, if you have no predispositions for emptiness from a former life, it seems that a thing which was in the hand has suddenly been lost. If you have predispositions, it seems that a lost jewel which had been in the hand has suddenly been found.[28]

What is experienced with a sense of loss at an early stage is later re-experienced with a sense of finding a treasure that had been lost.

Much of this system of spiritual education, or amplification, indeed can be viewed as aimed at overcoming this fear of one's own most basic nature. The strangeness of our own natural potential is a function of misconception, in this case of the basic nature of the mind, specifically the sense that afflictive emotions subsist in the nature of the mind. As the Zen master Enni (1202–1280) indicates, the source of suffering is the misidentification of afflictive emotions as the very nature of the mind:

> Those injured by this spirit of the afflictions, believing that their deluded thoughts are the original mind and taking delight in the seeds of desire, revolve through the four [kinds of] rebirth in the three evil [destinies]. [29]

As a remedy, the scholar-practitioners cited above call for reasoned affirmation of the basic purity of the mind, this being within the frequently reiterated context that well-reasoned faith is far stronger than unreasoned faith. However, this dictum may not take into account the power and effectiveness of faith that is built not on reasoning but on inklings, on glimpses; such faith is a central element in leading a practitioner, consciously and unconsciously, to profound experience. As the Sixth Patriarch Hui-Neng says in the Platform Sutra, "Your own minds are the Buddha, do not doubt this!"[30]

The frequent descriptions in the literature of Tibet's Old Translation School, as well as in East Asian Buddhism, of identifying one's own actual nature, one's own face, suggest that the sense of at-homeness, of "being set on mama's lap," reveals religion not as something separate but as eventually most familiar. The joy and sense of at-homeness that a child feels when (in a happy mood) he or she is set on mama's lap is an analog to highly developed yogis' sense of joyful naturalness when they identify in experience their own basic nature. The fundamental innate mind of clear light, when experienced by one who has overcome the initial, distorted fear and sense of annihilation, is most familiar, most comforting, most common, most ordinary. One might even question that such an experience is religious because of not having the quality of separateness and awe, but as we have seen, the experience of religious flourishing in this tradition is an acculturation to a state that is foreign only because of the afflicted state of the practitioner.

The practices of the beings of the three levels of capacity, though extensions of common experiences, pass through a phase of alienness but then culminate in a sense of familiarity, resulting from cultivation of the path. The agential path is the bridge between an original common endowment and expansive flourishing of such experience to a universal level; it opens a passageway by removing the obstacles creating the inability to withstand the implications of these profound states. This need for acculturation is reflected in the frequently repeated Tibetan oral teaching that "meditation" is actually "familiarization," a matter of getting used to, or adjusting one's mind to, the implications of profound realizations, as is evidenced by the fact that the term "forbearance" is used for levels of the path indicating an overcoming of unease with the ramifications of deeper states.

The path-experiences of beings of all three capacities can be so shattering that they are difficult to withstand. For, when these common experiences in their expanded meaning impinge on a consciousness not yet ready for them, they may indeed be dreadful, fraught with implications under-mining and threatening distorted postures of personality. To appreciate the significance of the agential challenge, we must realize how upsetting it can be to contemplate:

- the plight of transmigrations as animals, hungry ghosts, and hell-beings;
- the plight of cyclic existence in general;
- the needs of the endless number of sentient beings; and
- the implications of the basic nature of the mind.

The contemplation of these can be upsetting because they are in such great opposition to ingrained attitudes. When done effectively, the impact of such contemplations on the pursuit of present superficial pleasures and self-centered goals is indeed devastating, though ultimately beneficial, in demanding rearrangement of the personality.

Attachment is built on bias, and the extension of more homogeneous attitudes requires a dramatic withdrawal of the energy of attachment. Since the agential path toward expanded flourishing is relative to detach-ment from biased states—from viewing the afflictive emotions as the basic nature of the mind—it is fraught with dangers that should not be ignored in favor of the comfortably ordered layout of stages that com-municate little of the pain and clash between intimately held attach-ments and higher attitudes. Only when we see these implications can we place the agential struggle in the context of its liberative task. From this perspective we see the enormity and momentousness of this Buddhist endeavor.

To summarize, a genuine good life comes with a profound understand-ing of the interconnectivity of all phenomena, including all living beings; our intentions and the verbal and physical actions following upon them are the causes of the world and become the fundamental source of our human flourishing. In addition, by realizing that our lives are continually imperiled by our obliviousness to the fragility of life and the certainty of death, that this is due to the lack of stability brought on by securing only our own desires, and so on, we should develop renunciation by reducing craving so that we may effectively use our bodies as excellent vessels for attaining human flourishing through thoughtful behavior. Then, with heartfelt understanding of the sameness of myself and others in terms of each and every one of us wanting happiness and not wanting suffering, we should find ways to actively refrain from aggression, and practice nonviolence in daily interactions, which will eventually develop into compassion and loving-kindness.

Emphasis on the practical application of Buddha doctrine also is found in the Ch'an tradition. The *Records of the Transmission of the Lamp* offers an example of the importance of living up to the abovementioned principles. When Bai Juyi (772–846), a famous member of the literati, was the governor of Hangzhou, he visited the Ch'an master Daolin, who was often called Bird's Nest Ch'an Master, as he meditated upon a tree. Bai asked Daolin: "What is Buddha doctrine?" The Master answered, "Do not commit any evil, but practice all virtuous deeds." Bai pointed out that the Master's answer was way too easy, while enlightenment was not easy at all. He said, "Even a three-year-old boy would know it!" Daolin responded, "Even a three-year-old boy can surely understand it; but even an eighty-year-old man cannot accomplish it."[31] The knowledge and teachings of Buddhism are meaningful for one's flourishing life only when actually practiced.

Notes

1   Francis H. Cook, *Hua-Yen Buddhism: The Jewel Net of Indra* (Philadelphia: Pennsylvania State University Press, 1977), 2.

2   Cook, *Hua-Yen Buddhism*, 2.

3   From Ngag-wang-leg-dan's oral teachings. Jeffrey Hopkins, *Meditation on Emptiness* (Boston: Wisdom Publications, 1996), 354.

4   Bstan 'dzin rgya mtsho, Alison Anderson, and Marianne Dresser, *Beyond Dogma: Dialogues and Discourses* (Berkeley, Calif.: North Atlantic Books, 1996), 192. For further discussion, see José Ignacio Cabezón, "Three Buddhist Views of the Doctrines of Creation and Creator," in *Buddhism, Christianity and the Question of Creation: Karmic or Divine?* ed. Perry Schmidt-Leukel, 33–46 (Burlington, Vt.: Ashgate, 2006).

5   Shāntideva, "Engaging in Bodhisattva Behavior," Study Buddhism, by Berzin Archives, trans. by Alexander Berzin, accessed January 27, 2023, https://studybuddhism.com/en/tibetan-buddhism/original-texts/sutra-texts/engaging-in-bodhisattva-behavior; V.13–14. The material on the website is adapted from Alexander Berzin, *Engaging in the Bodhisattva Behavior (spyod-'jug, bodhisattvacaryāvatāra) by Shāntideva*, online publication, 2005.

6   Bhikkhu Nanomole and Bhikkhu Bodhi, trans., "Raṭṭhapāla Sutta (MN 82)," in *The Middle Length Discourses of the Buddha* (Boston: Wisdom Publications, 2009), 687–91.

7   Adapted from Gil Fronsdal, *The Dhammapada: Teachings of the Buddha* (Boston: Shambhala, 2008), 3.

8   See Hopkins' exposition on this topic in "A Tibetan Perspective on the Nature of Spiritual Experience," in *Paths to Liberation*, ed. Robert E. Buswell and Robert Gimello, 182–217 (Honolulu: University of Hawaii Press, 1992). The poem below is included in this volume.

9   The term "high status" refers to the elevated states of happiness as humans, demi-gods, or gods relative to animals, hungry ghosts, and hell-beings. These states, being created by karma, are all impermanent, eventually leading to rebirth in other states.

10   Bhikkhu Ñyāṇamoli and Bhikkhu Bodhi, trans., "Alagaddūpama Sutta (MN 22)," in *Middle Length Discourses*, 140–41.

11   There are a few extreme cases in this text of seeking and thereby removing the cause of desire from outside; for example, a monk cut off his penis to suppress his sexual desire. About this case, Buddha said, "When one thing [that is, desire] should have been cut off, that foolish man cut off something else [that is, his penis]." See Thanisaro Bhikku, trans., *The Buddhist Monastic Code II* (Valery Center, Calif.: Metta Forest Monastery, 2013), 126, https://www.accesstoinsight.org/lib/authors/thanissaro/bmc2.pdf.

12   Our translation; 佛說譬喻經, T04n21704_001, http://tripitaka.cbeta.org/mobile/index.php?index=T04n0217_001.

13   In a similar vein, in the Forty-Two Chapter Sutra, Buddha uses the same simile, explaining that seeking fortune and sensual pleasure is like a child's licking honey off a blade; the child is never satiated, and instead there is the danger of cutting one's tongue. See 四十二章經, T17n0784_001, http://tripitaka.cbeta.org/T17n0784_001.

14 Geshe Lhundup Sopa and Jeffrey Hopkins, *Cutting through Appearances: Practice and Theory of Tibetan Buddhism* (Ithaca, N.Y.: Snow Lion Publications, 1989), 69.

15 Lama Thubten Yeshe and Nicholas Ribush, eds., *The Essence of Tibetan Buddhism: The Three Principal Aspects of the Path and Introduction to Tantra* (Boston: Lama Yeshe Wisdom Archive, 2001), 17.

16 Adapted from Shāntideva, "Engaging in Bodhisattva Behavior."

17 Adapted from Shāntideva, "Engaging in Bodhisattva Behavior."

18 Bhikkhu Bodhi, trans., "Mallikā Sutta," in *The Connected Discourses of the Buddha: A Translation of the Saṃyutta Nikāya* (Boston: Wisdom Publications, 2000), 170–71.

19 Fronsdal, *Dhammapada*, 35.

20 Jeffrey Hopkins, *Compassion in Tibetan Buddhism: Tsong-ka-pa; Kensur Lekden's Meditations of a Tantric Abbot* (Ithaca, N.Y.: Snow Lion Publications, 1985), 183–84.

21 Fronsdal, *Dhammapada*, 50.

22 Chandrakīrti's "Supplement to (Nāgārjuna's) 'Treatise on the Middle,'" (I.3); translation from Hopkins, *Compassion in Tibetan Buddhism*, 83:

> Homage to that compassion for transmigrating beings
> Powerless like a bucket traveling in a well
> Through initially adhering to a self, "I,"
> And then generating attachment for things, "This is mine."

23 His Holiness the Dalai Lama, *For the Benefit of All Beings: A Commentary on the Way of the Bodhisattva*, tr. Padmakara Translation Group (Boulder, Colo.: Shambhala Publications, 1999), 64.

24 His Holiness the Dalai Lama, *For the Benefit of All Beings*, 65.

25 His Holiness the Dalai Lama, *For the Benefit of All Beings*, 65.

26 Reflection on the presentation of this ordered system itself induces advancement in religious perspective and spiritual experience.

27 The doctrine of three types of beings forms an integrated series of practices for one individual and also constitutes a typology supposedly applicable to all beings; anyone and everyone can be classified within this rubric. Most ordinary beings, including animals, are the low of the low capacity, since the scope of their concern is mainly limited to the temporary affairs of this lifetime; those who also employ religious means to achieve happiness in

this lifetime are the middling of the low; those who are about to generate a nonartificial form of an intention to leave cyclic existence in all its aspects are of middling capacity, as are all lower level practioners. Those who have generated the unusual compassion described above are, in turn, classified as beings of great capacity.

As a typology for humanity in general, this system has obvious faults. It cannot classify the most compassionate Christians, for instance, as any of these, since they are not mainly seeking either (1) "Buddhahood so that Buddhahood might be attained in the continuums of other sentient beings," as a being of great capacity would; (2) "liberation for one's own sake," as a being of middling capacity would; (3) "the mere happiness of a future lifetime," as a being of supreme low capacity would; (4) "the mere happiness of this lifetime through religious and non-religious means," as a being of middling low capacity would, or (5) "the mere happiness of this lifetime through non-religious means," as a being of low capacity would. The typology has similar, severe difficulties with Hindu systems, adherents to which, because of being considered not to recognize properly the process of cyclic existence, would probably be classified as beings of the middling low variety, outside the realm of religious practitioners.

Though the typology is aimed at including all beings, its failure to recognize other traditions as even within the count of religions suggests that a hidden agenda is to exclude practitioners of other religions from the count of religious beings. This is not surprising in a parochial culture, but such harsh exclusivity does run counter to the advocacy of universal compassion. Followers quickly learn to bifurcate their minds, such that they are deeply moved by calls to unbiased compassion and yet participate with vigor in exaggerated discrimination against other groups. At times, when confronted with such exclusivity, we have wondered whether it is just that a message of universal compassion is being wrapped in a package of parochialism or whether a message of parochial prejudice is being wrapped in the package of universal compassion. Nevertheless, the typology says much about the direction of the Indo-Tibetan Buddhist experience of religious flourishing and can be used within such a framework.

28 Ngag-wang-lo-sang-gya-tsho (1617–1682), *Instruction on the Stages of the Path to Enlightenment, Sacred Word of Mañjushrī* (Thimphu, Bhutan: Kun-bzang-stobs-rgyal, 1976), as found in Jeffrey Hopkins, trans., *Practice of Emptiness* (Dharamsala, India: Library of Tibetan Works and Archives, 1974), 17.

29 Carl Bielefeldt, "A Discussion of Seated Zen," in *Buddhism in Practice*, ed. Donald S. Lopez Jr. (Princeton, N.J.: Princeton University Press, 1995), 203.

30 John R. McRae, trans., *The Platform Sutra of the Sixth Patriarch* (Berkeley, Calif.: Numata Center for Buddhist Translation and Research, 2000), 90.

31 Our translation; *The Records of the Transmission of the Lamp*, T51n2076, http://tripitaka.cbeta.org/T51n2076_004.

3

A Ruist (Confucian) Vision

Bin Song and Stephen C. Angle

INTRODUCTION: THE RU TRADITION

Since Protestant missionaries arrived in China in the middle of the nine-teenth century, the Ru tradition has been prevalently labeled as "Confucian-ism" in English after the Latinized name of its founding teacher, Confucius (551–479 BCE), whose original honorary title in Chinese is Kongzi (孔子; Master Kong). However, contemporary scholars, particularly in the areas of comparative religion and philosophy, increasingly realize that this nomen-clature was created in a special time of human history; in this chapter we will refer to the "Ru" tradition rather than to "Confucianism."[1]

The character *Ru* (儒) was adopted by Kongzi's followers shortly after his demise to identify themselves in a period of "warring states" (战国, fifth century to 221 BCE). In this extremely combative and chaotic era, many schools of thought competed with one another. Although contem-porary scholars continue to debate the origin and meaning of the term *Ru*, we can discern its relatively stable semantics from the ways Ru wrote about it in the received Ruist classics.[2] From here, we find that a Ru can be defined broadly as a generally educated person who aims to harmo-nize the well-being of all involved beings in a civilization through inherit-ing, devising, and practicing appropriate (義, *yi*) familial, communal, and cultural conventions, which are termed as "rituals" (禮, *li*).[3] In this way, the literal meaning of the character Ru, "being soft" (柔, *rou*), indicates a distinctively humanistic path that Kongzi and his followers advocated in order to remedy human predicaments induced by the social turmoil of the times: there are intrinsically good, nonviolent dimensions of human nature, and through cultivating them, humans can build a humane (仁, *ren*) society in which all its participants can flourish.

This Ruist project of social reengineering was hardly successful during wartime. Nevertheless, when the wars ended and ancient Chinese civilization began to adopt the political pattern of unified empires in one dynasty after another, Ruism was soon established as state ideology sustained by a system of civil examinations, whose major purpose was to recruit officials from Ru literati to staff the empire's administrative bureaucracy.[4] Because of this close connection to politics, Ruist learning was significantly influenced by the social and political changes that took place throughout numerous dynastic cycles, which in turn led to considerable variations internal to the Ru school of thought.

In this broad context, to present a synthetic Ruist understanding of the good life—in which, as we will see, "joy" is a paramount component—two periods of Ruism are of primary significance. The first is surely its classical period, when Kongzi and his eminent followers such as Yan Hui (521–481 BCE), Mengzi (372–289 BCE), and Xunzi (?–238 BCE) helped to pass down classics from ancient times and composed new ones to address their current needs. These classics formed a seminal foundation for Ruism's later evolution. The second was largely concomitant with China's Song (960–1279 CE) through Ming Dynasties (1368–1644 CE), but geographically, in this later period Ruism also extended to other Asian countries such as Korea, Japan, and Vietnam. An intellectual feature of Ruism in this period is that while debating and incorporating ideas from other traditions such as Daoism and Buddhism, Ruism reorganized and reinterpreted its canon, developing a magnificent and largely self-coherent system that encompasses major aspects of philosophical and religious thought, such as spirituality, metaphysics, epistemology, ethics, aesthetics, and political theory. English scholarship normally designates Ruism in this period as "Neo-Confucianism," but for the purposes of this chapter we will simply refer to the Ruism of this period as Song-Ming Ruism, after the names of the relevant dynasties.

Per this brief introduction of the Ruist thought and history, we will mainly draw on resources in the aforementioned two periods of Ruism in the following ways. Firstly, we will locate the key texts in which classical Ruists discussed joy and the good life, as the nature and place of joy here provides a helpful platform upon which a broader vision can be set out. The focus on joy as the affective norm (life feeling right) reveals crucial insights into the normative commitments concerning the circumstances and conditions (life going well) and the actions and desires (life led well) of the good life. Secondly, by invoking commentarial thoughts upon these texts, we will appeal to the wisdom of both periods of Ruism to respond to the tripartite hypothesis of the good life.[5] We will argue that this tripartite framework is fit for analyzing its Ruist counterpart. However, the original vocabulary used to describe each dimension of the hypothesis will experience twists and turns while encountering the peculiarity of Ruist thought. While incorporating these specificities into the larger analytic framework, we hope Ruism's contribution to the volume will broaden our imagination and understanding of the good life.

THE JOY OF KONGZI AND YAN HUI (孔顏之樂)

To Ruists, it makes sense to explore their vision of the good life by asking about the place of joy within it, because this was a pivotal question asked by Ruists themselves at the beginning of Ruism's revival in the Song through Ming period:

> Once upon a time, we learned with Zhou Dunyi. Quite often, he required us to search for whence Yan Hui and Kongzi derived their joy. The question is, for what reason were they joyful?[6]

"We" here refers to Cheng Yi (1033–1107 CE) and Cheng Hao (1032–1085 CE). Together with their teacher Zhou Dunyi (1017–1073 CE), the Cheng brothers were acclaimed by the later Ru tradition as among the most prominent, pioneering Ru thinkers of the Song dynasty. Yan Hui refers to the student whom Kongzi thought of, among all his students, as being the best at learning.[7]

The question discussed by these three Ru masters on "the joy of Kongzi and Yan Hui" (孔顏之樂) hearkens back to texts composed in the classical stage of Ruism, such as:

> Kongzi said, "What a worthy man is Yan Hui! Living in a narrow alley, subsisting on a basket of grain and gourd full of water—other people could not bear their worries over such a hardship, yet Hui never changes his joy. What a worthy man is Hui!" (*Analects* 6.11)

> Kongzi said, "Eating plain food and drinking water, having only your bent arm as a pillow—certainly there is joy to be found in this! Wealth and eminence, if attained in an inappropriate way, concern me no more than the floating clouds." (*Analects* 7.16)

Here, Kongzi and his favorite student, Yan Hui, are depicted as both being able to remain joyful despite poverty.

Relying just on these terse descriptions, it is hard to decipher for what reason Kongzi and Yan Hui were joyful. However, by relying on other related texts, we can be certain that although the joy of Kongzi and Yan Hui arises despite poverty, it is not *because of* poverty. In other words, it is not an ascetic type of joy which denies normal human needs for economic security and the appropriate human pursuit for wealth. To the contrary, Kongzi's attitude towards wealth, if considered from a communal perspective, is realistic and practical; applied to individuals, his attitude is moderate. For instance, in *Analects* 13.9, when asked about how to govern the state of Wei with a large population, Kongzi provided a two-step proposal: firstly, to make people rich; and secondly, to have them educated. According to this view, a government is obliged to execute policies to secure economic prosperity for its people in order that the people can have a foundation to pursue their education and moral self-cultivation. When thinking about his own wealth, Kongzi said: "if a business is pursuable for the sake of wealth, then I would do it even if this means serving as a junior officer holding a whip at the entrance to a marketplace. If not, however, I will turn to do what I love" (*Analects* 7:12). Here, Kongzi's point is that the creation of personal wealth is vulnerable to uncontrollable external conditions. Rather than craving for wealth regardless, it would be wiser for people to focus upon doing what they intrinsically love.

Again, this does not mean that wealth, or other similar outputs of human activities, is inherently despicable. From Kongzi's biography, we know that he experienced extreme poverty and hardship, particularly when he wandered from state to state in order to promote (to no avail) his political philosophy. However, before that expedition, Kongzi once briefly occupied the highest office in his home state of Lu, and after he returned to Lu, his focus on teaching and scholarship also spoke to the fact that his life had enjoyed a certain degree of settlement and peace.[8] During these more stable periods of his life, Kongzi is described as loving food, relishing music, being a connoisseur of clothing, and remaining sociable and amicable while interacting with people.[9] Kongzi in these portraits can be seen as having a refined and sophisticated taste for life, and he would not mind living as a moderate *bon vivant* when conditions allow it.

Based on the analysis above, it is evident that Kongzi and Yan Hui were able to experience joy even amid poverty, while still being attuned to different forms of happiness. This highlights the profound nature of joy within the Ru tradition. By nurturing this feeling in a proper manner, it can remain a constant aspect of human life even in the face of changing circumstances. However, it is important to note that joy cannot be entirely disassociated from the specific circumstances of an individual's life. If we use the language of whole versus part, joy can be seen as a holistic feeling toward the whole world, one that is concerned with, while not being limited to, the concrete life situations that make up the world's changing parts. If we use the trope of transcendence versus immanence, we can say that this deeper dimension of human life transcends while simultaneously remaining immanent in its other dimensions. The traditional Ruist vocabulary to describe this contrast between the transcendent whole and its immanent parts is "what lies beyond shape" (形而上) versus "what lies within shape" (形而下). The former is furthermore described as referring to Dao (道, the Way), and the latter as *qi* (器, utensil-like things).[10]

"I Am with Zeng Dian" (吾與點也)

While frequently inquiring into the "joy of Kongzi and Yan Hui" using a dyadic framework of "what lies beyond shape" and "what lies within shape," Ru thinkers in the Song through Ming period also emphasized an additional passage in the *Analects*. In this passage, Kongzi expresses his attitude towards the feeling of joy and views about the desirability of the vision of the good life of another of his students, Zeng Dian. Compared to the above quotes on the joy of Kongzi and Yan Hui, Zeng Dian's words are embedded in a more specific context, and the drama of the passage also creates a richer space for Ru thinkers' varying interpretations. Since this passage is so central to later Ruists' discussion on joy and the good life, we quote it in its entirety and use it as another anchoring text for our discussion:

> Zi Lu, Zeng Dian, Ran You, and Gong Xihua were seated in attendance. Kongzi said to them, "Although I am older than any of you, please do not feel uneasy in responding to me. You, while living at home, often complain, 'No one appreciates me.' Well, if someone were to appreciate you, what would you do?" Zi Lu spoke up immediately. "If I were given charge of a state of a thousand chariots—even one hemmed in between powerful states, suffering from armed invasions and afflicted by famine—before three years were up I could infuse its people with courage and a sense of what is right." The Master smiled at him. He then turned to Ran You. "Ran You, what would you do?" Ran You answered, "If I were given charge of a state sixty or seventy—or even fifty or sixty—square *li* in area, before three years were up I could see that the people would have become wealthy. As for instructing its people in ritual practice and music, this is a task that would have to await the arrival of an exemplary person." Kongzi then turned to Gong Xihua. "Gong Xihua, what would you do?" Gong Xihua answered, "I am not saying that I would actually be able to do it, but my wish, at least, would be to learn how to do the following. I would like to serve as a minor functionary—properly clad in ceremonial cap and gown—in ceremonies at the ancestral temple, or at diplomatic gatherings."
>
> Kongzi then turned to Zeng Dian. "You, Zeng Dian! What would you do?" Zeng Dian stopped strumming his zither, and as the last sonorous notes faded away he set the instrument aside and rose to his feet. "I would love to do something quite different from any of the other three." "What harm is there in that?" Kongzi said, "We are all just talking about our aspirations." Zeng Dian then said, "In the last month of spring, once the spring garments have been completed, I should like to assemble a company of five or six young people and six or seven kids to go bathe in the Yi River and enjoy the breeze upon

the Rain Dance Altar, and then return singing to our residence."
Kongzi sighed deeply, saying, "I am with Zeng Dian!"

The other three pupils left, but Zeng Dian stayed behind. He
asked Kongzi, "What did you think of what the other pupils said?"
"Each of them was simply talking about their aspirations." "Then
why, Master, did you smile at Zi Lu?" "One cannot govern a state
without ritual-propriety. His words failed to express the proper
sense of deference, and that is why I smiled at him." "Was Ran
You's aspiration, then, not concerned with statecraft?" "Why did
something sixty or seventy—even fifty or sixty—square *li* in area
not constitute a state?" "Was Gong Xihua's aspiration, then, not
concerned with statecraft?" "If ancestral temples and diplomatic
gatherings are not the business of the feudal lords, what then are
they? If Gong Xihua's aspiration is a minor one, then what would be
considered a major one?"[11]

Several details about the context of the conversation need to be clarified
before we can offer our philosophical analysis.

First, since Kongzi described himself as "old" and the general mood
sounds relaxed, the conversation must have taken place when Kongzi had
finished his wandering and returned to his home state. The order of speaking among the first three students followed seniority. However, even if Zi
Lu was indeed the eldest among all the four, the fact that he did not look
at, and hence show his due respect toward, the others before speaking was
seen as violating a "proper sense of deference," leading to Kongzi's disap-
proving smile. And oddly, Zeng Dian was the last one to respond, even
though he was the second oldest.[12]

Second, the oddity of Zeng Dian's response is also manifested at other
points. First, the bearing of Zeng Dian's response was rather different.
Beginning from the fact that he was playing music, Zeng Dian dared to
deliver a very contrasting answer. Using a term from elsewhere in the *Analects*, Zeng Dian can therefore be called a "wild one" (狂者), one who har-
bors lofty aspirations without taking concrete and careful steps to realize
them.[13] What is more, the content of Zeng Dian's response was no less off-
beat. The original question of Kongzi's was about students' aspirations concerning statecraft if they had a chance to be appointed in government. In
contrast, what Zeng Dian aspired to was a purely quotidian and mundane,

albeit very joyful, activity that sounds like anything but statecraft. According to Zhu Xi's (1130–1200 CE) commentary, what Zeng Dian intended
was to largely follow an ancient custom called "Fu Chu" (祓除) at a special
season of the year and then enjoy a community field trip without much
planning in advance. According to Zhu Xi, the fact that Zeng Dian can
"enjoy the ordinariness of his everyday life" (樂其日用之常) in an "unhurried and restful" (從容) way is particularly commendable.[14]

Third, it is not difficult to connect the nature of ordinariness that
accompanies Zeng Dian's joy to the constant feeling of joy that Kongzi
and Yan Hui were described as being able to entertain despite external
conditions. However, as indicated by the oddities of Zeng Dian's response,
his answer must also have hinted at something extraordinary so as to win
Kongzi's concurrence. If we employ the original referent of "ecstasy" to
something that "stands out," we can even characterize Zeng Dian's joy as
having an ecstatic characteristic that transcends, while not being segre-
gated from, ordinary moments of life. This intricate interplay between the
ordinary and extraordinary dimensions of Zeng Dian's experience of joy
hearkens back to the above analysis about the relationship between a transcendent whole and its immanent parts as it is implied by the joy of Kongzi
and Yan Hui.

According to this analysis, the joy of Kongzi and Yan Hui refers to a
deeper, extraordinary dimension of human life, one which "lies beyond
shape." However, the joy deriving from this dimension transcends, while
being simultaneously immanent in, those more ordinary dimensions that
"lie within shape." Once again, Kongzi's attitude towards Zeng Dian's joy
confirmed this intricate relationship between transcendence and immanence. In the second half of the conversation, when others left Zeng Dian
to face Kongzi alone, Kongzi made clear his approval towards all the other
aspirations of which he had seemingly disapproved. If Zeng Dian's joy
"stands out" in contrast to those more normal aspirations for good life in
the first half of the conversation, it has to be "leveled off" later.

Therefore, what is extraordinary in Zeng Dian's joy? Why does the
extraordinary have to be eventually renormalized? For what reasons does
Kongzi both approve and disapprove of Zeng Dian's joy? Furthermore,
how can we correctly understand the relationship between "what lies

beyond shape" and "what lies within shape," so as to constantly embody a desirable, joyful, good life?

The Ru tradition in its Song through Ming period tries to unravel these puzzles. In our view, we can utilize the tripartite hypothesis to parse out the answers provided by those Ru thinkers.

The Concrete Circumstance:
How the World within Shape Is for Us

The joy of Zeng Dian and his related conversation with Kongzi can be read simply as an affective response to a certain set of circumstances. That is, if those four responses were indeed all about statecraft, the quotidian joy described by Zeng Dian can be seen as the result of commendable statecraft.

The other three aspirations all refer to varying aspects of civil life, and more importantly, there is an order of priority among them. In other words, in order to create a civil order within a state, first, as Zi Lu aspires, we must have a strong defensive army to secure peace among states; second, as Ran You says, people in the state must be economically well-off so that they can get access to culture and education; lastly, as Gong Xihua wills, there must be a system of social etiquette and cultural conventions so that people can interact each other in a ritually proper way. If all these preconditions are satisfied, the circumstance in a normal neighborhood can be created so that Zeng Dian and his younger human fellows can freely enjoy their quotidian life in an unhurried and restful way.[15]

Despite the fact that this purely circumstantial locus of Zeng Dian's joy has nothing to do with the transcendent dimension of life that "lies beyond shape," its underlying idea of political philosophy remains a matter of almost unchallengeable common sense among Ruist scholars. In general, to live a good, joyful private life in society, we need to have a peaceful, sufficiently wealthy, and orderly public life beforehand. This idea is clearly espoused by Kongzi when he proposes his two-step statecraft idea quoted above. We can also see this in the status of the civil examination as a major institutional engine of Ruism. The aspiration of contributing to such a civil foundation for people's daily happiness is universally shared by Ru learners.

Nevertheless, what stands out in later Ruists' discussions of *Analects* 11.25 is *not* this priority of circumstantial well-being. This is because for Ru to be dedicated to creating those civil preconditions for people's desirable, mundane lives, they must have already perceived that same sort of constant joy as that of Kongzi and Yan Hui, so that the state of their inner lives would not be affected by the unforeseeable fortunes or misfortunes which inevitably accompany their social and political endeavors. In other words, if not grounded in a deeper feeling of joy towards their ordinary lives, their pursuit of social activism would rather be driven by power, fame, or other external, selfish interests and, hence, would undermine the very foundation of Ruist statecraft. A classical Ruist text phrases this priority of a statesperson's self-cultivation over statecraft as "from the Son of Heaven (the emperor) to common people, we all should take the cultivation of self as the root."[16]

Because of this emphasis upon moral self-cultivation, the fact that Zeng Dian enjoys the ordinariness of everyday life can be interpreted in a very different way. Instead, the joy is seen as representing a way of human living whose quality surpasses the other three respondents', so that it can be taken as a foundation, rather than an expected result, of those social and political activities contributing to desirable civil life.

Therefore, the crucial question for us to understand the significance of Zeng Dian's joy for the Ru tradition is as follows: How is joy the foundation of good statecraft? Or, using the same terms once employed by Zhou Dunyi, whence does Zeng Dian derive his joy? As indicated by our above discussion, Ru thinkers' pondering over these questions is organized by the conceptual interplay between the extraordinary Dao (the Way) aspect of human living, termed as "what lies beyond shape," and the ordinary *qi* (utensil-like things) aspect, termed as "what lies within shape." If the purely circumstantial understanding of Zeng Dian's joy as an expected result of proper statecraft can be thought of as answering "how the world is for Zeng Dian's joy" when the world is understood in a "within shape" way, the next level of contemplation on the same question will have to view it from a "beyond shape" perspective.

THE ORIGINAL CIRCUMSTANCE:
HOW THE WORLD BEYOND SHAPE IS FOR US

According to those quoted Ru thinkers in the Song through Ming period, the reason that Zeng Dian, Kongzi, and Yan Hui were able to enjoy mundane moments of everyday life regardless of their personal fortunes is that they experienced the existential bond between their selves and the broadest circumstance that humans can ever conceive of: the eternally self-generating and evolving cosmos itself, which is termed Tian (天, cosmos).[17] As a result of this experience, while living and striving for the normal goals of life, these Ru succeed in finding their due position in the broadest realm of being, and thus, a constant feeling of joy—with its comprising affective nuances such as settlement (定), tranquility (静), contentedness (安), and vivacity (生意) — can arise to accompany all mundane moments of life.

A couple of verses from classical Ruism will suffice for us to empathize with this Ruist cosmic experience:

> Kongzi said, "What does Tian ever say? Yet the four seasons are put in motion by it, and the myriad creatures receive their life from it. What does Tian ever say?" (*Analects* 17.19)

> It is said in the *Book of Poetry*, "The hawks fly up to heaven; the fish leap in the deep." This expresses how this Dao is seen above and below. The Dao of an exemplary person may be found, in its simple elements, in the interaction of husband and wife; but in its utmost reaches, it shines brightly through heaven and earth.[18]

Tian is depicted here as an all-encompassing, constantly creative cosmic field from which all creatures are generated, each with a unique nature, while all are changing and evolving together. The essential feature of this cosmic field is characterized as "birth birth" (生生, *shengsheng*), or "creating creativity,"[19] and the all-encompassing togetherness of creatures is also frequently portrayed as the most sublime form of "dynamic harmony" (和, *he*).

Since Tian is where concrete, shaped things derive from, contemplation over the most generic features of this cosmic field will be, using the terms that we have introduced, to understand the Dao aspect of the world which is "beyond shape." Since Tian's creativity is always manifested in cosmic beings that have a shape, we can see that the cosmic power of Tian transcends, while simultaneously being immanent in all the world that is "within shape." In other words, it is an ontological commitment to the relationship between the original, root state (本體) of the world and its derived states that makes Ruists particularly favor the discourse on joy of Kongzi, Yan Hui, and Zeng Dian. It is also only when one experiences the unbroken bond between one's mundane life and the root state of the world that one can entertain the same transcendent feeling of joy while delving deeply into vivid moments of everyday life, just as Zhu Xi explained whence Zeng Dian derived his joy:

> The leisurely joy felt in Zeng Dian's heart vibrates together with all the myriad of things above and below, between heaven and earth. He perceives subtly the wonderous reality that each of these myriad things has its due position (in the cosmos), which is indescribable by human words.[20]

Despite the fact that devising a metaphysical ethics or ethical metaphysics by pondering the position of the human species within the entire realm of being is not unique to Ruism among the major spiritual traditions in East Asia, what is salient about the Ru tradition is that it admits both the unique nature of human beings vis-à-vis nonhuman beings, regarding our capacity of building an inclusive, co-thriving civilization, and the continuity between this human nature and the essential feature of the evolving cosmos.

Understood in this way, the Ruist ethical teaching that centers upon the cultivation of the virtue of "humaneness" (仁, *ren*) in varying human relationships, and the aforementioned Ruist political teaching that aims to create a sustainable civil order, both refer to the uniquely human activities that can manifest the harmonizing power of Tian in the human realm. This implies that the social activism entailed by the three aspirations of Zeng Dian's fellow students, if conducted properly, helps to realize the normative human nature whose ultimate origin is the process of "birth birth" of Tian's cosmic evolution. Because of this continuity of human nature with the broadest root state of the evolving cosmos, while commending Zeng Dian's joy as referring to an extremely high spiritual state of a Ru's self-cultivation,[21] Ruists would never downplay those human endeavors that are necessary to realizing this state in social activities conducive to a harmonious civilization. In other words, the joy of Zeng Dian, since it derives from a normative human nature which is endowed by the constantly creative power of Tian, strives for broadening its impact in the human realm and, thus, urges us to be dedicated to varying social endeavors to build a sustainable, humane civilization. We can find the connection between the spiritual joy of Zeng Dian and varying types of social activism through Zhu Xi's comment about the aforementioned broad and great cosmic Dao that makes "the hawks fly up to heaven; the fish leap in the deep":

> Many of those sages' sayings sound broad and great, but they all regathered themselves to pursue real and solid things. . . . Although they taught the original state of the world as such, they are solidly committed to the perfection of each thing whenever they are doing something, such as ritual and music, law and governance, culture and institution. All conceivable human affairs are about the original state of the world. Because the original state of the world reaches and completes everything, as long as some human affair has not been perfected, a piece of the original state will get lost.[22]

Quite obviously, a humanistic commitment to realizing what is transcendent in the immanent human world through human efforts can be taken as the major reason why, while facing Zeng Dian alone, Kongzi reemphasizes that those aspirations other than Zeng Dian's are all commendable.

Regarding the question of how the world is, such that an individual can feel a constant joy about his or her everyday life, Ruists will answer in two interrelated ways: if we are talking about the worldly preconditions that enable humans to enjoy their mundane life, we should be dedicated to creating a good civil order. If we are talking about a spiritual condition that designates a deeper dimension of life, we should realize the unbroken bond of human existence with the original state of the world and, furthermore, follow our uniquely human nature to manifest the ever-harmonizing and generating power of the cosmos in the human world.

JOY AS A PRIMER FOR ALL PROPER AFFECTIONS: HOW WE FEEL

Since the joy of Kongzi, Yan Hui, and Zeng Dian derives from the ontologically original state of the world as an ever-generative cosmic field and, hence,
refers to the broadest circumstance of human life, Wang Yangming (1472–
1529 CE) holds that "joy is the original state of the human heartmind" (樂是
心之本體).[23] The feeling of joy is different from emotions (情, qing). Kongzi,
Yan Hui, and Zeng Dian were joyful about the all-compassing, infinite,
cosmic whole that accommodates human individuals in each of their due
positions, while emotions arise from human reactions to concrete, finite life
situations and may or may not be appropriate.

Nevertheless, as entailed by the relationship between the transcendent
Dao and the immanent Qi discussed above, an ontological and spiritual
commitment to the cultivation of constant joy does not make Ruists disfa-
vor emotions. Quite the opposite: as long as emotions react appropriately,
with appropriateness understood here as being able to create harmonies
in evolving situations so as to realize the cosmic Dao in the human world,
they are thought of as desirable objectives for one's self-cultivation and,
thus, can be enjoyed as integral ingredients to the good life.

Two examples can illustrate Ruists' reflection on the relationship between
the constant spiritual joy and its derived mundane emotions: worry (憂, you)
and grief (哀, ai). We would not normally think that a worried or grieving
person can be simultaneously deeply joyful. However, Ruists think that we
can, so long as we are worried or grief-filled about the right things.

As indicated by the previous discussion on the original circumstance
of human life, whether the constantly harmonizing and generating power
of Tian can be realized in the human world in a uniquely humane way
depends upon human efforts. Kongzi once taught that "it is humans who
advance the Dao; it is not the Dao which advances humans."[24] In the same
way, when considering that the constant interaction of yin and yang vital
energies in the cosmos comprises the Dao that endows life and energy to
all creatures, the Appended Texts of the Classic of Change states that "Without human beings, Dao would not proceed automatically (in the human
world)."[25] These classical texts speak to the human responsibility of civiliz-
ing the human species so as to perpetuate the cosmic Dao.

This responsibility entails that a morally committed human would have to learn, deliberate, plan, experiment, and act on a daily basis so as to continually build and organize a functional society from its micro units of family and local community all the way up to the macro domain of states and all under the heavens. During this process, we would be regularly worrying about issues such as whether we have become learned enough, whether our plans were viable, or whether our human partners' interests were all treated with justice and balance. And this would mean that we should always be prepared for obstacles, failures, and even regrets, notwithstanding that we also try our best to overcome them. In a word, it is unavoidable for a morally motived human to be worried. The aspirations expressed by Zeng Dian's fellow students offer perfect examples, all of them referring to career planning and the necessary social and political preconditions of enjoyable mundane life.

Nevertheless, as Kongzi's affirmation of the value of these aspirations indicates, these worries are thought of as being just fine as long as they are directed to the right purpose and in an appropriate way. If we realize that the finitude of human beings entails that the emotion of worry cannot be eliminated from our life, then, when we try our best to fulfill the ultimate concern of human life, understood as "enlarging the cosmic Dao in the human realm," we can remain deeply joyful even when we have to be worried and concerned about mundane affairs. Crucially, Ru philosophers consistently distinguish between these appropriate worries and a different class of concerns of which we can and should rid ourselves. As Mengzi puts it, "An exemplary person has lifelong worries but not daily anxieties. The worries are like this: 'Shun was a person, and I am a person. Shun was a model for the whole world that could be passed down to future generations, yet I am still nothing more than an ordinary person.'"[26] Viewed in today's terms, if pursuits such as performing well in a job interview, acing a test, or making a good impression on a date lack moral motivation, the daily anxieties that accompany them are as nothing to an exemplary person. Instead, if these ordinary tasks contribute to the development of a moral and ultimately meaningful life, an exemplary person would joyfully worry over them.

This mood of humane and joyful worry, so to speak, is captured remarkably well by Zhang Zai (1022–1077 CE) when he comments about why even a sage, the perfect ideal of Ruist moral self-cultivation, still experiences the emotion of worry. Zhang Zai says:

> What Tian is capable of is [to impart] nature, while the deliberation and planning by human beings are what humans are capable of. A great person completes his or her human nature in a way that he or she would not take Tian's capability as human capacity. Instead, he or she would take deliberation and planning as what humans are genuinely capable of. In this sense, the *Classic of Change* teaches us "it is heaven and earth that sets up a position, while it is sages who complete the human capabilities."[27]

In other words, although the potential for planning and deliberation is imparted to the human species by Tian's cosmic evolution, it is still humans who determine whether to activate these potentials or not for serving a humane cause. Because of this, Zhang goes on to argue that

> the worry of a sage derives from her or his virtue of humaneness, whereas Tian cannot be said to have any emotion of worry whatsoever. Because it is sages who complete human capabilities, humans are different from heaven and earth [itself].[28]

Understood in this way, it would be the virtue of humaneness, which aims to enlarge the cosmic Dao in the human world, that enables a sage to be deeply joyful while simultaneously being rightfully worried.

Another emotion, grief, helps us to further understand why the spiritual joy of Kongzi, Yan Hui, and Zeng Dian can be taken as an existential primer of all proper human affections. Grief is normally understood as keen mental distress or suffering due to afflictions or loss, such as what one feels facing the loss of an immediate family member. Again, a grieving person would not normally be thought of as capable of being simultaneously joyful. However, according to Wang Yangming, this might indeed be the case. The following conversation between Wang Yangming and his student speaks to Wang's delicate view on this point:

> "[You taught us that] joy is the original state of human heartmind. However, when people's parents die, we will cry and grieve. Can we

still find joy here?" Master Wang answers: "[In this situation,] only after we have a loud cry, can we feel joyful. Without crying, we will not feel joy. [This also means that] while crying, our heartmind feels settled and peaceful. This is whence our joy derives. Therefore, the original state [of joy] has never been perturbed."[29]

In other words, as long as we grieve for the right cause and in an appropriate way, it manifests constant spiritual joy, rather than undermining it.

Actually, the relationship between the constant joy and appropriate worry and grief can extend to all emotions. According to the *Zhong Yong* (中庸, *Centrality and Commonality*), the state of human living to which the constant joy refers is named as being "centered," while the state in which varying emotions obtain their due measure is called "harmony": "When the emotions of happiness, anger, sorrow, and delight have not been aroused, this is called 'centered'; when these emotions are aroused and abide by their due measure, this is called 'harmony.' The state of being centered is the great root of all under the heavens, while the state of harmony is the extensive path for all under the heavens."[30] Since all emotions are essentially enjoyable once they are rooted in the constant spiritual joy of Kongzi, Yan Hui, and Zeng Dian, a *junzi* (君子, exemplary person)'s state of life is also depicted as: "a *junzi* is content wherever he or she goes."[31]

AGENCY AND CULTIVATING EFFORT 工夫: WHAT WE DO

According to our above discussion, the Ru tradition espouses the value of humanism and emphasizes the unique human responsibility of advancing the cosmic Dao in the human world. Therefore, apart from an ontological discourse about the original state of the changing world and how to theorize the world-human connection, the Ru tradition is dedicated to another practical discourse about what humans should do regarding the aforementioned responsibility. This practical discourse, which is termed the discourse on *gongfu* (工夫, cultivating effort), can be thought of as aiming for people's spiritual formation to achieve and maintain the joy of Kongzi, Yan Hui, and Zeng Dian in everyday life.

The Ru masters in the Song through Ming period developed detailed, interlocking theories and practices of *gongfu*, with some thinkers putting more emphasis on outward-focused practice while others stress inward-focused practice.[32] Virtually all Ruists of this era term the way that cosmic and human realities dynamically and harmoniously fit together as "Pattern" (理, Li). Some teachers, like Cheng Yi, argue that to realize the cosmically human joy of Kongzi, Yan Hui, and Zeng Dian, humans need to accumulatively learn Pattern as it is distinctively manifested in varying domains of human life, until eventually reaching the moment when one can envision the interconnection of all aspects of Pattern in the cosmos as an organic whole. At this moment one realizes how human nature is rooted in the Pattern of Tian, and by preserving this one entertains a constant feeling of joy in whatever concrete activities one needs to pursue.

According to Cheng Yi, there are three major kinds of cultivating efforts one can undertake in order to get a handle on Pattern:

> Underlying each thing or affair, there is a Pattern; in each case we need to completely investigate its Pattern. The ways of investigating Pattern are varying: we discuss and understand the meaning of texts when we read books; we dispute about famous persons in ancient and recent times, and hence, distinguish right and wrong; we react appropriately when we deal with varying human affairs. All of these are ways of investigating Pattern.[33]

Since on this account the process of rediscovering the ontological bond between the cosmos and humans, whence constant joy arises, is accumulative, we can view the approach to *gongfu* recommended by Cheng Yi as in some ways "externalist," requiring human agents to continually learn and abide by Pattern. In contrast, since the connection between humans and the cosmos is ontologically original, an alternative approach insists that the realization of it does not depend upon accumulative, externalist endeavors of knowing. Instead, according to thinkers like Wang Yangming, we should focus upon reaching our "good knowing" (致良知), an ability innate to the human heartmind that keeps human thoughts and deeds from straying away from the Pattern that is entailed by the original existential bond between humans and the cosmic Dao. In this sense, all those endeavors described by Cheng Yi are considered not as preconditions, but as stimuli of the realization of "good knowing" upon which the constant spiritual joy rests.

According to Wang Longxi (1498–1583 CE), an eminent student of Wang Yangming, there are three major ways to reach "good knowing" and, thus, to becoming aware of the ontological bond between humans and the cosmic Dao:

> An exemplary person's learning becomes praiseworthy only once they have achieved awareness (悟, wu). If the gate to awareness is not open, we have no way to confirm what has been learned. There are three ways someone might achieve awareness: some achieve it through words, some achieve it through quiet-sitting, and some achieve it through effort and practice amidst the changing circumstances of daily living.[34]

This path of cultivating efforts towards the realization of the constant spiritual joy is often understood to be more internalist and intuitive, though it is striking that here, too, reflection on words (i.e., texts) and attention to acting correctly in daily life both play roles, as they did for Cheng Yi. Indeed, although there were heated debates among the Song through Ming Ru masters, the disputants also shared a largely common set of ontological, spiritual, and moral commitments. Furthermore, many of the practical ways of spiritual and moral cultivation that they articulated were also common property (with various underlying understandings), such as devoted reading, quiet-sitting meditation, ritual performance, contemplating artworks such as painting and calligraphy, and so on.[35]

If we were to furnish our own reflection about these two paths of cultivating efforts, it would be as follows: Because the finite situations of human life are not ontologically severed from the infinite whole of the cosmos, a nonaccumulative, intuitive grasp of the original ontological bond should be the only viable account that we can give about how we can be aware of the bond upon which the good life, a life of constant joy, relies. However, as we discussed above, the ever-generative power of the cosmic Dao transcends, while simultaneously being immanent to, details of the mundane world. This implies that the vision of the good life of Kongzi, Yan Hui, and Zeng Dian, and the centrality of constant spiritual joy therein, requires us to return to mundane moments of everyday life and, thus, try our best to perpetuate the cosmic harmony of Tian in the human world. Further, this will unquestionably demand our grasp of the ways that Pattern pertains to varying life situations and, thus, urge us to continue to learn and act in order to pervade and enrich our deeply inspired spiritual joy within evolving life situations. In short, the Ruist path to the good life demands a subtle combination of both approaches, internal and external, to cultivating efforts towards the realization and maintaining of the constant spiritual joy of Kongzi, Yan Hui, and Zeng Dian.

AGENCY, JOY, AND THE STATE OF BEING 境界：WHERE WE LIVE

Another Ruist discourse that is closely related to "cultivating effort" focuses on *jingjie* (境界, state of being). The literal meaning of *jingjie* is a territory (境) with a boundary (界). However, for understanding Ruism, especially in its Song through Ming period, we need to realize that the term *jingjie* primarily refers to how the wholeness of the world appears to humans because of their varying spiritual inner statuses.[36] For example, facing the same bamboo tree, a scientist will perceive a plant which grows according to biological laws, while to a poetic eye, the tree may appear to be full of cosmic vital energies interconnected with humans so that the tree's aesthetic quality can be earnestly appreciated. In this way, despite living in the same physical world, the world, with its objective and nonmanipulable qualities, appears differently to the scientist and the poet. Thus, using the Ruist term *jingjie*, we can characterize these two perceivers as living in different *jingjie*. In English-language scholarship, *jingjie* is comparable to the "level" of human needs discussed by Abraham Maslow or the "dimensions" of human life theorized by Paul Tillich. Because *jingjie* designates the holistic awareness, feeling, or sense of a person towards his or her world, we prefer to translate *jingjie* as "state of being."

If the Ruist discourse on the original state of the world investigates the most generic, ontological traits of the evolving cosmos and the position of human beings within it, and the discourse on cultivating effort points out the practical paths of self-cultivation made possible by those ontological traits, then the significance of the discourse on the state of being consists in its illuminating the goal of self-cultivation. The world relates differently to us because of the varying efforts that we have made to better our life. In this sense, the discourse on the state of being is highly relevant to the central topic of the volume, since it concerns the degrees of desirability of varying types of the good life: the higher the *jingjie* in which one's life resides, the more desirable the goodness of his or her life is.

Inspired by terms used by the modern Ru philosopher, Feng Youlan (1895–1990 CE), in his work of "A Rediscovery of Humanity" (新原人), we would like to characterize the Ruist conceptions of the good life as referring to four different kinds of *jingjie* according to the above-quoted conversation between Kongzi, Zeng Dian, and the other students.

The *jingjie* that Zi Lu and Ran You's aspirations represent is a utilitarian state of being (功利境界). This is because these aspirations attend to the basic biological needs of the human species, such as physical security and economic prosperity. People living in this state of being will perceive the world as an exploitable resource for human flourishing, and therefore, the feeling of joy that they may consequentially entertain depends upon whether they secure maximal utilities from the worldly resource.

The *jingjie* which Gong Xihua's career path represents is a moral state of being (道德境界). This is because Gong Xihua's primal concern is to have humans interact with each other in a ritually proper way according to conventional moral standards. People dwelling in a moral state of being will be dedicated to coordinating people's biological needs for the sake of a functional society, and in this sense, the joy they may feel about their moral accomplishments depends less upon the limitedness of earthly resources and the resulting changeability of human fortunes. However, just as Gong Xihua's moral sense derives from his meticulous obedience to social conventions, people in a moral state of being have not yet found the ultimate origin of morality and thus cannot liberate their feeling of joy from preoccupation with social conventions.

The *jingjie* that Zeng Dian lives out during his late spring field trip along the river of Yi is a heaven-and-earth state of being (天地境界). People dwelling in this state of being will perceive the original existential bond of human beings with the constantly creating cosmos and, hence, obtain the ultimate power and meaning of life while living through its everyday mundane moments. Since these people connect to a source of human agency which is more original than moral conventions, their morality would not be realized in the form of a meticulous obedience to rules and customs. Instead, it will be out of one's freedom—with freedom understood here in the sense of "fulfilling one's human nature endowed by the cosmic Dao"—that they interact morally with their fellow humans and with all in the cosmos. Because of the realization of genuine freedom in the heaven-and-earth state of being, people's spiritual bearing in this state is typically depicted by Ru literature as "悠然" (restful and delightful), "灑脫" (easygoing), "從心所欲" (following the flow of one's desire), "無累" (not being restrained), and so on. As a consequence, the joy felt by people in this state of being can transcend fortunes and vicissitudes and, thus, show its resilience and sustainability in comparison to those depending on joys in the two aforementioned states.

Nevertheless, the heaven-and-earth state of being is still not the most desirable type of good life. This is because if people indulge themselves in the joy of Zeng Dian too much, they may risk slacking off on cultivating themselves diligently so as to fulfill their responsibility of realizing the cosmic Dao in the human world. As discussed before, the relationship between Tian and humans is intricate in Ruist metaphysics: on the one hand, the cosmic creativity of Tian transcends while remaining immanent in evolving cosmic occasions; on the other hand, whether Tian's creativity can be manifested in the human world in a uniquely humane way totally depends upon human endeavors. Therefore, despite the fact that the realization of the initial ontological bond between Tian and humans gives rise to the genuine freedom of human agents, the implementation of this freedom entails that we should be continually dedicated to learning, planning, deliberating, and acting so as to create more appropriate patterns of human sociality for establishing a sustainable and harmonious civilization. In this sense, the joy of Zeng Dian and its corresponding goodness of life may be said as "extremely high and bright," since it dwells in the heaven-and-earth state of being. However, the joy would not genuinely benefit the human world if it is not redirected to the normal paths of human agency, which, as represented by the other three aspirations, all aim to create preconditions for enjoyable everyday life.

Therefore, we would characterize the highest state of being for the good life as one of "centrality and normality" (中庸境界), which aims to bring the ultimate power and meaning of human life perceived in the heaven-and-earth state of being into all concrete and evolving mundane situations of everyday life. In this sense, a genuinely joyful person would not only appear to be "restful," "easygoing," and "not restrained." She or he should also be "cautious and reverent" (謹敬) and enjoy a lifestyle which appears to be "normal and ordinary" (平常). Using the words of the *Zhong Yong*, the highest state of being for humans' good life can be termed as "Standing Extremely High and Bright, yet on a Central and Normal Path,"[37] which could well serve as an alternative title of this chapter.

Conclusion

In this chapter, we focus on the conversation between Kongzi, Zeng Dian, and his other students, as well as related texts on the joy of Kongzi and Yan Hui in the *Analects*, to parse out the Ruist understanding of joy and the good life. While responding to the tripartite hypothesis of the good life, we incorporate three Ruist categories of discourse into our discussion. In order to clarify the broadest circumstance of human life, that is, how the world is for us, we need to introduce the Ruist metaphysics on the "original state" (本體) of the world. While explaining what we should do as human agents to achieve and maintain constant joy and a desirable good life, we need to adopt the Ruist discourse on "cultivating effort" (工夫). Furthermore, the goal of self-cultivation is thought of by the Ru tradition in a discourse of "state of being" (境界). Correspondingly, the relationship between the constant spiritual joy and other proper affections should also be reconsidered as being ontological and depending practically upon our cultivating efforts. If we need to use one concise statement to generalize the Ruist understanding of joy and the good life, we would say: for a Ruist, to live a joyful good human life is to know the original state of the world (識本體), to make efforts to cultivate oneself (做工夫), and to reach one's due state of being (達境界).

Recommended Primary Texts

Chan Wing-Tsit. *A Source Book in Chinese Philosophy*. Princeton, N.J.: Princeton University Press, 1963.

Hagen, Kurtis, and Steve Coutinho, trans. *Philosophers of the Warring States: A Sourcebook in Chinese Philosophy*. Peterborough, Ontario: Broadview Press, 2018.

Hutton, Eric L., trans. *Xunzi: The Complete Text*. Princeton, N.J.: Princeton University Press, 2016.

Ivanhoe, Philip J., and Bryan W. Van Norden. *Readings in Classical Chinese Philosophy*. 2nd ed. Indianapolis: Hackett, 2005.

Johnston, Ian, and Wang Ping, trans. *Daxue & Zhongyong (English and Taiwanese Chinese Edition)*. Hong Kong: Chinese University Press, 2012.

Slingerland, Edward. *Confucius Analects with Selections from Traditional Commentaries*. Indianapolis: Hackett, 2003.

Tiwald, Justin, and Bryan W. Van Norden, eds. *Readings in Later Chinese Philosophy: Han to the 20th Century*. Indianapolis: Hackett, 2014.

Van Norden, Bryan W., trans. *Mengzi: With Selections from Traditional Commentaries*. Indianapolis: Hackett, 2008.

Wang, Yangming. *Instructions for Practical Living and Other Neo-Confucian Writing*. Translated by Wing-tsit Chan. New York: Columbia University Press, 1963.

Zhu, Xi, and Lü Zuqian. *Reflections on Things at Hand: The Neo-Confucian Anthology*. Translated by Wing-tsit Chan. New York: Columbia University Press, 1967.

Zhu, Xi. *Zhu Xi Selected Writings*. Translated and edited by Philip J. Ivanhoe. New York: Oxford University Press, 2019.

Notes

1   An explanation of the history on the nomenclature of "Confucianism" vis-à-vis the "Ru" tradition can be found in Tony Swain, *Confucianism in China: An Introduction* (London: Bloomsbury, 2017), 3–22, and Anna Sun, *Confucianism as a World Religion: Contested Histories and Contemporary Realities* (Princeton, N.J.: Princeton University Press, 2013), 45–76. In this chapter, "Confucianism" will be written as "Ruism" or the "Ru tradition," and "Confucian" or "Confucianist" will be written as "Ru" or "Ruist." When used as a noun, the plural of "Ru" or "Ruist" is "Ru" or "Ruists."

2   Examples are "The Achievements of Ru" (儒效) in the *Xunzi* and "The Deeds of Ru" (儒行) in the *Classic of Rites*.

3   Alternative translations could be "etiquettes" or "civilities." This chapter employs the term "ritual" in its broad, Ruist sense.

4   We are summarizing many centuries of historical changes here; our description applies most accurately to the later dynasties of imperial China, beginning around 1000 CE.

5 The tripartite hypothesis concerns the circumstances, the affective dimension, and the practical or agential aspect of the good life; for more details, see this volume's introduction.

6 Cheng Hao 程顥 and Cheng Yi 程頤, *Works of Cheng Brothers* 二程集 (Beijing: Zhong Hua Shu Ju, 1981), 16. If not specified, translations of Ruist texts in this chapter will be our own.

7 The *Analects* 6.3. Passage numbering of the *Analects* follows Edward Slingerland, *Confucius Analects with Selections from Traditional Commentaries* (Indianapolis: Hackett Publishing Company, 2003). All translations are our own.

8 A classical account of Kongzi's biography is available from the chapter of the "The Great Family of Kongzi" in Sima Qian's *Records of the Grand Historian*. For an English translation, see Burton Watson, trans., *Records of the Grand Historian of China* (New York: Columbia University Press, 1961).

9 See *Analects* 10.8, 7:14, 10.6, 10.13, and other related verses.

10 All these vocabulary originally derive from the *Appended Texts of the Classic of Change* 易經 繫辭, such as "what lies beyond shape is called Dao, and what lies within shape is called a utensil-like thing" (Wang Bi 王弼, Han Kangbo 韩康伯, and Kong Yingda 孔穎达, *Commentaries on Thirteen Classics: the Rectified Meaning of Zhou Yi* 十三经注疏 周易 正义, [Beijing: Beijing Da Xue Chu Ban She, 1999], 292). We will have a more detailed analysis of this text below.

11 *Analects* 11.26.

12 About the order of seniority among these four students, please see Cheng Shude 程樹德, *Collected Commentaries on the Analects* 論語集釋 (Beijing: Zhong Hua Shu Ju, 1990), 797.

13 See *Analects* 13.21.

14 Zhu Xi 四書章句集注, in *Complete Works of Master Zhu* 朱子全書, vol. 6 (Shanghai: Shanghai Gu Ji Chu Ban She, 2002), 165.

15 An example of this reading can be found at Zhang Lüxiang 張履祥 (1611–1674 CE), *A Memorandum* 備忘錄, which is quoted by Cheng, *Collected Commentaries*, 816.

16 Compare Wing-Tsit Chan, trans., "The Great Learning," in *A Source Book in Chinese Philosophy* (Princeton, N.J.: Princeton University Press, 1963), 87.

17 See Stephen C. Angle, "Tian (天) as Cosmos in Zhu Xi's Neo-Confucianism," *Dao: A Journal of Comparative Philosophy* 17, no. 2 (2018): 169–85.

18 Compare Chan, trans., "Centrality and Commonality," in *Source Book in Chinese Philosophy*, 100.

19 As the *Appended Texts* of the *Classic of Change* says, "Birth and Birth, this is called change," in Wang, Han, and Kong, *Commentaries on Thirteen Classics*, 271.

20 Zhu Xi, *Complete Works*, 6:165.

21 The use of "spiritual" in the context of Zeng Dian's joy is not premised upon any ontological conception about the existence of spirits or ghosts. Rather, it refers broadly and vaguely to the pervading cosmic context in which Zeng Dian's joy is ultimately rooted.

22 Zhu Xi, *Complete Works*, 16:2070.

23 A discussion of this statement will be detailed in the following.

24 *Analects* 15.29.

25 Wang, Han, and Kong, *Commentaries on Thirteen Classics*, 316.

26 Mengzi 4B:28. Shun 舜 was an ancient legendary sage-king before the time of Kongzi and Mengzi.

27 Zhang Zai, *Collected Works of Zhang Zai* 張載集 (Beijing: Zhong Hua Shu Ju, 2008), 21.

28 Zhang, *Collected Works*, 189. "Heaven and earth" here refer to the nature of the nonhuman world.

29 Wang Yangming, *Complete Works of Wang Shouren* 王守仁全集 (Shanghai: Shang Hai Gu Ji Chu Ban She, 2006), 112.

30 Chan, *Source Book in Chinese Philosophy*, 97.

31 Chan, *Source Book in Chinese Philosophy*, 101.

32 Historians sometimes use categories like "Cheng-Zhu school of Pattern (理學)" and the "Lu-Wang school of heartmind (心學)" to refer to these different approaches, but such reductionist categories are historically and conceptually misleading; see Stephen C. Angle and Justin Tiwald, *Neo-Confucianism: A Philosophical Introduction* (Oxford: Polity, 2017), ch. 1.

33 Cheng and Cheng, *Works of Cheng Brothers*, 188.

34 Wang Longxi, *A Complete Work of Master Wang Longxi* 王龍溪先生全集, Kuai Ji Mo Shi 會稽莫氏: 道光2年 (1822), vol. 17, 卷十七, available online at https://ctext.org/library.pl?if=en&res=88271. For Wang Longxi, what one needs to be aware of in *wu* and in one's good knowing are the same. Therefore, we translate *wu* as "awareness" in this context. Alternative translations of *wu* include "awakening" or "enlightenment."

35 See Angle and Tiwald, *Neo-Confucianism*, ch. 7 for more details and references.

36 About the use of *jingjie* in the intellectual history of Chinese thought, as well as its cases in Song through Ming Ruism, please see Fu Changzhen 付长珍, *The Discourse of Jingjie in Song Ruism* 宋儒境界论 (Shanghai: Shanghai San Lian Shu Dian, 2008), 24–32.

37 Chan, "Centrality and Commonality," 110.

4

A Jewish Vision

Yonatan Y. Brafman and Alan Mittleman

The principal code of Jewish law, the sixteenth-century Shulḥan Arukh, begins with the following charge: "a person should strengthen himself like a lion to arise in the morning to serve his Creator." From one's first moment of wakefulness until one falls asleep, one should be focused on the infinite ways one should serve the Infinite One. One serves, ideally, with a lion's courage, with a will determined to overcome all opposition, and with a firm cognitive grasp on the inherited, authoritative ways the tradition fleshes out the meaning of serving God.

In this chapter, we consider this core conception of the good life in Judaism: *human flourishing as service to God through fidelity to God's covenant and its commandments (mitzvot)*. This conception derives from the Bible, where it coexists with other ideas of human flourishing that we will consider briefly below. It becomes dominant after the destruction of the Temple in 70 CE in the Judaism of the rabbinic leaders of the Jewish people whose interpretations set the tone for all subsequent Judaism. It remains alive in all variants of Judaism today, from the most traditional to the most acculturated. As we unpack the meanings of "service to God" and "fidelity to covenant and commandments," we aim not only to describe but to advocate for this vision, if not in its full traditional version at least in a contemporary philosophically attuned form. We will not claim that it is better than the visions of other traditions but only that it has its virtues and is rationally defensible. It is, at least for Jews, choice-worthy.

It will be useful to explicate Jewish ideas of human flourishing by reference to three criteria: the role of agency in realizing a good life, the real-world circumstances in which agents find themselves and to which they must adapt, and the place of feelings—the affective dimension of human experience—by which human beings sense whether life is "going well" or not.[1] A number of questions immediately arise: Who has agency in the Jewish core conception? Does Judaism focus primarily on individuals and their efforts to live good lives, on the Jewish people in its entirety, or, in a rich way, on both? Are the circumstances in which agents operate primarily personal or collective? That is, how much weight should be given to the historical vicissitudes of the Jewish people and how much to the individual's situation? Finally, what role does joy (*simḥah*), the key affective component of the good life, play in Judaism? Is joy possible, given historical vicissitudes such as exile and persecution? How is the joy individuals sometimes achieve related to the joy (or joylessness) of the Jewish people? Given that people have an innate capacity for feelings such as joy, satisfaction, contentment, etcetera, how does "religious" joy relate to spontaneous, "natural" joy? Another question, perhaps peculiar to Judaism, is also salient. The Bible commands that Jews, in serving God on the festivals, experience joy. How is that possible? Can joy be *commanded*? These questions find their answers in Judaism's holistic vision of a good life. Individual and community, the personal and the public, the present and the imagined past, and the full complex range of human cognition and emotion are all brought together in the life of service to God.

AGENCY

Animals—at least some of them—have desires and pursue goals. Higher animals might have thoughts about the objects of their desires, perhaps even making choices among which objects to pursue. They can sometimes figure out how to overcome obstacles to the fulfillment of their desires, that is, they can navigate the constraints imposed by circumstances. But can they be said to have agency? Perhaps not. *Agency implies a mind capable of reflection.* If an animal desires food and food is present, the animal will do what it can to get the food. If a human being desires food and food is available, the human being might rush, like the famished Esau to get the "mess of porridge" (Gen 25:29–34), but even when seized by hunger, human beings think about what they are doing. In the biblical example, Esau accedes to Jacob's request that he forfeit his rights as the firstborn son in exchange for Jacob's lentil stew, which he craves. "I am at the point of death," Esau reflects, "so what use is my birthright to me?" This is what agency (although not wisdom) looks like. For human beings, at least, agency involves self-awareness, reflection on not merely the fact of desire, but the meaning and weight of desire, the significance of desire x vis-à-vis desire y, the place of the desiring dimension of oneself in the overall project of one's life. Agency, especially as it grows robust, is the dimension in which we experience freedom from animalistic desire through the critical incorporation of desire into the lifelong cultivation of selfhood. Agency is more than a matter of fulfilling desires and harnessing reason to assist. It is a fundamental part of living what we hope to be worthy, flourishing lives.[2]

Agency figures prominently in biblical approaches to the good life. In the wisdom literature (a genre of biblical works that includes Proverbs and Ecclesiastes, among others), with its universalizing, practical, rather "secular" tone, human beings are responsible for determining how they want their lives to go, sizing up their situations, pursuing their self-interest; attaining worldly success through having a large family, wealth, and a successful position in the royal court; and for feeling satisfaction in their accomplishments. In this literature, attaining the good life is not mysterious; it requires discipline, "wisdom," and some luck. Although thoughtful, wisdom is somewhat naïve.[3] Its confidence is subjected to devastating criticism in the Book of Job, where the protagonist, although he has done everything right, finds that his life has gone horribly wrong. The bond between agency and outcome, wisdom and desert has been shattered. In rabbinic Judaism, practical wisdom is transformed into moral reflection on the ideals of character and conduct that contribute to human flourishing.

In the priestly conception of human flourishing, most prominently on display in Leviticus, the good life has to do with punctilious ritual performance in the presence of the Holy God. Divine holiness is understood in quasiphysical terms as an energetic, potentially quite dangerous presence, which abides in the wilderness shrine or, later, in the Jerusalem Temple. The presence can only abide in a ritually clean, pure place. Extreme care is required to keep the place—and the Israelite people—suitable for divine visitation. Human flourishing, on this view, has to do with dwelling in the presence of God, with living in a realm where divine power radiates outward from a cultic site into a holy (separated, pure) people and land. It is the responsibility of, first, the priests to guard the holy place and ensure the ongoing connection with its divine resident and, second, the entire people to bring sacrifices to God. This requires intensely focused agency. Purity is both possible to achieve and impossible to maintain. Sacrifices and other rituals are needed to overcome inevitable accretions of impurity. With the destruction of the First Temple (in 587 BCE by the Babylonians) and then the Second (in 70 CE by the Romans), the priestly conception of flourishing is assimilated into rabbinic Judaism. Its archaic idea of holiness shifts into a moral and legal register where Jews, both as individuals and as a people, pursue holiness through ritual and ethical commitments that set them apart from non-Jews and help them to serve God.

The conception on which we will focus—the one that emphasizes divine service through fidelity to the covenant and its commandments—is most securely rooted in Deuteronomy. Its most well-known expression, which became the pivotal part of the daily liturgy (the Shema), is Deuteronomy 6:4–9:

> Hear (Shema), O Israel! The LORD is our God, the LORD alone. You shall love the LORD your God with all your heart and with all your soul and with all your might. Take to heart these instructions with which I charge you this day. Impress them upon your children. Recite them when you lie down and when you get up. Bind them as a sign on your hand and let them serve as a symbol on your forehead, inscribe them on the doorposts of your house and on your gates. (translations from the New Jewish Publication Society version, 1985)

After a "metaphysical" declaration of the uniqueness of God, the Israelites are told to *do* something, namely, to love God in a holistic way, with heart, soul, and strength. This commandment represents a robust picture of agency. Doing involves cognitive and affective dimensions. One must believe something—that God is "one" or unique—and one must respond to that putative fact with love. The love should be fulsome, unstinting, filled with devotion, even to the point of self-sacrifice. One should bring one's children into the circle of lovers—the covenantal community. One should deepen one's awareness of the Beloved by daily ritual practices—reciting biblical words, binding them to arm and forehead, fixing them to the portal of one's home.

The commanding verbs are all in the singular and, indeed, address the individual whose agency is required. But the subject of the commandments is also the Jewish people. The people have entered into a covenant, a binding agreement of love and loyalty between God and a portion of humanity. The collective covenantal bond is only possible because individuals, through their representatives, agreed to enter into it. God made an offer of protection and solicitude to a group and awaited a thoughtful, voluntary response from agents who were at liberty to consider God's proposal:

> The LORD called to him [Moses] from the mountain, saying, "Thus shall you say to the house of Jacob and declare to the children of Israel: 'You have seen what I did to the Egyptians, how I bore you on eagles' wings and brought you to Me. Now then, if you will obey Me faithfully and keep My covenant, you shall be My treasured possession among all the peoples. Indeed, all the earth is Mine, but you shall be to Me a kingdom of priests and a holy nation.' These are the words that you shall speak to the children of Israel." Moses came and summoned the elders of the people and put before them all that the LORD had commanded him. All the people answered as one, saying, "All that the LORD has spoken we will do!" And Moses brought back the people's words to the LORD. (Exod 19:3–8)

Although the people might have weighed the pros and cons of the offer, fully exercising their rational agency, they did not. But other peoples, according to the ancient rabbinic interpretation known as *midrash*, did. The midrash pictures God as going from people to people offering them the covenant (Sifre Devarim para. 343). Each people asks what is in it and, finding the requirements onerous (What? We can't kill, fornicate, or steal?!?), rejects it. Israel is presented as jumping at the chance without full deliberation, thereby showing its keenness and ardor. The absence of deliberation in the biblical text, marked as a virtue by the midrash, does not undercut the role of agency, however. The people had recently experienced God's deliverance from slavery in Egypt and miraculous rescue from Egyptian pursuit. God reminds them that he brought them out on "eagles' wings." Hesitation and bean counting, under these circumstances, would have been mean and unworthy.

The biblical text, in its descriptions of committing to the covenant, stresses the freedom of human beings to accept or reject God's offer of fidelity. On acceptance, loyalty—the exclusivity of love—becomes mutual. The basic idea of Israel as God's covenant partner underwrites the Jewish people's strong sense of uniqueness. Judaism comes to believe that God loves them passionately, not to the exclusion of other nations, but in a peculiarly intense way. (Other nations may also enter into relationships of fidelity with God. The idea of the "covenant of the sons of Noah" is how rabbinic thought deals with the question of what a flourishing life for non-Jews is like. We return to this in the conclusion.) Frequent defection on the part of Israel from equally passionate love of God causes divine censure and rebuke. The prophet Hosea, for one, constructs the relationship between the covenant partners as a marriage in which Israel, through its worship of other gods, becomes as if a prostitute, abandoning her husband for other lovers. Once committed to God through covenant, no divorce is possible, or defection permitted. Israel remains free, but only free to love or free to sin, with horrendous consequences if she chooses the latter course. Here, then, we get a sense of what the command to love God means. It refers less to an emotional state or feeling—although it includes them—than to practices that manifest devotion and care. Negatively, it means not worshipping other gods. Positively, it means serving God daily through actions constitutive of the covenant, such as worship (through prayer, not sacrifice), honest dealing, charity, respect toward others, refraining from "unfit" food, honoring God in public through upright behavior, and much else. We will focus much more on how feelings can be commanded in our treatment of joy below.

The entire project of Judaism, as it were, rests on assumptions of robust human agency. Matters incontestably beyond human control can remain in God's hands, but responsibility is expected of us within our own personal and public sphere: "Concealed acts concern the LORD our God; but with overt acts, it is for us and our children ever to apply all the provisions of this Teaching [Torah]" (Deut 29:28). The degree of control that classical Judaism expects us to have over our own lives is more than many moderns, beset by concerns of genetic, neuroscientific, and psychological or sociocultural determinism, would allow. Is Judaism's tendency to heighten the scope and power of human agency defensible? Does it have a realistic assessment of the constraints on agency and a plausible response to them? The premier medieval biblical commentator, Rabbi Shlomo Yitzḥaki (Rashi), suggests an answer. Addressing the verse above, in which we are told to love God with all our heart, soul, and might, Rashi observes that the Hebrew term for heart (*levav*) is somewhat anomalous. "Heart" is ordinarily spelled in Hebrew with one "v" (*lev*); why does the Bible double the letter in this verse? Rashi alludes to the ancient rabbinic teaching that there are two contrary impulses that pull at the human heart, the "good inclination" and the "evil inclination." The doubled "v" is a reference to this: we should serve God with both our good and our evil inclination. He doesn't say that we should vanquish our evil inclination, but that we should direct it—in an intentional, agential way—to loving service of God. That view, in philosophical terms, is a version of compatibilism.

In the face of deterministic pressure, we win a measure of freedom of will, full human agency, by integrating our desires into a consciously chosen project of life. Leaving the biological or metaphysical underpinnings of human action to God, so to speak, human beings themselves retain responsibility for how well they make use of whatever freedom they have. One of our principal challenges is to work toward integration of all the elements of our rational and emotional lives, developing a coherent selfhood oriented toward the ideals and values we deem worthy. Judaism offers a complex of ideals and values worthy of a lifetime's focus. Its literary sources are cognizant of the obstacles, internal and external, that impede their realization. That goes to the realism, indeed, the excellence of the Judaic vision of the good life, in our view.

CIRCUMSTANCES

Judaism takes the circumstantial dimension of human life seriously. It will not do to insist dogmatically that the social, historical, political, or economic conditions that impinge on a person's agency don't ultimately matter. The American myth of rugged individuals who, by dint of grit and strength of will, "pull themselves up by their own bootstraps" regardless of humble origins is self-serving if not disingenuous. There is an exaggerated focus on the strength and status of individuals here. As robust as Judaism's conception of agency is, it is not dismissive of the severe constraints that circumstances can impose—especially if they are products of injustice. Judaism's "master narrative" is the Exodus. Israel as a people on the stage of history, rather than as an extended kinship group, was forged in Egypt under conditions of maximum humiliation and subjugation. The intolerable circumstances of slavery were not just miserable for the individuals involved, severely constraining their opportunities for flourishing. They were a stain on humanity; an historic injustice that called for rectification.

When Moses goes to Pharaoh to demand the liberation of his people, he speaks not in the name of individual or human rights—that is not the Bible's conceptual vocabulary—but in terms of God's expectations for Israel: Israel is My first-born son. I have said to you, "Let My son go that he may worship [literally, serve] Me" (Exod 4:22–23). Human flourishing under slavery is not possible, because men and women are forced to serve a false master; they are not free to serve their ultimate master, who seeks their good and in service to whom they find their own good. Israel is the servant of God and can truthfully serve no other (Lev 25:55). It is significant that the liberty God wants for the people is a covenantal liberty, a "fettered freedom," in which their task will be to serve the Ultimate by building a society that rejects the false absolutes and dehumanizing practices of Egypt. In Isaiah Berlin's language, the covenantal liberty the Exodus enables is both "freedom from" and "freedom to."[4] It is freedom from oppression and its endless humiliations, but it is also freedom to fulfill a higher project than individual liberty, full stop. Berlin finds a whiff of totalitarianism in this, as if societies should not have substantive ideals or normative ends.

The Exodus story is a token of the moral seriousness of Judaism. The subject of the flourishing life must not be just the individual, taken in isolation. Contemplative depth, mystical transcendence, and wrestling with the ontic limitations imposed by the human condition as such (finitude, mortality, etc.) are not disallowed, but they are not the heart of the matter. Judaism has worldly concerns. Indeed, the Torah provides a framework for the governance of a complete society. Its legislation ranges from the laws of marriage and divorce to property damage, personal injury, and murder, and on to judicial process, punishment, and the conduct of warfare. The

Talmud develops these laws, harmonizing them and filling in their gaps. By the medieval period, Maimonides can present them in his great code, the Mishneh Torah—literally the restatement of the Torah—as a comprehensive philosophical, legal, and political scheme. Maimonides begins with the foundations of belief, proper character traits, and modes of worship. He then covers the full range of Jewish law, concluding with the laws of courts and kings. Although Maimonides is strongly influenced by Aristotle's approach to eudaimonia (the good life or human flourishing), as a Jewish thinker he sets the project of individual flourishing within that of building a good society.

A good many of the Torah's social, political, and economic injunctions are motivated by the oppression of the Israelites in Egypt. Based on their firsthand experience of suffering, injustice—the insult to human dignity visible on every page of history—is intolerable. It must be addressed. Their ultimate rectification awaits a messianic age in which the Torah's vision for a redeemed society can be fully realized. But although the work is great, we "are not free to desist from it" (Pirke Avot 2:21). Agency directed toward the amelioration of objective circumstances is, as the modern Jewish thinkers Hermann Cohen and Emmanuel Levinas put it, an "infinite task." The possibility of despair in the face of what might seem like a Sisyphean task was already limned by the prophet Jeremiah, who, writing to the exiles in Babylonia, told them to "build houses and live in them, plant gardens and eat their fruit. Take wives and beget sons and daughters . . . And seek the welfare of the city to which I [God] exiled you and pray to the LORD in its behalf; for in its prosperity, you shall prosper" (Jer 29:4–7). Judaism is a religion of hope, which reinforces agency despite circumstances that threaten to diminish or negate it.[5]

Individual circumstances vary endlessly, but Judaism urges that Jews integrate their life stories into the story of their people. "Do not separate yourself from the community" (Pirke Avot 2:5) is the watchword of a small, scattered, and beleaguered people. But it is also a sound bit of wisdom for enabling human flourishing. We are, as the philosopher Alasdair MacIntyre put it, "dependent, rational animals." We need one another; our flourishing is unthinkable without webs of love, support, affirmation, assistance, and mutuality. "Either companionship or death," the Talmud asserts, emphasizing the radical need for human togetherness (B. Ta'anit 23a). The Talmud cautions against those who would sit in their own homes eating and drinking while the community suffers calamity; calamity will catch up with them, their illusion of self-sufficiency notwithstanding (B. Ta'anit 11a). Indeed, the identification of one Jew with another is also transgenerational. The participants in the ritual narration of the Exodus story during the holiday of Passover exclaim that "in each generation, each person is obligated to see himself or herself as though he or she personally came forth from Egypt."

For the past two millennia, until the founding of the State of Israel in 1948 and continuing in some sense even afterwards, Jews characterized their collective circumstances as Exile (*galut*). Exposed to the depredations of hostile nations, their ancient state and thus a worldly political context for fully enacting divine law destroyed, their Temple—the site of the divine presence—in ruins, they struggled with how to make sense of catastrophe—with how to continue to love and serve God. We do not wish to explore questions of theodicy at this point, since space and focus do not permit. Rather, our concern is to understand how this long-enduring circumstance shaped the affective dimension of Jewish life. True, they followed Jeremiah's advice and worked to build good lives in a far-flung diaspora, but was joy possible under conditions of exile, oppression, and injustice? The emerging rabbinic leadership of the post-Destruction Jewish people thought long and hard about this question. Accordingly, we turn to the next criterion of the Judaic vision of the good life, the rabbinic idea of the "joy of the commandments."

THE AFFECTIVE DIMENSION: JOY

The etymology of the main term in biblical Hebrew for joy (*simḥah*) neatly brings together ideas of agency, affect, and human flourishing. Philologists postulate that the proto-Semitic ancestor of *simḥah* had the root meanings "to grow or flourish," "to shine," and "to rejoice." There is a conceptual connection embedded in the semantic range among flourishing (especially with respect to the verdant growth of plants), radiance (with respect to vitality and its manifestation in appearance), and joy. At the level of etymology, the Hebrew language itself attests to the integral role that joy plays in flourishing.[6]

The Pentateuch contains eleven texts that command the Israelites to "rejoice before the Lord" on the festivals.[7] This raises the question as to how an emotion could be commanded. In most of these texts, however, it is not the emotion as such that is commanded but rather *ritual actions* that support an emotional state.

"Rejoicing before the Lord" involves bringing a sacrifice, having it slaughtered, and eating it communally with family and others. As the Talmud (B. Pesaḥim 109a) later says, "Joy means nothing other than eating meat." The emphasis of the texts is not on commanding an emotion as such, but on commanding an action. This is within the capacity of the agent to achieve. Doing something leads, the Bible assumes, to feeling something. The behavioral-ritual complex makes emotions such as joy likely. Yet *both* ritual and emotion, doing and feeling, are important. The ritual act is not merely instrumental; it has value in and of itself as a mitzvah, a way of serving God.

The upshot of this is that joy, on the most authoritative biblical view, is not only or primarily an "inner state" facilitated by an outer, behavioral performance. From a modern point of view, nourished by the Romantic and Christian antinomian traditions, the inner is higher than the outer. Biblical religion and subsequent Judaism, however, see a whole. Both "spirit" and "flesh," love and law are necessary for a comprehensively flourishing life. In the biblical context, the sacrifice and communal meal on the festivals constitute rejoicing in a *normative, legal sense*. Rejoicing becomes a legal category, a mitzvah, to be fulfilled by appropriate ritual behavior and complemented by appropriate feelings. One should feel joy, but also gratitude, love, and satisfaction in that one has been blessed by God with sufficient means to give something precious back to God in thanksgiving. The ritual complex engenders a sphere where holiness feels palpable; where one feels the presence of God. Individuals participate in this numinous order, but it is also society-sustaining. Public rituals, sacred times and places, as students of religion know, play crucial roles in maintaining meaningful, cohesive group life. Sustaining the world of ritual, both within biblical Israel and, after the destruction of the Temple and the sacrificial system, in formative Judaism, was fundamental to the survival of the Jewish people. Indeed, we cannot see how continued Jewish survival is possible without fidelity to the basic practices stemming from the ancient covenant as reconstructed by rabbinic Judaism.

How was joy possible after the destruction of the Temple? Destruction and exile cast a long pall over the prospects for joy in formative Judaism. Neither individuals nor the whole people could bring sacrifices. The rabbis reinterpreted the commandment to rejoice on festivals by substituting the drinking of wine for the eating of sacrificial meat:

> It was taught . . . that Rabbi Yehuda ben Beteira says: When the Temple was standing, rejoicing (*simḥah*) was only through the eating of sacrificial meat, as it is stated: "And you shall rejoice before the Lord your God" (Deut 27:7). Now that the Temple is no longer standing, and one cannot eat sacrificial meat, he can fulfill the mitzvah of rejoicing on a Festival only by drinking wine, as it is stated: "And wine gladdens (*yisamaḥ*) the heart of man" (Psalm 104:15). (B. Pesaḥim 109a)

Drinking four cups of wine during the Passover ritual meal (*seder*)—a well-known custom in which the majority of Jews participate today—discharges the obligation to rejoice on the festival, as does sanctifying the festivals through a ritual declaration over wine. Other biblical practices that constituted rejoicing, such as anointing with oil, wearing festal clothing on holidays, having sexual relations with one's spouse, especially under the marriage canopy, and verbally praising God, continued into postexilic times. Nonetheless, the absence of the Temple and the impossibility of sacrifice and communal feasting raised haunting questions as to the *propriety* of joyousness. The search for the proper place and role for joy in Judaism remained salient.

Rejoicing in the legal sense, thanks to rabbinic interpretation, remained possible. But was joy in the complementary, emotional sense permitted under conditions of exile and persecution? This became a serious question for rabbinic Judaism. What should human flourishing mean in times of distress? Is there something out of joint or morally erroneous about seeking joy when one's people is immiserated? How much of the fullness of life is it right to seek? If Judaism were simply a path of individual spirituality, these questions might not have arisen. But insofar as Judaism describes the spiritual path of a nation, the questions became pressing for Jewish leadership.

The rabbis held on to joy and all that it implies for the imperative of cultivating a full, flourishing life, but they focused it on service to God through fidelity to God's commandments. They were wary of ordinary joy, of the kind urged by the author of Ecclesiastes, for whom joy is found in "the humble pleasures that sustain life amidst its struggles: eating, drinking, working, sleeping, being with one's beloved (Eccl 2:24–26; 3:12–13, 22; 5:17–19; 7:14; 8:15; 9:7–10; 11:7–12:1)."[8] In the wisdom tradition, which Ecclesiastes exemplifies, because so much of human life is beyond human control, opportunities for joy—which are given by God—must be seized and enjoyed.[9] The rabbis pivoted away from this outlook and developed the concept of *simḥah shel mitzvah*: the joy of the commandment(s). They give joy, the native disposition of human emotional life, which Ecclesiastes celebrates, a religious intention and a Jewish specificity. Joy is related to the performance of the commandments. One should perform the *mitzvot* joyously, that is, willingly and happily—not mechanically, glumly, or for ulterior motives.[10] Serving God through responding to the Covenant Partner's will should be a joyous affair. The Jewish daily prayer book affirms, early in the statutory morning service, "Happy are we; how good is our portion; how pleasant is our destiny; how beautiful is our inheritance. Happy are we who rise early and go to sleep late so that we can recite the Shema every day!" If it is beyond one's present cognitive and emotional grasp to feel joy in the performance of commandments, one can grow into it through continued exertion.[11]

One can—indeed, as an agent one *ought* to—develop virtuous habits and a second nature. Responding to God with love and joy, spontaneously and unstintingly, is part of personal development. It is also an acculturation into the norms of Jewish civilization. The process civilizes. It puts in place a form of life that builds on but replaces a "natural" life, a life untutored by the Torah. Ordering one's desires, feelings, and intentions toward fulfilling the commandments is a commitment to virtues such as patience, fortitude, dedication, loyalty, and love. It elevates and integrates the natural proclivities of the soul toward holistic excellence. It is a form of life that would be recognizable, in its formal properties, to Aristotle.

To return to the rabbinic concept of the "joy of the commandments," what does it include and exclude? That is, what do the rabbis take to exemplify Jewish "religious" joy? What remains of naïve, natural joy? Is it excluded by the rabbinic focus on the commandments, as well as by the dark times in which exilic Jews lived? As to what the joy of the commandments includes, the rabbis claim that biblical prophecy only occurred if the prophet was in a mood of joyous receptivity:

> [T]he Divine Presence rests [upon an individual] neither through gloom, nor through sloth, nor through frivolity, nor through levity, nor through talk, nor through idle chatter, but rather through a matter of joy associated with a commandment [*davar simhah shel mitzvah*] . . . Rabbi Judah said: And so too for a matter of *halakha* [Jewish law]. (B. Shabbat 30b)

Closeness to God, exemplified by prophetic inspiration, is only possible with joy. Given that condition, study and prayer—rabbinic vehicles for experiencing the presence of God—are likewise only possible in a state of joy. As Rabbi Judah claims, encounter with God's word, the Torah, especially with the study of its normative dimensions, which rabbinic Judaism praises above almost all else, requires a state of profound joy.

This is also true of prayer: "Our Rabbis taught: One should not stand up to pray while immersed in sorrow, or idleness, or laughter, or chatter, or frivolity, or idle talk, but only with the joy of the commandment [*simhah shel mitzvah*]" (B. Berakhot 31a). While there are times of anguish when one must pour out one's heart in prayer, the normal, daily condition should be one of joy. For "happy are we who rise early and go to sleep late to recite the Shema."

The above text makes a clear division not just between joy and sorrow but between joy and its natural cousins. Laughter and levity are ephemeral. They need to be oriented toward true joy, which is coordinate with, paradoxically, seriousness. The joy of prayer must coexist with sobriety and awe. The Mishnah (B. Berakhot 5:1) rules categorically, "One may only stand up to pray in a serious frame of mind [*koved rosh*]." How can this be reconciled with joy?

> [S]aid Rabbi Nahman ben Isaac: We learn it from here: "Serve the Lord with fear and rejoice with trembling (Ps 2:11)." What is meant by "rejoice with trembling"?—Rabbi Adda ben Mattena said in the name of Rav: In the place where there is rejoicing there should also be trembling. (B. Berakhot 30b)

Apparently, joy and seriousness should condition one another. The serious frame of mind required for prayer should be tempered by rejoicing. Rejoicing should be of the proper sort, however: cognizant of its holy purpose. Prayer is both an occasion for joy ("the place where there is rejoicing") and of seriousness and awe ("there should also be trembling"). The moral psychology of the rabbis is not simplistic.

Given the affective complexity of the joy of the commandments, the Talmud discourages or prohibits *excessive* joy (*badah tuva*). Joy is a necessary component of the good life, but in pre-messianic times at least, it has its limits. Excessive joy of a frivolous kind undermines seriousness. But circumstances matter. If one is wearing phylacteries, excessive joy is permissible. On the other hand, excessive joy is prohibited at weddings, even though they are religiously significant occasions. Rashi suggests a rationale for this distinction. Excessive joy is permitted while wearing phylacteries because, given the content of the scrolls they contain, "they are a testament to the rule and service of [the] Creator." That awareness, he assumes, weighs upon the wearer and keeps joy tied to seriousness. Excessive joy at a wedding, in contrast, is not accompanied by a similar testament and is therefore prohibited.[12] The problem with excessive joy is that it is liable to overwhelm awareness of the sovereignty of God. Excessive joy would displace seriousness and awe rather than be held in balance with them.

This rabbinic effort to reinterpret, channel, and facilitate joy notwithstanding, doubts remain in rabbinic literature about the degree to which it is possible in an age of exile. Perhaps circumstances undermine both joy and the good life, our best efforts notwithstanding. The Talmud records a statement of Rabbi Yoḥanan in the name of Rabbi Simeon bar Yoḥai:

> It is forbidden to a man to fill his mouth with laughter in this world, because it says, "Then will our mouth be filled with laughter and our tongue with singing" (Ps 126:2). When will that be? At the time when "they shall say among the nations, the Lord hath done great things with these [the Jews]" (Ps 126:2).[13]

In this opinion, not until the Jewish people are redeemed from exile is it permissible to fill one's mouth with laughter. Until then, joy is suspect. Midrash Tanḥuma states "Once Jerusalem was destroyed, 'All gladness is obscured;

the joy of the whole earth had departed.'"[14] Correspondingly, Midrash Zutra records the radical statement by Rabbi Joshua bar Ḥaninah that "since the day that the Temple and Jerusalem were destroyed there is no joy for the Holy Blessed One until Jerusalem is rebuilt and Israel is returned to it."[15] In a recollection of bygone rejoicing in the Temple during the Feast of Booths, the Mishnah (Sukkah 5:1), which was codified after the destruction, states simply but poignantly, "Anyone who has never seen the rejoicing at the place of [water] drawing [a ritual on the last days of the festival], has never seen rejoicing in all his days." The message to its readers is that they have never experienced true joy.

For all of this agonizing about whether joy, and by implication human flourishing, is possible in a hostile world, the need to fulfill the commandment to rejoice precluded giving way to despair. The joy of the commandments saved the possibility of joy. The Talmud states:

> Our Rabbis taught: A man is obligated to make his children and his household rejoice on a Festival, for it is said, "And you shall rejoice on your festival, [you and your son, and your daughter, etc.]" (Deut 16:14). With what does he make them rejoice? With wine. R. Judah said: Men with what is suitable for them, and women with what is suitable for them. "Men with what is suitable for them": with wine. And women with what? R. Joseph teaches: in Babylonia, with colored garments; in the Land of Israel, with ironed linen garments.[16]

The obligation for the individual to rejoice rescues him or her from the threat of despondency and orients him or her toward a duty to help others rejoice. Maimonides amplifies this. Following rabbinic precedent, he rules that it is obligatory to rejoice on the festival and that, although this originally involved offering sacrifices in the Temple, it may be fulfilled in the home. Men should eat meat and drink wine; they should also cause the members of their family—women and children—to rejoice by giving them appropriate gifts. Moreover, they should bring joy to others outside of their household. Indeed, Maimonides links the commandment of rejoicing on the festivals with the requirement that joy should have practical, moral, and affective consequences. In "Laws of the Festivals," he writes,

> And while one eats and drinks himself, it is his duty to feed the stranger, the orphan, the widow, and other poor and unfortunate people, for he who locks the door to his courtyard and eats and drinks with his wife and family, without giving anything to eat and drink to the poor and the bitter in soul—his meal is not rejoicing in a divine commandment (*simḥat mitzvah*), but a rejoicing in his own stomach. (6:18)

Despite its material expressions, rejoicing on the festival must be oriented toward the fulfillment of God's commandments. Indeed, in distinguishing such joy from excessive or extreme expressions of folly, he describes it as "the kind of rejoicing which partakes of the worship of the Creator of all things" (6:20). This entails that it cannot be focused solely on the self but must be extended to include one's family and the poor. Proper joy must overflow; it must cause others to rejoice. By doing so, one practices virtues such as liberality. Further, one models the graciousness and generosity of God, the ultimate exemplar of virtue. We are to "walk in the ways" of the One "who is good and does good."

Conclusion: Criticisms and Responses

Judaism, we have maintained, presents an account of human flourishing as service to God through fidelity to God's covenant and its commandments. This agential expression of its view of the good life applies both to the individual Jew and to the Jewish people. As such, its circumstantial condition is not limited to the situation of individuals. For the principal Jewish version of the good life to be fully achievable, the people must be able to order its collective life according to the social, legal, and political framework of the Torah and to draw near to God at the Jerusalem Temple. Only then can true joy, the affective expression of the good life, be fully experienced. Prior to the Messianic Age, this side of redemption, joy can be experienced only intermittently, but still significantly, during the performance of the commandments and especially in the celebration of the festivals.

Regarding the Jewish account of human flourishing offered here, several objections suggest themselves. First is a charge of irrationality: many of the commandments, for example the prohibition of wearing a garment composed of wool and linen, seem to have no discernible reason and thus no role in the promotion of the good life; acting according to them would thus seem to be irrational. Second is the related charge of heteronomy: performance of the commandments, especially if they are not supported by reasons, seems to be indistinguishable from blind obedience. Freedom, an important component of many other accounts of human flourishing, appears to be lacking from the Jewish vision. Third is the charge of monomania. Following Susan Wolf's criticism of "moral saints," individuals solely concerned with fulfilling their moral duty, Judaism's focus on service to God might prevent the pursuit and cultivation of other human goods, like intellectual knowledge, artistic virtuosity, or even exemplary friendship.[17] Last is the charge of particularism: given the centrality of God's covenant with the Jewish people, it could be argued that Judaism fails to offer an account of *human* flourishing. Indeed, it leaves most of humankind without any guidance as to how to lead a life worth living.

These objections are neither new nor alien to Judaism. They express certain problematics that arise due to the structure of its account of human flourishing, and so there is already an existing and continuous tradition of reflection and argument about them. Indeed, much of their force is dispelled when the implications of the account we have offered are appreciated. First, conceiving of the commandments as the expression of a covenantal relationship between the Jewish People and God that realizes human flourishing already sets them in a context in which their performance can be rationally understood and reflectively endorsed. They can be seen, not as motivated by a bare intention to serve an arbitrary God, but as diverse ways in which God and the Jewish people work to express the intimacy of their relationship and, ultimately, to perfect humanity.

Despite both Christian and Enlightenment caricatures, the Jewish people have seldom understood themselves to be obeying senseless commandments. Indeed, there is a tradition of reflection on the "reasons for the commandments" (*ta'amei ha-mitzvot*), which originated in classical rabbinical literature, fully developed as a domain of inquiry in medieval Jewish philosophy and mysticism, and continues into the present. The commandments have been variously understood as a means for reinforcing philosophical knowledge, inculcating ethical virtues and even hygienic techniques, and (in mysticism) affecting the internal dynamics of divine life. These diverse accounts cannot be reconciled with each other, and many of them do not merit endorsement by contemporary Jews; they rely on dubious metaphysics, offer outdated medical recommendations, promote objectionable visions of moral character, or just fail to rationalize the commandments. Yet, their existence attests to the commitment that the commandments, and thus their practice, admit of rational endorsement. Although some of these accounts fail, some merit further attention. Maimonides' sweeping adaptation of the commandments to an Aristotelian virtue ethics has become timely, given the rebirth of virtue-oriented ethics in the last few decades.[18]

Abstracting from their details, accounts of the reasons for the commandments often share an important structural similarity. Based on a biblical verse (Lev 18:4), rabbinic literature (*Sifra,* Lev 18:4, para. 140) draws a distinction between two different types of commandments: statutes (*hukkim*) and ordinances (*mishpatim*). Ordinances are those commandments whose purposes are apparent, such as the prohibitions of murder and idolatry, the prescription to establish courts of justice, or the duty to thank God for the undeserved blessing of life. Statutes are those commandments whose purposes are opaque, such as the prohibition of, again, wearing garments made of wool and linen or the prescription of ritual slaughter. Crucially, the tradition rarely maintained that the statutes have no reason whatsoever. The statutes instead are usually connected with Jewish historical experience or with divine ends, which transcend but do not contradict human reason. Indeed, the distinction between ordinances and statutes is a way of articulating the dialectic between human philosophical and ethical commonality and Jewish religious distinctiveness, between, as it is often labeled, universalism and particularism. The commandments are understood to include and supplement the conditions for universal human flourishing.

Based on an appreciation of the prevalence and structure of accounts of the reasons for the commandments, a response to the charge of heteronomy becomes available. If, as the general and Jewish philosopher Emil Fackenheim argued, autonomy requires that each individual create his or her own moral code, then of course Judaism is heteronomous, but so are most moral systems and religious traditions. Rather, autonomy should be understood only to require that each individual could reflectively endorse those norms to which he or she is committed. The project of providing reasons for the commandments should then be understood as transforming obedience into freedom. This entails showing how everyone has reason to acknowledge the ordinances and how the Jewish people have reason to accept the statutes. The particularity of the statutes infringes neither on their rationality nor on the acceptance of them with autonomy.[19] They represent what makes sense for the Jewish people to do, in view of the Jews' specific history and relationship with God. To insist that all norms and practices must be evaluated at the bar of abstract reason is an imperialistic universalism. Indeed, we suggest that it is one of the strengths of the Jewish view of human flourishing that it articulates both the norms that every human society should acknowledge and promulgates determinate laws for the Jewish people.

This feature of the Jewish tradition is expressed most fully in the Noahide Laws, which, the contemporary Jewish philosopher David Novak argues, express a form of Jewish natural law. While the ordinances are those commandments that everyone can acknowledge as reasonable, a subset of seven of them, the Noahide Laws, are understood by the rabbis to *apply* to everyone. As articulated in the rabbinic tradition, they include prohibitions on idolatry, blasphemy, murder, theft, sexual immorality, eating flesh torn from a living animal, and the prescription to establish courts of justice.[20] They can be understood more abstractly as the Jewish view on the minimal conditions for any society to make human life possible and thus serve as preconditions for human flourishing.

This multilevel normative structure responds to the last two charges. Judaism does not demand that the individual be exclusively focused on service to God, because the commandments are not solely focused on that end; they have a variety of purposes. Some are universal moral principles, others are specific legal or political determinations, and still others express, commemorate, and teach about the Jewish experience in history and relationship with the divine. And these too are diverse: the joy of the festivals is different from the despair of mourning; even the love expected and cultivated in marriage diverges from the loving-kindness mandated toward fellow Jews. Despite the polemics of the modern Jewish thinker Yeshayahu Leibowitz, the performance of these commandments need not be accompanied by the bare intention to serve God. Indeed, as we have illustrated in the context of the festivals, to do so would be to neglect a crucial component of their performance—joy. The Jewish tradition is better represented by his contemporary Joseph Soloveitchik, for whom experiential commandments, those whose performance should be accompanied by various emotional states, are central. In this view, Judaism does not require the sacrifice of all goods to the austere demands of God; but rather, sanctifies these goods, in their proper season, through the divine-human relationship.

Lastly, Judaism does not neglect the universal human good in favor of the particular good of the Jewish people. First, any individual who desires to enter the covenant with God and is willing to accept the commandments upon himself or herself is admitted into the Jewish people. But historically Judaism neither demanded nor sought converts, precisely because it did not see itself as the *sole* means of human flourishing. Instead, through the idea of the Noahide Laws, it developed minimal standards for any human society while leaving those societies the normative freedom to develop their own specific political, legal, and religious laws in view of their experiences in history and relationship with the divine. This combination of universalism and particularism is another attractive feature of the Jewish vision of the good life. For it articulates the substantive goods of Jewish life—individual and communal service to God through fidelity to the covenant and its commandments—as well as standards necessary for any plausible approach to human flourishing.

Jewish reflections on agency, circumstance, and affect, although originating thousands of years ago in biblical thought, display a kind of modernity. The autonomy of the individual agent, who is nonetheless embedded in a communal world that should be continuously striving to achieve a good society despite historical vicissitudes; the endorsement of a life rich in human connections, solidarity, and emotional experience; the orientation toward larger purpose, toward transcendence—these ideals have not been obliterated by our secular age. They still draw people toward the Jewish way of life, the Jewish path toward human flourishing.

Notes

1   These criteria track those of Aristotle in assessing the characteristics of a
     well-lived life. See Anthony Kenny, *What I Believe* (London: Continuum,
     2006), 151. Kenny, commenting on Aristotle's conception of eudaimonia,
     stresses three elements, which correspond roughly to the threefold ana-
     lytic framework used in this chapter: contentment (the affective state of
     happiness), welfare (the quality of one's objective circumstances), and
     dignity (the agency to exercise control over one's situation).

2   Harry G. Frankfurt, *The Reasons of Love* (Princeton, N.J.: Princeton Uni-
     versity Press, 2004), 18–21.

3   For scholarly perspectives on the good life in biblical, especially Wis-
     dom literature, see Brent A. Strawn, ed., *The Bible and the Pursuit of
     Happiness* (New York: Oxford University Press, 2012), 117–35; and
     Hava Tirosh-Samuelson, *Happiness in Premodern Judaism: Virtue,
     Knowledge, and Well-Being* (Cincinnati, Ohio: Hebrew Union College
     Press, 2003), 55–100.

4   Isaiah Berlin, *Two Concepts of Liberty* (Oxford: Clarendon Press, 1958).

5   On the role of hope as a support for agency, see Adrienne Martin, *How
     We Hope* (Princeton, N.J.: Princeton University Press, 2016). For a study
     of the dynamics of hope in Judaism, see Alan Mittleman, *Hope in a Dem-
     ocratic Age* (Oxford: Oxford University Press, 2009).

6   Akkadian *šamāḫu* has all three of these meanings. Hebrew *s-m-ḫ* has
     "shine" and "rejoice." The sense of "grow" or "flourish" comes from a
     related root, *ṣ-m-ḫ*. For a review of the literature, see Gary A. Ander-
     son, *A Time to Mourn, A Time to Dance: The Expression of Grief and Joy
     in Israelite Religion* (State College: Pennsylvania State University Press,
     1991), 51–53. See also Alan Cooper, "III. Joy: Judaism," in *Encyclope-
     dia of the Bible and Its Reception*, vol. 14 (Boston: Walter de Gruyter,
     2016), 823–24; and Yochanan Muffs, *Love & Joy: Law, Language, and
     Religion in Ancient Israel* (New York: Jewish Theological Seminary of
     America, 1992), 122; 144–45.

7   Lev 23:40; Num 10:10; Deut 12:7, 12, 18; 14:26; 16:11, 14, 15; 26:11; 27:7.
     For analysis, see Anderson, *Time to Mourn*, 18–26.

8   Eunny Lee, "Joy: I. Hebrew Bible/Old Testament," in *Encyclopedia of the
     Bible and Its Reception*, vol. 14 (Boston: Walter de Gruyter, 2016), 819.

9   Lee, "Joy," 819.

10 On the joy that should accompany the performance of the command-
    ments, see B. Berakhot 31a. Significantly, this Talmudic citation distin-
    guishes the required joyfulness not only from sadness and distractedness
    but from frivolity and levity. Joy is more elevated, like bliss, than those
    affective states.

11 The Talmud states that if one performs a mitzvah in a less than whole-
    hearted way, one will, through ongoing practice, come to perform it for
    the right reasons; see B. Pesaḥim 50b.

12 B. Berakhot 30b, Rashi (ad loc.), s.v. *tefilin menihana.*

13 B. Berakhot 31a.

14 Midrash Tanḥuma (Buber), Parshat Pekudei 8, citing Isaiah 51:3.

15 Midrash Zutra (Buber), Lamentations 1:7.

16 B. Pesaḥim 109a.

17 See Susan Wolf, "Moral Saints," *Journal of Philosophy* 79, no. 8 (1982):
    419–39.

18 For a study of the history of Jewish ethics, including the construal of the
    commandments as a mode of ethical practice directed toward human
    flourishing, see Alan Mittleman, *A Short History of Jewish Ethics: Con-
    duct and Character in the Context of Covenant* (Chichester: Wiley
    Blackwell, 2012).

19 A fine study of the role of autonomy in Jewish moral and legal thought is
    Kenneth Seeskin, *Autonomy in Jewish Philosophy* (New York: Cambridge
    University Press, 2009).

20 See David Novak, *The Image of the Non-Jew in Judaism: The Idea of
    Noahide Law*, 2nd ed. (Oxford: Littman Library of Jewish Civilization,
    2011).

5

A Christian Vision

Matthew Croasmun, Ryan McAnnally-Linz, and Miroslav Volf

Dreams are rarely modest. The dreams you have for your life inevitably spill over its boundaries. If you dream of working a particular job, as an engineer or a baker or lawyer or a teacher, you are also dreaming of clients, ingredients, a whole legal system, or students and a school. Dream of a home, and you will find yourself inevitably dreaming of some combination of neighborhood, geography, a physical structure, things both comforting and useful, and, crucially, other *people* inside and outside the home that make it what it is. Hope for joy, and you will find that joy, too, is woven into the tapestry of a *world* over which it would be right to rejoice.[1]

When we dream a life, we dream a world.

And so, for Christians, a vision of flourishing life is not a vision of any one life, but rather a vision of a whole world fully flourishing. Jesus called this world the "kingdom of God," the world as God would have it be. But to evoke a world as God would want it is not so much to answer the question of the shape of flourishing life but to restate it in a theological register. What kind of world would fully reflect the rule and reign of God, after all? Jesus was always a bit indirect about this. He offered a number of parables—the kingdom of God is like a mustard seed, he would say, or treasure hidden in a field or a measure of yeast—but these are more evocative than definitive.

The ancient traveling preacher, Saint Paul (we'll just call him "Paul"), who along with Saint John was the most seminal thinker in the entire Christian history, did dare to offer what we might call a "definition" of the kingdom of God. It comes in the midst of a letter he wrote to the early churches in Rome, trying to help them sort out their priorities. They are in danger, Paul thinks, of placing too much weight on a minor question about what food they should or should not eat. In response, Paul advises them to allow a variety of different eating practices in their community: "For the kingdom of God is not food and drink but righteousness and peace and joy in the Holy Spirit" (Rom 14:17, NRSV here and below).

Flourishing life is righteousness, peace, and joy in the Holy Spirit. It is not merely about the *means* of life—food, drink, money, safety, health, and the like. Flourishing includes these things, but it orients them toward life led well (righteousness), life going well (peace), and life feeling as it should (joy).

We will consider each of these in turn to try to get a sense of how Paul imagines flourishing life in each of its aspects. But first we need to attend to a major problem. If fully flourishing life is possible only in a fully flourishing world, what hope do we have to live in such a world? Or to put it another way: Suppose we could describe in every detail the shape of flourishing life; why should we suppose that we could live such a life? Like most Christians, Paul tells a rather extraordinary story about the world—a big, cosmic Story of Everything—that offers nuanced answers to these questions.[2]

THE STORY OF EVERYTHING

The whole arc of Paul's Story of Everything is grounded in love. God is love.[3] God creates out of love. God intends us to imitate God's love. God redeems for the sake of love. God draws all things together in a world of perfect love. Love is the thread that holds the whole story together (1 Cor 13:13). Love is the foundation of all things. Love is the goal at which all things aim. Love is what is lost and betrayed when we live as we ought not. Love is the possibility of the good that nevertheless lies at hand even in the midst of injustice, deprivation, pain, and loss (Rom 8:39).

Creation: The World Is a Gift

Paul's story begins at the very Beginning of all things, when God creates the world (Gen 1–2). Flourishing is possible, first of all, because God is good, and the world God created is good. "The earth and its fullness are the Lord's," Paul declares in the words of the spiritual poetry of his people, the Jewish people (1 Cor 10:26, Ps 24:1). He also writes, "Ever since the creation of the world God's eternal power and divine nature, invisible though they are, have been seen and understood through the things God has made" (Rom 1:20). The created world reveals the very nature of God.

When it comes to God's nature, most important for Paul is that God is a giver of good gifts. The creation is such a gift—the first and foundational good gift. But God did not stop giving good gifts once the creation was established. God keeps (and will always keep) giving them.

As a result, for Paul, the fundamental character of flourishing life, when and where it is possible, is that of a *gift*. We don't achieve flourishing life. We receive it as a gift. The main way Paul talks about this is by using the language of *grace*, to which we will return in a moment.

This "economy of grace"—a whole way of thinking about the world in which the best things are not achieved, but rather received as gifts—can be quite disorienting for those of us who are used to valuing things in proportion to how hard we had to work to get them.[4] Understanding Paul's vision of flourishing life may entail changing how we think about *gifts* versus *earnings*. For Paul, gifts are better and richer sources of joy than anything we earn. (Plus, Paul's pretty pessimistic about what exactly we've *earned* in life; "What do you have that you did not receive?" he asks rhetorically and expects the answer to be "nothing." Moreover, our sin [about which, more below] "earns" us death; that we receive better is by virtue of God's grace.)

Now, God created the world good, but God did not create it *mature*.[5] Creation's goodness still needs to grow and unfurl in order to fully flourish. In the meantime, there's something inevitably "partial" about life in this world (1 Cor 13:9). The goodness of this world is still growing, still developing, still on its way. There's a time coming when the world will be complete, but that's the End of the story, and we're not there yet. In the meantime, whatever we experience of flourishing life here and now points to a yet greater fulfillment in a world of perfect love. This fact ought both to restrain Christian enthusiasm for plans to build social utopias in the present but also to deepen Christian appreciation for the goodness of the present creation, which is not only good in itself but also abounding with foretastes of the perfect world to come.[6]

Fall: The World Is Broken

The possibilities of flourishing life, however, are not just constrained in the here and now because God's good creation is maturing. Left to our own devices, flourishing life is largely out of reach because of what Paul calls *sin*.

We sin. All of us. Created to receive and express God's love, we fall short in both respects. We do not know ourselves as loved by God. And we do not love as God loves. In fact, in Paul's language, we make ourselves God's enemies (Rom 5:10) and enemies of the creation God loves.

Created to act as agents within the created order, we misuse our agency. Intended to care for the creation, we dominate and destroy it. Intended to love one another, we cheat each other instead. We lie. We seek our own interest at the expense of others. Created to honor one another's bodies, we instead use them for our own purposes. Created to honor one another's agency, we abuse the agency of others. We oppress people; we make it impossible for them to flourish as agents.

As a result, we suffer at one another's hands. The consequences of our misuse of our *agency* become the *circumstances* of the lives of others. When we fail to *lead* our lives well, life *goes* poorly for others. Of course, these cycles of sin and suffering don't unfold uniformly. Some perpetrate more violence, and some suffer more of it. Paul is concerned to attend to these disparities. But he also insists that all of us are caught up together in this dynamic. Wrong begets wrong.[7]

It's not just that we sin; it's that we are "addicted" to sin. Paul describes vividly what it is like to live within this addiction. "I do not understand my own actions," he says (Rom 7:15a). "I can will what is right, but I cannot do it. For I do not do the good I want, but the evil I do not want is what I do. Now if I do what I do not want, it is no longer I that do it, but sin that dwells within me." (Rom 7:18b–20) It's not just that we sin, but rather that we are under sin's dominion. We are dominated by sin. Sometimes it seems like we should use a capital letter when naming it: *Sin*, a power who often seems to act in our place. Left unchecked, Sin dominates our individual and social lives (Rom 6:12). Our sinful attitudes, decisions, and actions give rise to unjust social structures. Those social structures constrain our individual lives, reenforcing the same thoughts and behaviors that buttress unjust ideologies, practices, and institutions. The cycle is self-perpetuating.[8]

As a result, Sin, even more than the immaturity of a good creation still on its way to full flourishing, severely limits the possibilities of flourishing life here and now. Simply put, because of Sin, flourishing life is not possible for us in the here and now.

Redemption: A New World Is Coming to Be in Christ

And yet, despite our enmity, God nevertheless pursues us in love (Rom 5:6, 10). For Paul, it is especially important that we understand that God pursues the creation in love through the ways God relates to *the people of God*, the Jewish people. God's purposes for the flourishing of the whole world begin with and have always to do with the Jewish people. God reveals Godself to the Jewish people. God gives the Jewish people laws by which they might flourish in the midst of a broken world, bearing witness to a world yet to come. The story of this self-revelation of God, God's laws, the stories of a people living by and living in rebellion against these laws, the poetry of these people, the voices of prophets calling the people back to the laws of God by which they might flourish—all these are contained in the Hebrew Bible, Paul's holy scriptures (Christians' "Old Testament"). Most importantly for Paul, the Hebrew scriptures point to a king through whom God's rule and reign (the kingdom of God) will come to be established.

Paul believes that Jesus of Nazareth is that promised king—the "anointed one," in Paul's Greek, "the Christ" (Rom 1:1–4). Jesus established the long-awaited kingdom of God in an unexpected way. By exercise of Divine power, Jesus did what we—even the best of us—cannot do (Rom 8:3–4): Jesus lived a flourishing life in this world that is not yet fulfilled and still under the sway of Sin. Most centrally, Jesus *led* his life well. His was a life of love, an expression of Divine love in a human life the likes of which the world had never seen.

Living a flourishing life in a world like ours had consequences. Jesus' flourishing life was met with lethal opposition from sinful people and from the systems of Sin in the context of which he lived (chiefly, the Roman Empire). But, Paul insists, God raised Jesus from the dead, vindicating his life as the life toward which the whole creation has been and is now oriented. All this, Paul insists, is plain from the Hebrew Bible, at least once you know what to look for. This story is what Paul preached in the churches he started across the ancient Eastern Mediterranean: "For I handed on to you as of first importance what I in turn had received: that Christ died for our sins in accordance with the scriptures, and that he was buried, and that he was raised on the third day in accordance with the scriptures" (1 Cor 15:3–4).

Now, because lives spill over into worlds, and Jesus' life was something genuinely new compared to the Sin-stricken world he entered, Jesus' life, death, and resurrection create a new world (2 Cor 5:17). If our sinful lives, inevitably shaped by the unjust systems within which we live, end up reenforcing those same systems, Jesus' life does just the opposite. Jesus' life of love inaugurates a new world of love—God's kingdom.

This world is "new" in two senses. First, it is new in the sense of being quite different than the world as dominated by Sin. It is "renewed," reformed from the deformation, the distortions, that sin brought about in God's good creation. Second, it is new in the sense of being the presence of that perfect, mature creation at which God's original good creation was always aimed.

Thinking of the life of Jesus as bringing a "new creation" helps Paul make sense of the ways that the flourishing life Jesus offers to us often runs deeply counter to the way the world as we know it works. God's wisdom ends up looking like foolishness to us. God's strength looks like weakness. The cross—the instrument of imperial death upon which Jesus died—captures both. The cross appeared to be foolishness and weakness—the failure of Jesus' mission to inaugurate a world of love. But, in fact, the cross is God's strength and wisdom—both in the sense of embodying God's enduring commitment to love in the face of violent opposition, and in that God vindicated Jesus' commitment to love in raising Jesus from the dead (1 Cor 1:18–25).

The new world coming to be in Christ means that flourishing life is possible for us in ways it would not be otherwise in a world dominated by Sin. Jesus offers his life to us so that we can participate in his flourishing life by sharing in his Spirit (1 Cor 6:17). Paul's language mirrors the way he described participation in sin: "it is no longer I who live, but it is Christ who lives in me. And the life I now live in the flesh I live by faith in the Son of God, who loved me and gave himself for me" (Gal 2:20). The indwelling Spirit of Christ animates the Christian, making possible a new way of life.

All of this, Paul says, is a gift. We didn't earn it. It's a matter of grace. Christ lived and died for our sake, in order to make possible the flourishing life for the sake of which God created the world. Paul puts it this way: "For while we were still weak, at the right time Christ died for the ungodly. Indeed, rarely will anyone die for a righteous person—though perhaps for a good person someone might actually dare to die. But God proves his love for us in that while we still were sinners Christ died for us" (Rom 5:6–8). The possibility of flourishing life is a gift.

And this is perhaps one of the most distinctive features of Paul's account of flourishing life. Strictly speaking, flourishing *is not possible* for us on our own. We don't *achieve* flourishing life; we *receive* it as a free gift from God. Inasmuch as flourishing life includes—indeed, in some ways, is *centered* in—our agency, that life will transform and include our agency. So, Paul can seem to talk out of both sides of his mouth about *whose* work it is when it comes to leading our lives well. "Work out your own salvation with fear and trembling," Paul advises one church community, "for it is God who is at work in you, enabling you both to will and to work for [God's] good pleasure" (Phil 2:12b–13). But however we make sense of this interworking of human and Divine agency, the simple fact for Paul remains: what was impossible for us is now possible—as a gift (grace), received from Christ, and still limited by the constraints of a not-yet-fulfilled world still profoundly shaped by Sin.

Consummation: All Things Will Be Summed Up in Love

But there remains one more crucial movement in Paul's Story of Everything: the End. In the end, love remains (1 Cor 13:13). The whole creation is transformed into a world of perfect love, glorious and free from decay. Paul writes, "The creation itself will be set free from its bondage to decay and will obtain the freedom of the glory of the children of God" (Rom 8:21). Freedom from decay means no more war, no more strife—and no more death (1 Cor 15:26, 54–56). The world of perfect love is a world of reconciled relationships— across dividing lines of ethnicity, class, and gender (Gal 3:28) and between God and the creation itself. In the end, the world is suffused with God's presence; God is "all in all" (1 Cor 15:28).

To be sure, there is something new about this world of perfect love. It is different from the world as we know it. It's got a different shape, a different "form," as Paul calls it. Power and wisdom work differently, for example. Power doesn't dominate or oppress; knowledge doesn't tear anyone down, but rather builds people up. As a result of this newness, there are important discontinuities between this world and the new creation that is coming to be in Jesus. As the new world dawns, the form of this world "is passing away" (1 Cor 7:31). "Every ruler and every authority and power" that have made themselves the enemies of God will be destroyed (1 Cor 15:24). Our bodies themselves, Paul says, will have to be changed. Our flesh and blood simply "cannot inherit the kingdom of God" (1 Cor 15:50). We will need to be transformed (1 Cor 15:51).

But there is also continuity. The metaphors Paul uses to describe the change coming at the End of all things point to continuity even as they describe what's new. Paul likens this change to what happens as a seed becomes a mature plant (1 Cor 15:42–43). There is an organic relationship of growth and maturation. The world to come is not a replacement for this world, but a fulfillment of it. Perhaps Paul's most common metaphor is that of putting on clothing. We will "put on imperishability" (1 Cor 15:53, cf. 2 Cor 5:4); our fundamental human identity will not change.

Perhaps the most striking sign of this continuity is the fact that, for Paul, this new world has already begun. Paul describes himself and his readers as those "on whom the ends of the ages have come" (1 Cor 10:11). The ages are turning, right now. And those of us who live between the resurrection of Christ and the end of all things live in an overlap between the creation and the new creation.

Paul believes this doubly hemmed-in expectation of a world of perfect love—coming to be through the life and Spirit of Jesus, but not yet fully present—should make us skeptical of extreme claims about the good life. We should be skeptical of utopian social projects (including Christian ones!) that purport to be able to realize the perfect in the here and now. The perfect, the fully mature, is still yet to come. Being clear-eyed about that is itself *a mark of maturity* in the here and now.[9] But we also ought to be skeptical of any sort of spiritual quietism that would perpetually defer all hope for social transformation to some heavenly hereafter. The world of perfect love has come upon us in the world-making life, death, and resurrection of Jesus Christ and the continued work of the Spirit of Christ in the world.

Participating in Christ involves participating in that new world of perfect love that is coming to be in his presence.

In summary, for Paul:

- Flourishing is not an accomplishment, but a gift. Flourishing is not possible for us on our own; we simply can't pull it off, (a) because we live in a world still maturing into its fullness and (b) because we live in a world ruled by Sin.

- Nevertheless, flourishing *is* possible for us by participating in the life of Jesus Christ, who makes his life available to us through the gift of his Spirit.

- That flourishing life is never complete in the here and now. Nevertheless, we can live in anticipation of the fully flourishing life that is possible in the world of perfect love begun in Jesus' life, death, and resurrection. That life awaits us in its fullness at the End of all things, but we can live into it in this world even though this world is incomplete and marred by Sin. We just have to keep these constraints and this "Story of Everything" in mind.

THE SHAPE OF FLOURISHING LIFE

The "Story of Everything" informs the structure of Paul's Christian vision of flourishing life. But what is its content?

Life Led Well: Righteousness

First, Paul says, flourishing life—life in the kingdom of God—is marked by righteousness, which we might also translate as "justice." Flourishing life is in step with God's law, laid out in God's covenant with God's people. In that covenant, the people have responsibilities—and so does God. Along with most Jewish theologians of his day, Paul argues that our lives flourish in the context of this loving covenantal relationship.[10] To lead our lives well is to act in line with the good intentions of this covenantal relationship. This is what "righteousness" or "justice" means for Paul.

But what does that look like in practice? Along with many Jewish thinkers, ancient and contemporary, Paul insists that God's law can be summed up in love—particularly in loving one's neighbor (Gal 5:14; Rom 13:8-10). Whatever we might do, Paul says, if we do it apart from love, it is of little value:

> If I speak in the tongues of mortals and of angels, but do not have love, I am a noisy gong or a clanging cymbal. And if I have prophetic powers, and understand all mysteries and all knowledge, and if I have all faith, so as to remove mountains, but do not have love, I am nothing. If I give away all my possessions, and if I hand over my body so that I may boast, but do not have love, I gain nothing. Love is patient; love is kind; love is not envious or boastful or arrogant or rude. It does not insist on its own way; it is not irritable or resentful; it does not rejoice in wrongdoing, but rejoices in the truth. It bears all things, believes all things, hopes all things, endures all things. (1 Cor 13:1–7)

If this sort of love sums up the covenant responsibility of God's people, so too does it describe God's faithfulness to God's people. In fact, it is God's faithful love that best demonstrates for Paul what love looks like in the midst of a world marred by sin and still awaiting full completion. In this world, love often *suffers*. For Paul, God's love in this world is made known in particular through Jesus the Messiah, "who loved [us] and gave himself up for [us]" (Gal 2:20), and did so "while we still were sinners," while we were still God's "enemies" (Rom 5:8–10). The fact of God's faithful love even in the midst of the world's brokenness provides a profound sense of assurance:

> What then are we to say about these things? If God is for us, who is against us? He who did not withhold his own Son, but gave him up for all of us, will he not with him also give us everything else? Who will bring any charge against God's elect? It is God who justifies. Who is to condemn? It is Christ Jesus, who died, yes, who was raised, who is at the right hand of God, who indeed intercedes for us. Who will separate us from the love of Christ? Will hardship, or distress, or persecution, or famine, or nakedness, or peril, or sword? As it is written,
>
> "For your sake we are being killed all day long;
>   we are accounted as sheep to be slaughtered."
>
> No, in all these things we are more than conquerors through him who loved us. For I am convinced that neither death, nor life, nor angels, nor rulers, nor things present, nor things to come, nor powers, nor height, nor depth, nor anything else in all creation, will be able to separate us from the love of God in Christ Jesus our Lord. (Rom 8:31–39)

To be sure, the love of God does not guarantee that one's life will go well. In fact, life in imitation of Jesus' self-giving love quite often brings about the same misunderstanding and violent opposition that Jesus faced. If in Jesus Christ the power and wisdom of God's love looked like weakness and foolishness, then we should expect the same of *our* love (1 Cor 1:18–31). If in Jesus Christ, the cost of love was death, we ought to be prepared for the same (Rom 8:17).

So, love may look different in this life than it did at the dawn of creation and certainly looks different than it will when God has made all things right, but love is equally the measure of flourishing agency *throughout* Paul's big story. This gives agency a unique place in Paul's vision of flourishing life. Love persists throughout the big story in ways that peace and joy—the definitive markers of flourishing circumstances and affect—do not. So, for example, while Paul says, "rejoice always" (e.g., Phil 4:4), he never says "rejoice only." While he advocates always *pursuing* peace, he does so not because one pursuing flourishing life should expect always to be *at peace* in this life (quite the contrary in many cases!). Rather, one ought to always pursue peace because the pursuit of peace is what love looks in a world often *not* at peace. In this life, there are many injustices with which it would be wrong to be at peace (this is the moral insight in the protest slogan, "no justice, no peace"). Similarly, there are circumstances over which it would be *evil* to rejoice. But for Paul, there is no condition under which it is wrong to love. The rule "always and only love" works in any and every moment of Paul's big story. We may not be able to pull it off, but love is always the right ideal to aim at.

Life Going Well: Peace

Second, Paul says, flourishing life is a life at *peace*. Peace, for Paul, is primarily about right relationships. Relationships are the most important of life's circumstances, and the context in which the value of other circumstances (food, money, etc.) become clear. For Paul, life is going well when we live at peace with God, with one another, and with the whole creation.

The foundation of life going well is peace with God. God has "reconciled us to himself through Christ" (2 Cor 5:18). Ultimately, when Christ's mission is fully realized at the end of all things, the world will be fully suffused with God's presence and become the home of God.[11] Then God will be "all in all" (1 Cor 15:28).

For Paul, God being all in all doesn't crowd out the world, but rather sets all the world's relationships right—beginning with those "in Christ," that is, those who take up Christ's way of life in baptism and live into the new creation coming to be in the wake of his world-making life. In this new community, "there is no longer Jew or Greek, there is no longer slave or free, there is no longer male and female; for all of you are one in Christ Jesus" (Gal 3:28). This life of perfect peace across lines of class, gender, and ethnicity is not possible in the here and now. But the basic principles of unity in diversity and mutual belonging with one another are foundational for the way of life Paul advocates. Captives are set free (1 Cor 7:22). Honor is extended to those on the margins (1 Cor 12:23–24), and all seek to outdo one another in showing honor (Rom 12:10). This is how the Church is supposed to live, which Paul often describes as being like a single body with many different but equally valuable members (1 Cor 12), or like God's family, each member an adopted child of a loving heavenly father (Rom 8:15).

Ultimately, the peace established in God's adopted family extends beyond the bounds of the human community entirely. For Paul, what begins with the family of God extends to the entire creation, as all are woven together as the home of God. If sin suggests the illusion of human life independent of the rest of the natural world, Paul's account of the shape of fully flourishing circumstances makes clear that full human flourishing is bound together with the full flourishing of the entirety of the creation. Peace that begins with the church ends in the whole creation at peace: the world at home in having become the home of God.

It is in the context of this whole world at peace that the true value of material goods becomes clear. Because "the earth and its fullness are the Lord's" (1 Cor 10:26), raw materials, human labor, and the products humans craft are valuable (as is the money they use to exchange these more fundamental goods). And because they are valuable, it is important that these material goods be equitably distributed. Paul is insistent that his churches "remember the poor" (Gal 2:10) and encourages them to set aside money to care for those less fortunate (1 Cor 16:2).

Being generous with material goods distributes them to those who need them. Such generosity is also an antidote to one's own obsession with obtaining, controlling, and enjoying material goods. After all, even if material goods have an important role to play in the circumstantial dimension of flourishing life, flourishing is not reducible to them; even flourishing circumstances are not reducible to material goods. This is part of what Paul is trying to say in Romans 14:17 when he insists that "the kingdom of God is not food and drink." Flourishing life is not reducible to life's circumstances—much less is it reducible to just a small set of circumstances narrowly understood. There are those in Paul's world who advocate for just such a vision of life—those whose "god is their belly" (Phil 3:19), who would subject their whole life and all material goods to their appetites. It is not difficult to imagine modern parallels: those who might imagine that "the good life" is precisely a life of conspicuous wealth and consumption.[12] The mistake both then and now is not simply that people overestimate how important material goods are, but also that they relate to material goods exclusively through their "belly." They see those goods through the lens of their own appetite for consumption. The value of material goods is reduced to what they do for us: temporarily satisfy a craving or mark our superiority in a game of social comparison, for example.[13] For Paul, such a vision completely misconstrues the set of relationships with which Paul is concerned: with creation, inasmuch as bellies and the good things that fill them are misunderstood as gods, rather than gifts of God; with human persons, inasmuch as devotion to our own appetites erases our neighbors from view, except perhaps as mere objects of desire or means to get what we want; and with God, inasmuch as God is ironically displaced by God's own good gifts.

Such distorted understandings of what it might be to live "at peace" highlight for Paul the extent to which, under the conditions of sin and incompleteness, peace is not always possible, or even good. It would be wrong to live at peace with a vision of life that reduces life to material wealth or to live fully at peace within an economic system where some starve while others waste nearly as much food as they consume. While we ought to pursue genuine peace, we ought to beware of false peace. After all, it is the propagandists of the Roman empire—not the Christians—whose slogan is "peace and security," and Paul cites the slogan to shame those who fall prey to their deception (1 Thess 5:3).

In this life, all is not at peace—and it will never be. In contrast to the imperial propagandists, Paul expects his ministry to elicit opposition (not peace) and boasts about the extent to which his own ministry has brought on the sorts of suffering that Jesus' ministry did (2 Cor 11:23–33). Flourishing life in this world is lived for the sake of a peace that we will never find in its fullness this side of the new creation. Nevertheless, Paul says we should live as peacemakers, as reconcilers of ruptured relationships between humans and one another, humans and God, and humans and the rest of the natural world. And we should accept that we may be hated precisely *because* we are peacemakers. Precisely *because* we pursue the peace of all, we may not in fact live at peace. Sometimes, to the extent to which we lead our lives well, for just that reason our lives will not go well. But this, too, can be good news, because for Paul, any hardships we undergo for the sake of love are just further evidence that we are living in the midst of the big story he preached. And the end of that story is a world where love endures, where God and the creation will be at peace and at home with one another.

Life Feeling as It Should: Joy

Paul has a lot to say about joy. The emotion appears more than forty times in Paul's letters.[14] In his letters, Paul expresses joy, hopes for joy, even *commands* joy. Paul describes himself and his fellow ministers as "joy workers" (2 Cor 1:24).[15] "Joy" clearly describes the affective dimension of flourishing life for Paul.

We might define joy this way: joy is an emotional response to something—especially something un-earned and un-owed—we recognize as good. (Gifts are especially fertile ground from which joy may spring.) We don't simply rejoice in the abstract; we rejoice *over* something we construe as being as it ought to be. Paul for his part rejoices over both salutary circumstances and flourishing agency when he recognizes it in others.[16] In the context of a fully flourishing life, joy is the "crown" of the good life: if we are formed in love, when circumstances in life are as they should be, we naturally rejoice over it; joy is the appropriate response of the righteous person in a world at peace.[17]

And yet, as we have said, this life is not always a life of peace. Consequently, if we want our lives to be disciplined by love, there is much over which we ought not rejoice. A key characteristic of love, according to Paul, is the way it regulates the causes of joy: love "does not rejoice in wrongdoing, but rejoices in the truth" (1 Cor 13:6). And so, while we ought to anticipate a perfect world of love and peace to which we ought always to respond with *joy*, in this life it is more important that our emotional lives are indexed to the truth of the world as it is. In short, it is more important to feel *rightly* than to feel *good*. Wrongdoing ought to elicit sorrow or perhaps anger. The suffering of another should elicit compassion. Indeed, *feeling with* others—emotional solidarity—is a key marker for Paul of a flourishing emotional life in an as-yet-unfulfilled world marked by sin: "Rejoice with those who rejoice, weep with those who weep" (Rom 12:15). This call to solidarity demands that we resist modern tendencies to weep over those who rejoice (e.g., Instagram's FOMO) and rejoice over those who weep (e.g., Twitter's schadenfreude). In a broken world like ours, not all joy is worthy of the name. Allowing love to norm our emotional lives helps us resist these corrupt forms of joy.

There is, however, an omnipresent cause for righteous joy, even in this life: God. Inasmuch as the goodness of every good thing is tied up in its relatedness to God, God is the cause of *every* joy.[18] But even when life's circumstances are plainly not as they ought to be, there is still God, whose loving presence can and ought to be the cause of joy. It is for this reason that Paul can command joy: "Rejoice in the Lord always; again I will say, Rejoice" (Phil 4:4).

How does Paul expect his hearers both to "rejoice in the Lord always" and to "weep with those who weep"? This puzzle points us in a familiar direction: the command is to rejoice *always but not only*. There will be a day in the world of perfect love when we are able to rejoice always and only, but in this life our joy often must be mixed with sorrow. Rejoice in the Lord, but lament over injustice. Rejoice in the Lord, but weep with a neighbor in pain. This is simply what joy looks like this side of the fulfillment of all things. Even when we rejoice over some small part of the world that is at some moment at peace, our joy over this ought to be mixed with sorrow over the fact that this precious pocket is not yet woven into a tapestry of fully flourishing life: the world at home in having become the home of God. In this broader context, joys—whether small like the joy of a sweet strawberry or large like the joy of a long-estranged relationship mended at last—are also always *longings*, as they inevitably reach for a world in which they might extend to embrace and include one another in an unending web of joy. Our joys, Paul insists, ought to be as immodest as our dreams. They ought to have a whole world as their horizon.

***

As integral as joy and peace are to Paul's vision of fully flourishing life, one can still identify a priority *in this life* for love. In this world, flourishing life is:

(1) always *and* only a life of love,

(2) always *but not* only a life of joy, and

(3) *neither* always *nor* only a life at peace.

In the end, all three are woven together, but in this life, in which there are circumstances with which it would be wicked to be at peace and over which it would be evil to rejoice, love must come first.

Love leads the way to a world of joy and peace. However, love is no mere means to the ultimate end of a world fully at peace or replete with unending joy. Love is its own good. It is good for humans to love one another, to love God and God's good creation. The world to come does not do away with love. Certain religious practices—even practices central to the worship life of Paul and his community—will come to an end in a world of perfect love we can barely imagine. But love will remain (1 Cor 13:8–13).

When we dream a life, we dream a world. A world of love, peace, and joy, in harmony with one another: life led well, going well, and feeling as it should—this is the world Jesus' life summons into being. It lies beyond this immature and evil-stricken world. And yet it summons us, even in the midst of conditions that make it impossible.

Fully flourishing life "haunts" our lives in the here and now. From creation itself, life has been oriented toward a fullness of flourishing beyond what the creation was (yet) capable of. Now, marred by sin, aspects of our world can seem to be little more than parodies of the full flourishing at which all life ultimately aims. The same trajectory toward a world at home with God and with one another remains, but the gap between the ideal and the real has grown and taken on a different character. What once felt like growing pains now feels like tragedy. What we might have experienced as simple hope for a yet fuller expression of what we already experience as good is now often a pained yearning for a life that somehow seems both ours by right of nature ("how things were meant to be") and yet hard for us even to imagine.

Paul affirms this yearning, this hunger. It is a sign that we were indeed made for more than the lives we can experience here and now. And yet it also points to the fact that some foretaste of that life is embedded here. This is, after all, still God's good creation. It is still a gift. And the good gifts of God are at hand all around us: never complete, never untouched by sin's corruption, but here. In little pockets of peace in communities marked by love, there are yet grounds for joy. Grounds that help us see every good thing around us as a gift from God.

And, in the end, that's just what Paul promises when it comes to flourishing life: it is a gift. We can't make it happen, can't will our way to it. Love, peace, and joy describe flourishing life as Paul understands it. They are also the first three components of the "fruit of the [Holy] Spirit," Paul famously describes in Galatians 5:22–23. They are gifts, as is flourishing life—fruit of God's work within us. A gift from a God of love who gives good gifts, whose greatest gift is God's presence within and among us, calling us to be at home.

Notes

1   This argument is adopted from one advanced by Matthew Croasmun and Katie Grosh in "River Retreat: Seeking the Shape of Flourishing Life," a guided reflection written for the Grace Farms Foundation, 2022, https://gracefarms.org/wp-content/uploads/2022/02/River-Retreat-PDF.pdf.

2   For the cosmic scale of Paul's theological narrative, see Beverly Roberts Gaventa, "The Cosmic Power of Sin in Paul's Letter to the Romans: Toward a Widescreen Edition," *Interpretation* 58, no. 3 (2004): 229–40.

3   "God is love" is not Paul's own phrase. It comes from a different book of the Christian Bible, known as First John. It nevertheless pithily expresses Paul's conviction that love is supremely characteristic of God (see, e.g., 2 Cor 13:11).

4   We borrow the phrase "economy of grace" from Kathryn Tanner, *Economy of Grace* (Minneapolis: Fortress, 2005).

5   The Greek word Paul uses is *teleios*, which can variously be translated as "perfect," "complete," or "mature." Each translation presents potential misunderstandings. If we say that the creation is not yet "perfect," it can sound like God made mistakes when creating the world; God did not. If we say that the creation is not yet "complete," it can sound like God left something out that is waiting to be added; God did not. If we say the creation is not yet "mature," it can sound like the creation is simply in the early stages of a natural process of growth, whereas Paul's understanding is that the transition from this world to the world to come is in many ways more radical than that. The technical theological term in English closest to *teleios* is "consummated," which suggests a rich sense of fulfillment—the world and its creator having found themselves at home with one another. To avoid such technical terminology, we will use the language of "maturity" and "immaturity," which rightly conveys the sense that, at the moment of creation, the world is entirely good but not yet all that it is intended to be.

6   For discussion of this latter dynamic in the Gospel of Luke (one of the ancient accounts of the life of Jesus), see Matthew Croasmun and Miroslav Volf, *The Hunger for Home: Food and Meals in the Gospel of Luke* (Waco, Tex.: Baylor University Press, 2022).

7   For further reflection on these dynamics, see Howard Thurman, *Jesus and the Disinherited* (Boston: Beacon University Press, 1996).

8   It is not difficult to imagine how large societal maladies like patriarchy and white supremacy might fit the dynamics Paul is talking about. See Matthew Croasmun, *The Emergence of Sin: The Cosmic Tyrant* (New York: Oxford University Press, 2017).

9   We discuss the subtle ways Paul uses language of "maturity" in Miroslav Volf and Matthew Croasmun, *For the Life of the World: Theology That Makes a Difference* (Grand Rapids: Brazos, 2019), 153–63.

10   New Testament scholar E. P. Sanders describes this first-century Jewish theological common sense as "covenantal nomism" in his *Paul and Palestinian Judaism* (Minneapolis: Fortress, 1977).

11   For our elaborations of this theme, see Miroslav Volf and Ryan McAnnally-Linz, *The Home of God: A Brief Story of Everything* (Grand Rapids: Brazos, 2022); Croasmun and Volf, *Hunger for Home*.

12   One of our colleagues once taught a philosophy course about "the good life." At the end of the semester, one of her students confided in a course

review that they thought a course on the good life would have had a lot more to say about *yachts*.

13 See Volf and McAnnally-Linz, *Home of God*, 199–201.

14 More precisely, in Paul's *undisputed* letters. Most modern scholars hold that some of the books in the New Testament that bear Paul's name were not written by Paul himself.

15 This is our translation. The Greek literally says "we are co-workers of your joy."

16 For Paul rejoicing over good circumstances (relational peace), see 2 Corinthians 7:4, 7; Philippians 2:2, 4:1; 1 Thessalonians 2:19–20; 3:9. For Paul rejoicing over agential flourishing, see Romans 16:19, 2 Corinthians 7:9, and Philemon 7.

17 Miroslav Volf, "The Crown of the Good Life: A Hypothesis," in *Joy and Human Flourishing: Essays on Theology, Culture, and the Good Life*, ed. Miroslav Volf and Justin E. Crisp (Minneapolis: Fortress, 2015), 127–36.

18 Kathryn Tanner, "Religious Joy, Natural Joy, and Human Happiness," unpublished paper for Yale Center for Faith & Culture consultation on "Joy, Human Nature, and Human Destiny" (September 12–13, 2014).

6

A Muslim Vision
On the Truly Happy Life

HRH Prince Ghazi bin Muhammad and Ismail Fajrie Alatas

INTRODUCTION

Islam's full view on what it takes to live a truly happy life cannot be fully covered in the limited space allotted to this tract. Literally millions of texts and commentaries on the Qur'an have been written over the course of Islamic history about Islamic life, true happiness, and spirituality, and only their surface can be scratched here. Nevertheless, what follows is a basic sketch of life and happiness and what they entail, starting with their definitions from the Qur'an and the *ahadith* (the sayings of the Prophet Muhammad ﷺ; singular: *hadith*).

This tract is divided into two halves that mirror each other, starting with the negations and then the definitions of life and happiness, respectively. Then it explains these definitions systematically, starting from the other five circumstantial questions of the English language: "why," "when," "where," "how," and "who." These will deal with *existential*, *circumstantial*, *agential*, *affective*, and *anthropological* aspects of life and happiness, respectively. There are many citations in the text, particularly from the Qur'an (presented in italics, with both the chapter names and numbers, and verse numbers, in brackets) and the *ahadith*, but references are placed in the text itself. In order to be accessible to everyone, the tract contains no footnotes or endnotes (and no technical jargon—apart from the five terms in italics above).

137

PART I: LIFE

(I)(A) What Is Not Life?

Human life

By "life" in this tract we mean "life lived by human beings," and so "human life." So, even though the definition of life that we will later give applies to all forms of life, we are concerned here only with human life. But even with human life, there is a difference, in the Qur'an, between life *in* the world and life *of* the world (i.e., life that is too "worldly").

Now obviously life *in* the world is immeasurably precious because it is a unique opportunity for goodness and righteous deeds (and these endure eternally), but the life *of* the world is in itself ultimately pointless. In the Qur'an, God gives the following parable of the two kinds of life:

> And strike for them the similitude of the life of this world as water which We send down out from the heaven, and the vegetation of the earth mingles with it, and it then becomes chaff, scattered by the winds. And God is Omnipotent over all things. / Wealth and children are an adornment of the life of this world. But the enduring things, the righteous deeds—[these] are better with your Lord for reward and better in [respect of] hope. (*Al-Kahf* 18:45–46)

True human life

As regards "positive" life, the word "True Life" (*al-Hayyawan*) is mentioned only once in the Qur'an, and it is in the context of paradise:

> And the life of this world is nothing but diversion and play. But surely the Abode of the Hereafter is indeed the [True] Life (al-Hayyawan) if they only knew. (*Al-'Ankabut* 29:64)

Evidently, however, life in the world that leads to paradise, can be seen as part of it.

False human life

By contrast, the life of the world (*al-hayat al-dunya*) is mentioned around seventy-five times in the Qur'an, at least seventy of them in a negative context. It is never seen as "real" life, but rather as false and subhuman life and a beastly existence. God says in the Qur'an (referring to religious hypocrites and disbelievers):

> Surely the worst of beasts in God's sight are those who are deaf and dumb, those who do not understand. (*Al-An'am* 8:22)

The reason they are subhuman is precisely because they do not use their human intellect (*aql*) or (spiritual) hearts (*qulub*), these being—as will later be discussed—precisely what sets them apart from animals in the first place. God says in the Qur'an:

> . . . They have hearts, with which they do not understand, and they have eyes with which they do not perceive, and they have ears with which they do not hear. These, they are like cattle—nay, rather they are further astray. These—they are the heedless. (*Al-A'raf* 7:179)

Because they are heedless of God and their true selves, like animals they are led by their own caprices and desires—to the extent of effectively *worshipping* these desires. God says in the Qur'an:

> Have you seen him who has taken as his god his own desire? Will you be a guardian over him? / Or do you suppose that most of them listen or comprehend? They are but as the cattle—nay, but they are further astray from the way. (*Al-Furqan* 25:43–44)

Moreover, the subhuman existence of constant, blind, impulsive self-gratification naturally leads to perdition. God says in the Qur'an:

> . . . As for those who disbelieve, they take their enjoyment and eat as the cattle eat; and the Fire will be their habitation. (*Muhammad* 47:12)

A choice between two kinds of human life

In summary then, human beings have a choice between a negative, worldly life that is futile and subhuman—and not real life, and a positive, fully human life of enduring goodness and righteousness. The first is like the life of cattle, and the second is real human life. In the Qur'an, God summarizes this critical situation as follows:

The likeness of the life of this world is only as water, which We send
down from the heaven, then the plants of the earth mingle with it,
whereof mankind eat, and cattle [eat] until, when the earth has taken
on its ornaments, and has adorned itself, and its inhabitants think
that they are masters of it, Our command comes upon it by night or
day, and We make it as reaped corn, as though the previous day it had
not flourished. Thus do We detail the signs for a people who reflect.
(*Yunus* 10:24)

(I)(B) What Is Life?

What is a quality?

The first thing to say here is that "the Living" (*Al-Hayy*) is one of God's
Names and essential Attributes. It is mentioned five times in the Qur'an (in
the following verses: *Al-Baqarah* 2:255; *Aal Imran* 3:1; *Ta Ha* 20:111; *Al-
Furqan* 25:85, and *Ghafir* 40:65). The Divine Name "the Giver of Life" (*Al-
Muhiy*) is a Divine Name mentioned in gerund and verb form in the Qur'an
(in the following verses: *Al-Rum* 30:50 and *Fussilat* 41:39, respectively) and
as a noun in the *ahadith*. Consequently, life in itself is a quality given by and
derived from those Divine Attributes. What we mean by "quality" is simply
an indivisible element, wherever it be found.

What is the quality of life?

As regards life, God says in the Qur'an:

. . . We made, from water, every living thing. Will they not then
believe? (*Al-Anbiya* 21:30)

Now water, coming as it does from the clouds and bringing new life, is both
a symbol and tangible manifestation of Divine Mercy. God further says in
the Qur'an (referring to rainwater):

So behold the effects of God's mercy, how He revives the earth after it
has died. Surely He is the Reviver of the dead and He has power over
all things . . . (*Al-Rum* 30:50)

So, the first thing to be said about life—the life of every living created thing,
at least—is that it is an effect of Divine Mercy. But then God also says in the
Qur'an:

> There is no creature on the earth and no bird that flies with its wings, but they are communities like to you. We have neglected nothing in the Book; then to their Lord they shall be gathered. (*Al-An'am* 3:38)

So, all creatures on the earth and in the sky form "communities." Now communities "communicate" with each other precisely, and we know from science that this is true of fish, trees, plants, and indeed anything that reproduces sexually. God alludes to this in the Qur'an in His saying:

> Glory be to Him Who created all the pairs of what the earth produces, and of themselves, and of what they do not know. (*Ya Sin* 36:36)

Moreover, anything that maintains itself through homeostasis—including the simplest organisms—communicates within itself. What communication and internal communication have in common is self-awareness of some sort. Self-awareness is not yet knowledge (which requires particulars and objects), as is proved precisely by the existence of bacteria and their like, which do not know anything but can maintain themselves and reproduce. Consequently, our definition of the "quality" of life will be simply: something that, as a mercy from God, is self-aware (at certain times and in certain ways, at least). Indeed, this is essentially the same as the definition of life given by the great Islamic scholar, logician, theologian, and mystic Abu Hamid Al-Ghazali (d. 505 AH / 1111 CE) in his book *Moderation in Belief* (*Al-Iqtisad fil-I'tiqad*), where he says (in the Second Treatise):

> We do not mean by "living" anything other than someone [or something] that is aware of himself and realises his essence and [the difference between it and] that which is other than himself.

Human life

Human life, however, is not simply any life. It is characterized by the *existential* human condition as such. In the Qur'an, the human condition is characterized by human beings fundamentally being two things:

(1) God's vicegerents of the earth (*Al-Naml* 27:62), and

(2) God's servants, for "there is none in the heavens and the earth, but he comes to the Compassionate One as a servant." (*Maryam* 19:93)

God's vicegerents

It is in virtue of human beings being God's vicegerents (a "vicegerent" is a kind of steward or deputy, the Arabic word being *khalifah*) on the earth that people enjoy their extraordinary faculties. Now in the Qur'an, every person is seen to be composed of three main dimensions:

(1) a body;

(2) an individual soul (which has a personal ego—that can be purified— and a conscience), and

(3) a (supraindividual) spirit, which God blew into Adam ﷺ.

The body's faculties are well known and include the five senses. The soul also has certain obvious faculties, such as an intelligence capable of knowing the truth, a will capable of controlling the ego's pride and passions, sentiment capable of generous and altruistic love, speech capable of imparting knowledge and guidance, an imagination capable of picturing a future and abstract ideas, and a memory capable of remembering the past. The spirit is beyond the whole individual personality, and so, little can be said about it in words. God says in the Qur'an:

And they will question you concerning the Spirit. Say: "The Spirit is of the command of my Lord. And of knowledge you have not been given except a little." (*Al-Isra'* 17:85)

The soul is the individual "inner witness" of the body. The spirit is the supraindividual "inner witness" of the body and the soul taken together. Moreover, human beings also have a "spiritual" heart, which is a kind of "seat" of the spirit and a doorway to it, so that it is through this heart that they "see" or know spiritual realities. (This heart is of course in addition to— and different from—the physical heart that pumps blood around the body.) God says in the Qur'an:

Have they not traveled through the land with hearts to comprehend, or ears to hear? Indeed it is not eyes that are blind, but the hearts within the breasts. (*Al-Hajj* 22:46)

All these faculties together—body, soul, mind, heart, and spirit—are, when we think about it, truly miraculous gifts that we ordinarily, rather ungratefully, take for granted. This is especially clear when we consider the physically or mentally disabled, who lack some of these faculties. God says in the Qur'an that it is He

> Who perfected everything that He created. And He began the creation of man from clay, / then He made his progeny from an extract of a base fluid, / then He proportioned him, and breathed into him of His spirit. And He made for you hearing, and sight and hearts. Little thanks do you give. (*Al-Sajdah* 32:7–9)

The ultimate purpose of these extraordinary faculties is to do good and to worship, know, and love God, as will be later discussed. They comprise the sacred Trust that God gave human beings, which sets them apart even from the heavens themselves:

> Indeed We offered the Trust to the heavens and the earth and the mountains, but they refused to bear it and were apprehensive of it; but man undertook it. Truly he is a wrongdoer, ignorant. (*Al-Ahzab* 33:72)

God's servants

In addition to being God's vicegerents, human beings are also his servants or slaves (the Arabic word being *abd*). Anyone who balks at this idea should consider the following: you are born without choosing it; you are helpless as a child; you are ignorant as a youth; you are dominated by pride and passions as an adult; and you are dominated by illness and pain as you get older—and that is if you are fortunate enough to be free from worse woes inflicted by people. All the while you have to breathe, walk on something stable, drink, eat (and in most cases earn a livelihood), keep yourself and family safe and warm (but not too warm), maintain your body through difficult exercises, and sleep, and you have to constantly go to the bathroom and clean yourself (and these necessary activities alone will consume at least half your life). You also have to constantly jostle and negotiate your place and life, with 7.5 billion other people just like you who also inhabit this earth, in the face of which you are another speck, no different at all than countless others. Moreover, only one in 1 million or so will live to be 100 years old, and no one lives to be 125. Worse still, at any time, you can (and likely will) be inflicted with horrible calamity and suffering and can perish and die. Whatever you want, you will never get *all* that *you* want out of life, because you do not ultimately control even your own destiny. What could be more slavish than this existential predicament in which we all find ourselves?

The human condition

To be alive, as we have said, means to be self-aware. So, it follows that to be alive as a human being means to be aware of our double predicament of being God's vicegerents and His servants. Indeed, the human condition—human life as such—flows naturally from these two inherent characteristics of human beings—being God's vicegerents and His servants—taken together. As the great Islamic mystic poet Jalal al-Din Rumi (d. 672 AH / 1273 CE) famously said:

> A human being's situation is like this: an angel's wing was brought and tied to a donkey's tail so that perhaps the donkey might also become an angel, thanks to the radiation of the angel's company. (*Fihi ma fihi*, chapter 26)

In other words, as we are bowled through life, time, and space, with physical necessities constantly nipping at our heels and coming closer and closer to death, we have to do our best using the wondrous faculties we have been given to worship God and be good to others as best we can. God says:

> O you who believe, bow down and prostrate yourselves, and worship your Lord, and do good that perhaps you may succeed. (*Al-Hajj* 22:77)

(I)(C) Why Is Life?

The reason for human beings' existence

From the Islamic point of view, the question "why is life?" is tantamount to asking, "why did God create human beings?" This is, of course, the greatest—and perhaps the most ancient—of all the questions thinking human beings face. The answer to it explains the reason for the human condition being the way it is, as described above. Happily, the Qur'an provides a powerful and coherent answer. God says in the Qur'an:

Had your Lord willed, He would have made mankind one community, but they continue to differ, / except those on whom your Lord
has mercy; and for this He created them . . . (*Hud* 11:118–19)

The Prophet Muhammad's ﷺ cousin (and student) Ibn 'Abbas ؓ said that
the word "this" here refers to "mercy." In other words, God created people
for His Mercy.

This corresponds with God's words elsewhere in the Qur'an:

And I did not create the jinn and mankind except that they may worship Me. (*Al-Dhariyat* 51:56)

Referring to this verse, Ibn 'Abbas ؓ said: "Worshipping God" means "knowing Him." "Worshipping God," however, is more inclusive than "knowing God,"
because it includes those with blind faith in, but little knowledge of, God. It also
means that God created us to love Him: how can anyone worship God without loving Him? Or for that matter, how can anyone know God without loving
Him? And loving God necessarily means being loved by Him. God promises:

. . . God will assuredly bring a people whom He loves and who love
Him . . . (*Al-Ma'idah* 5:54)

In other words, God created us to worship Him and to love Him, so that He
could be merciful to us and love us. For love is a special and more particular
kind of mercy.

Righteous deeds and kindness to others

Worshipping God necessarily means love of other people as well. God says
in the Qur'an:

Truly the Compassionate One will give love to those who believe and
do righteous deeds. (*Maryam* 19:96)

Indeed, in over fifty other passages in the Qur'an, the phrase "those who
believe" is immediately followed by the phrase "and do righteous deeds,"
showing that the two are inseparable. And the Prophet Muhammad ﷺ said:

By Him in whose hand is my soul, you shall not enter paradise until
you have faith, and you will not have faith until you love each other.
(*Sahih Muslim*)

In other words, worshipping God is not just through prayer. People are not supposed to live permanently in isolation, praying and fasting. That is perhaps part of why the Prophet Muhammad ﷺ said: "there is no monasticism in Islam" (Ibn Kathir, *Al-Nihayah*). There cannot be real piety without kindness towards other people in one form or another. For people were created to be kind to others as part of their love for God. Indeed, God says in the Qur'an:

> It is not piety that you turn your faces to the East and to the West [in prayer]. True piety is [that of] the one who believes in God and the Last Day and the angels and the Book and the prophets, and who gives of his wealth, for the love of Him, to kinsmen and orphans and the needy and the traveler and beggars, and for slaves, and who observes prayer and pays the alms, and those who fulfil their covenant when they have engaged in a covenant, those who endure with fortitude misfortune, hardship, and peril are the ones who are truthful, and these are the ones who are God-fearing. (*Al-Baqarah* 2:177)

So worshipping God *necessarily involves* virtue and kindness towards others, all others. And kindness itself is the fruit and result of love. The Prophet Muhammad ﷺ said:

> God is Kind, and God loves kindness (*rifq*) in all things. (*Sahih Bukhari*; *Sahih Muslim*)

(I)(D) When Is Life?

Is life always worth living?

Is "life" always life as such? In other words, when is life "truly life"? When is life worth living for human beings? This is the *circumstantial* aspect of life: it deals with the circumstances necessary for a worthwhile life. This question follows on nicely from the previous one, since having established the purpose of life, it is then necessary to establish its conditions.

Patience and steadfastness

Now the general answer to this question is simple. Human beings are required to endure whatever they cannot avoid of hardship, trials, pain, illness, sorrow, need and difficult circumstances. In patience and steadfastness (the two things together are called *sabr* in Arabic), there are incalculable blessings. God says in the Qur'an:

> . . . God loves the patient and steadfast. (*Aal 'Imran* 3:146)

> Truly the patient and steadfast will be paid their reward in full without any reckoning. (*Al-Zumar* 39:10; see also *Al-Baqarah* 2:153–56; *Al-Baqarah* 2:249; *Al-Anfal* 8:46; *Al-Anfal* 8:66).

Accordingly, the Prophet Muhammad ﷺ said:

> The believer's state is truly wondrous: all that befalls him [or her] is good. That is something that is not true for anyone but a believer. If something pleasing befalls him [or her], he is thankful, and that is to his good. And if something harmful befalls him [or her], he is patient and steadfast, and that is to his good. (*Sahih Muslim*)

Of course, it is understood that the first recourse under duress—after prayer and supplication for relief—is to try to avoid difficulty, or remove it or relieve it. God says in the Qur'an:

> . . . God desires ease for you and does not desire difficulty for you . . . (*Al-Baqarah* 2:185)

So, people have every right to try to lighten their burdens and alleviate their problems. Only if it is not possible to do so—as it often is not—must they then have patience and steadfastness.

Unbearable circumstances

Nevertheless, there is a recognition in the Qur'an that there are circumstances and situations that cannot be alleviated and which even the strongest human beings cannot bear. In the Qur'an, the most blessed woman ever created is the Blessed Virgin Mary. God recalls in the Qur'an:

> And when the angels said, "O Mary, God has preferred you, and made you pure; He has preferred you above all women of the worlds." (*Aal 'Imran* 3:42)

And yet in the Qur'an, even the Blessed Virgin, during the pain of contractions, prayed:

". . . Would that I had died before this, and was as nothing, utterly forgotten!" (*Maryam* 19:23)

That is to say, there are conditions where people can and do suffer intolerable pain through no fault of their own, be it in illness, in injury, in thirst or starvation, in fear, in heat or cold, in humiliation, in physical disability, in old age, in sadness or loneliness, in madness, or, as in this case, simply in childbearing or birth.

Moral absolution

Mercifully, under such unbearable circumstances people are no longer accountable. Now different people have different capacities, strengths, and weaknesses, and so degrees of moral responsibility will vary accordingly. But everyone is completely morally absolved of what they cannot endure or do. God says in the Qur'an:

God does not burden a soul save to its capacity . . . (*Al-Baqarah* 2:286)

Moral responsibility

In short, in Islam adults are morally responsible for their own lives. This responsibility is not conditional upon favorable circumstances. There are, however, unbearable circumstances under which people are absolved of moral responsibility. Individuals simply have to deal with things as best they can. As will later be seen, *society* as such (and, a fortiori, Islamic society) *is* responsible for certain basic human rights that all human beings require in order to flourish. But as regards people's *individual* moral responsibility before God, Islam reflects the principle of Divine Mercy. This principle is simply that people must try to remain patient and steadfast under difficult circumstances, but if these become unbearable, they are no longer morally responsible for what is beyond their capacity to bear or to do.

(I)(E) Where Is Life?

Sociology

We have already seen that there is no isolationism or monasticism in Islam. We have also seen that communities—and therefore the societies that these communities make up—are integrally part of life itself, at least all complex life. It remains to be said that human life exists where human societies flourish. Indeed, human life requires functioning human societies. Functioning human societies in turn require a number of things. Now this is a complex subject and essentially involves the whole discipline of sociology. It deals with the *agential* aspect of life. In fact, it is generally accepted that the Arab, Islamic fourteenth-century CE scholar 'Abd Al-Rahman Ibn Khaldun (d. 808 AH / 1406 CE) was the "father" of the whole discipline of sociology as we know it, and the seminal work in the subject was his *Muqaddimah* (*The Introduction* [to History]). In it, Ibn Khaldun writes:

> The power of the individual human being is not sufficient for him to obtain (the food) he needs, and does not provide him with as much food as he requires to live . . . . Consequently, social organization is necessary to the human species. Without it, the existence of human beings would be incomplete. (First prefatory discussion, trans. Franz Rosenthal)

The bases of society in the Qur'an

The many bases of functioning human society are mentioned in the Qur'an itself. For example:

(1) As regards social organization, God mentions in the Qur'an:

> Those who, if We empower them in the land, maintain the prayer, and pay the alms, and enjoin decency and forbid indecency. And with God rests the outcome of all matters. (*Al-Hajj* 22:41)

(2) As regards food and (drink), God orders in the Qur'an:

> O people, eat of what is in the earth, lawful and wholesome; and follow not the steps of Satan; he is a manifest foe to you. (*Al-Baqarah* 2:168)

(3) As regards the arts and crafts, God mentions in the Qur'an that some of these originate in Divine inspiration:

> And We taught him [David ﷺ] the art of making garments for you to protect you against your [mutual] violence. Will you then be thankful? (*Al-Anbiya* 21:80)

(4) As regards skills and knowledge, God says in the very first Revelation revealed in the Quran:

> Recite: In the Name of your Lord Who created, / created man from a blood-clot. / Recite: and your Lord is the Most Generous, / Who taught by the pen— / taught man what he did not know. (*Al-'Alaq* 96:1–5)

(5) As regards cooperation with other people, God enjoins in the Qur'an:

> . . . Help one another to righteousness and piety; do not help one another to sin and enmity. And fear God; surely God is severe in retribution. . . . (*Al-Ma'idah* 5:2)

There are, of course, other necessary bases for society (and therefore human life) mentioned in the Qur'an, but we cannot hope to cover them all here. It is enough to say that these include marriage, clothing, tools and utensils, housing and shelter, government, law and order, security, defense, justice and rights (as will later be discussed), medicine and health care, literacy, sciences, agriculture and animal husbandry, irrigation and hydrology, transport, communication, education and religious education, employment opportunity, social welfare, economy, commerce, industry, care for the environment, cultural exchanges, diplomatic exchanges, and so on—in short, everything one might expect for a great civilization like Islam that has continued down to the present time. Indeed, Islamic scholars have always found in the Qur'an a basis for each of these in at least one passage in the Qur'an (and most often in the *ahadith* as well).

(I)(F) How Is Life?

How does life feel?

This question deals with the *affective* aspect of life. How does life feel? How will it always feel? God answers this very simply in the Qur'an:

> We certainly created man for toil and trial. (*Al-Balad* 90:4)

In other words, it is going to feel tough—at least sometimes—for everyone, no matter how strong, healthy, wealthy, clever, or pious.

The trials of life

The trials of life are not something that happen by accident and without meaning. Life is *supposed* to have these trials. This is part of the human condition, as mentioned earlier: it tests our sincerity (and hence our patience and virtue), both as God's servants and as His vicegerents. God says in the Qur'an:

> Do people suppose that they will be left to say, "We believe," and they will not be tried? / And certainly We tried those who were before them. So God shall surely know those who are sincere, and He shall surely know those who are liars. / Or do those who commit evil deeds suppose that they can elude Us? Evil is that which they judge! / Whoever hopes to encounter God, [should know that] God's [appointed] term will indeed come. And He is the Hearer, the Knower. / And whoever struggles (*jahada*), struggles (*yujahid*) only for his own soul. For truly God is Independent of [the creatures of] all the Worlds. (*Al-'Ankabut* 29:2–6)

In fact, it is the trials of life and our struggle (*jihad* in Arabic) with our own egos that determine the state of our own souls.

The meaning of the term *jihad*

This brings us to the issue of the meaning of the term *jihad*. Many people who do not know Arabic think that *jihad* means "Islamic religious war" or "holy war." This is not true and leads to dangerous misconceptions about the nature and purpose of *jihad*, making *jihad* a goal rather than a means. Actually, the term *jihad* in the Arabic language does not in itself originally have anything to do with war. The Arabic term for war is *harb*, and the term for military combat is *qital*. *Jihad* comes from the root *juhd*, meaning making an effort and, consequently, struggling and contending. In other words, military combat is not the essence of *jihad*; *jihad* simply means "to struggle."

The two kinds of *jihad*: The "greatest *jihad*" and the "lesser *jihad*"

In the Qur'an and the *ahadith*, the word *jihad* is used in (at least) two quite different ways, and so there are (at least) two kinds of *jihad*. The Prophet Muhammad ﷺ said, on returning from a military campaign:

> "We have returned from the lesser *jihad* to the greatest *jihad*." They said: "What is the greatest *jihad*, O Messenger of God?" He said ﷺ:

"The struggle against the ego [*nafs*]." (*Sunan al-Bayhaqi*; Al-Khatib al-Baghdadi, *Tarikh Baghdad*)

We are not concerned here with the "lesser *jihad*." Rather, we are concerned with the "greatest *jihad*," which is the internal struggle against the ego, which all believers are called on to wage and which is the sine qua non of spiritual life. The Prophet Muhammad ﷺ said:

The [true] warrior [*mujahid*] is the one who wages *jihad* against his own ego in obedience to God Almighty. (*Sunan Abu Dawud*; *Sunan Al-Tirmidhi*; *Musnad Ahmad*)

It is this "greatest *jihad*" that is endemically part of the human condition. Over and above the external trials and tribulations of life, the greatest *jihad* is—or at least should be—the internal occupation of every adult at every moment of their waking lives. God says in the Qur'an:

But as for such who feared standing before their Lord and restrained their soul from base desires / Paradise will be their abode. (*Al-Nazi'at* 79:40–41)

The components of the soul

Earlier, it was mentioned that every individual soul has: "a personal ego—that can be purified—and a conscience." To be more specific, in the Qur'an, the soul is seen to have three distinct major parts—or perhaps three "modes" (since the soul remains one). There is (1) *the soul which incites to evil* (*Yusuf* 12:53). It is "the ego." Then there is (2) *the self-reproaching soul* (*Al-Qiyamah* 75:2). It is what we usually call "the conscience." Finally, there is (3) *the soul at peace* (*Al-Fajr* 89:27).

The internal struggle within the soul

In fact, the whole "greatest *jihad*" mentioned above is nothing other than the internal struggle between the two or possibly three modes of the soul. Ghazali explains:

Know that your bitterest enemy is your own ego between your sides [i.e., inside you]. It was created to constantly incite ill. It is predisposed to evil and to fleeing from the good. You are under orders to purify it, to reform it and to make it worship its Lord and Creator through the chains of force. You must prevent its appetites and wean it from its pleasures. If you neglect it, it rears up and strays, and you will not be able to vanquish it after that. But if you persist in rebuking it, reproaching it, censuring it and blaming it, your soul will become the *self-reproaching soul* [*Al-Qiyamah* 75:2] by which God has sworn. If you [further] aspire for it to become the *soul at peace* [*Al-Fajr* 89:27] that is called to join the servants of God *well pleased and well pleasing* [*Al-Fajr* 89:28], then do not neglect for one moment to remind it and chase it up. Do not work on preaching to others, unless you have first dealt with your own ego. (*Ihya 'Ulum al-Din*, Book 38, Chapter 6)

The ego

But what is the ego exactly? The ego is the tendency for self-preservation gone mad. Consequently, the ego is always saying "me, me, me"; always seeking itself and only itself; always looking for attention and recognition; always puffing its own self up under whatever excuse it can find; always boasting and showing off at the slightest opportunity; always arrogant and wanting leadership or domination; always insisting on its own arbitrary ways; always remembering and savoring its little victories; always trying to prompt flattery from others; always brooding and fuming over perceived or imagined slights and insults; envious of others; selfish; callous towards people's needs and feelings; caring nothing really for the good; wishing no one well; easily irritable, resentful, and quick to fly into a rage and use harsh words or violence (if it feels it has enough power); secretly hating others who do not pander to it, and wanting to crush them; always wanting food, sex, and comfort; always wanting to own and hoard things; greedy; insatiable; never satisfied; never still; incapable of patience; lazy; lying without thought; believing in nothing; living in fantasies, yet secretly cowardly and never wanting to leave its comfort zone, nor oppose its own whims and caprices; and at last, given to absolute terror at the thought of death.

Anyone can observe the ego within themselves with a little bit of silence, solitude, prayer, fasting, and concentration, and the habit of observing it is the beginning of the "greatest *jihad.*" God says in the Qur'an:

So fear God as far as you can, and listen, and obey and spend; that is better for your souls. And whoever is shielded from the meanness of their own souls [egos], will be the successful ones. (*Al-Taghabun* 64:16)

Constant vigilance

The constant struggle with the ego explains why human life—that is, life lived with any degree of self-awareness—generally feels like constant toil: when there are no external struggles with trials and tribulations (and in fact even when there are), there is always the constant struggle within us, to restrain ourselves. In real life, after childhood, there are in fact very few moments—if any—of complete abandon, like those we see at the end of movies, with happy, fade-out background music. As soon as we let our guard down, the ego rears its head and makes us do something that makes us internally uneasy and from which we will later suffer. Human life is the self-awareness of the soul. It is a vigilant wake over—and struggle with—our own egos.

(I)(G) *Who Is Alive?*

False life

From all that we have said above, it follows that there is a "false life" and a "true life." The "false life" is the life of the ego that does not look beyond itself and allows itself full rein to work its evil. However, in reality there is not merely the futility of the life of the ego, but also the meeting with God after death and then the awful payback of our own sins. God summarizes all of these realities together in a single verse in the Qur'an:

> And as for those who disbelieve, their works are like a mirage in a plain which the thirsty man supposes to be water until he comes to it and finds it to be nothing, and he finds God there, Who pays him his account in full; and God is swift at reckoning. (*Al-Nur* 24:39)

So, the life of the ego is a mirage, an illusion of life. It is a false life, and it inevitably ends badly. The ego is never truly alive.

True life

Earlier we said that human beings were created to worship, know, and love God and to love others, be kind to them, and do good deeds. We later discussed *the soul at peace*, which is, as it were, the opposite of the ego, and said that true life lies in the self-aware soul. It remains to be said that it is only the *soul at peace* which has—and will have in eternity—true life. God says in the Qur'an:

> That which is with you will come to an end, but that which is with God remains. And He shall surely pay those who were patient their reward according to the best of what they used to do. / Whoever acts righteously, whether male or female, and is a believer, him verily We shall revive with a goodly life. And We shall surely pay them their reward according to the best of what they used to do. (*Al-Nahl* 16:96–97).

The "goodly life" (*hayatan tayyibah* in Arabic) mentioned here requires belief and virtue but is true life. It is true because it is the life that the *soul at peace* will have in eternity. That is why we have called this tract "On the Truly Happy Life."

PART II: HAPPINESS

(II)(A) What Is Not Happiness?

The religion of Islam is meant (in principle at least) to lead to happiness. God says to the Prophet Muhammad ﷺ in the Qur'an:

> Ta Ha. / We have not revealed the Qur'an to you that you should be miserable. (*Ta Ha* 20:1–2)

But what is happiness? Before answering this question, we have to clarify what it is not. In the Qur'an, there is a clear distinction between the quality of "happiness" (*sa'adah*) and the three sentiments often confused with it: "enjoyment" (*mut'a*), "joy" (*farah*), and "contentment" (*rida*). A close reading of the Qur'an shows that each of these terms has a deliberate, specific, and noninterchangeable meaning and is only used in an appropriate context. Understanding the differences between each of these, then, becomes the key to answering the all-important question: *what is happiness?*

Enjoyment

In the Qur'an, enjoyment (*mut'a*) tends to denote taking pleasure (*istimta'*) in a stimulus that originates from the physical senses, or that comes via the physical senses. Human beings share this kind of pleasure with animals. God says in the Qur'an:

> . . . As for those who disbelieve, they take their enjoyment and eat as the cattle eat . . . (*Muhammad* 47:12)

Though powerful, the problem with this kind of pleasure is that it is short-lived, because apart from anything else, the body—and worldly life itself—are brief. Indeed, in the Qur'an, God asks believers:

> . . . Are you so content with the life of this world, rather than with the Hereafter? Yet the enjoyment of the life of this world compared with the Hereafter is but little. (*Al-Tawbah* 9:38)

So, pleasure never leads to happiness. It is a *feeling*, and it does not last. This perhaps also explains why a lot of religious rules—such as fasting—are precisely about controlling physical pleasures or being patient in the face of their absence or their opposite (pain).

Joy

The *Oxford English Dictionary* (2014) defines "joy" as "a feeling of great pleasure and happiness." In the Qur'an, however, joy (*farah*) is something slightly different: it is a "happy" feeling, possibly with great pleasure, but it is not the same thing as happiness.

In fact, there are two kinds of joy mentioned in the Qur'an. One is positive and the other is negative. Negative joy is basically worldly joy. God says in the Qur'an:

> They rejoice in the life of this world, yet the life of this world in the Hereafter, is but [a brief] enjoyment. (*Al-Ra'd* 13:26)

Positive joy, on the other hand, is rejoicing in God, or because one sees something as coming from God. God says in the Qur'an:

> Say: "In the bounty of God, and in His mercy in that let them rejoice: it is better than what they hoard." (*Yunus* 10:58)

Both kinds of joy seem to depend on being given something: on *getting* or *receiving*. The difference between them is not so much what one receives, but how one sees it. In other words, when one receives something—say food, clothing, a home, a car, or any reasonable material benefit—if one rejoices in it merely for the sake of increasing one's worldly acquisitions, then that is "negative joy." If, however, one rejoices in it as a gift from God and for the good it may do, then that is "positive joy." But in both cases, joy, like pleasure, is not permanent. It fades either when the gift fades or when its novelty fades. It is not happiness.

Contentment

The *Oxford English Dictionary* (2014) defines the adjective "content" as "willing to accept something; satisfied." This is not very different from contentment (*rida*) as understood in the Qur'an. However, as with joy, there are two kinds of contentment in the Qur'an, one negative and one positive. The negative one is contentment with the world:

> Truly those who do not expect to encounter Us, and are content with the life of this world, and feel reassured in it, and those who are heedless of Our signs ... (*Yunus* 10:7)

The positive one is contentment with what God gives:

> If only they had been content with what God and His messenger have given them, and had said, "Sufficient for us is God ..." (*Al-Tawbah* 9:59)

Both kinds of contentment depend on a certain situation: on *having* something. Like joy, the difference between them is not so much what one has, but how one sees it. And, like joy, it is dependent on—or at least relative to—something external. Of course, if what is external is permanent and wonderful—as it will be in heaven—then contentment means never experiencing fear, suffering, privation, or want. God says of the blessed:

> Their reward with their Lord will be Gardens of Eden underneath which rivers flow, wherein they shall abide forever. God is content with them, and they are content with Him. That is [the reward] for him who fears his Lord. (*Al-Bayyinah* 98:8)

But this still does not make contentment exactly the same thing as happiness. Contentment is still something more contingent and perhaps also more passive.

In summary, the sentiment of "pleasure" comes from *feeling*, the sentiment of "joy" comes from *getting*, and the sentiment of "contentment" comes from *having*. And yet none of these are exactly the same thing as "happiness."

(II)(B) What Is Happiness?

Defining "happiness" from the Qur'an

The Arabic word for "happiness" (*sa'adah*)—or rather, its derivatives—occurs only twice in the Qur'an. It describes a sentiment, a quality, and a permanent state. It never describes a state of human beings in this world. Both times occur in the following passage, referring to paradise:

> The day it comes, no soul shall speak except by His permission. Some of them will be wretched, and some happy. / The wretched ones will be in the fire, sighing and groaning. / Remaining there as long as the heavens and the earth endure, unless your Lord wills. Your Lord does what He wills. / And as for those who are happy they shall be in paradise, remaining there for as long as the heavens and the earth endure, unless your Lord wills—uninterrupted giving. (*Hud* 11:105–8)

How does this define "happiness?" To answer this, we need to know that often in the Qur'an, definitions or clarifications are given immediately after a concept is named. Here we note that the "happiness" mentioned here is associated with "uninterrupted giving." Now the word for "giving" in Arabic (*ata*), together with its derivatives, only occurs fourteen times in the Qur'an, and nowhere else in the Qur'an is "uninterrupted giving" mentioned. So, we can conclude that happiness comes from "uninterrupted giving": God gives uninterruptedly to people in heaven, just as they gave uninterruptedly on earth.

Consequently, we can perhaps define human happiness as the following: the sentiment and quality which, as a mercy from God, comes from *uninterrupted giving* of something positive with a good intention. This is in a sense

obvious, since it is the insatiable ego that makes people unhappy, and "unin-
terrupted giving" is precisely the abandonment and emptying of the ego.
And when the ego is gone, the soul naturally returns to God and paradise.
As cited (in part) earlier, God says in the Qur'an:

> O soul at peace! / Return to your Lord, pleased, pleasing. / Then enter
> among My servants! / And enter My paradise! (*Al-Fajr* 89:27–30)

The "Pursuit of Happiness"

The 4th of July, 1776, United States of America's Declaration of Indepen-
dence drafted by Thomas Jefferson famously says:

> We hold these truths to be self-evident, that all men are created
> equal, that they are endowed by their Creator with certain unalien-
> able Rights, that among these are Life, Liberty, and the pursuit of
> Happiness.

Ever since then—and no doubt before—people (Muslims included) have
overtly assumed that it is quite natural, if not commendable, to strive to
be happy, or rather to make that the whole goal of their lives. Many people spend their whole lives "chasing" happiness. But it should be noted that
Jefferson wrote "the pursuit of Happiness," not "pursuing Happiness." This
is important because "pursuing Happiness" might suggest that happiness is
extrinsic, and indeed that is precisely the error of capitalist culture and con-
sumer societies: they look for happiness in and through extrinsic, imper-
sonal objects. "The pursuit of Happiness" does not suggest that at all, but
rather suggests a personal quest.

Indeed, happiness, as we have seen, comes from the activity of giving,
not from the activity of getting or having (or enjoying). Therefore, happiness
comes from our own activities (together with the right intentions). Consequently, pursuing passions, material acquisitions, and selfish actions can
never lead to happiness. But giving as much as we can all the time in some
way to someone or something that needs it (or to God, Who does not need
it) can lead to happiness. This means giving not just money and material
things, but our time, energy, knowledge, and care—in short, ourselves, to
the detriment of our egos.

Everyone can do that, to some extent, as so many disabled, handicapped, hungry, sick, and elderly people prove every day, simply by being patient. After all, patience is a kind of generosity towards destiny and therefore towards God's Will.

Among enabled people, no one understands this more than mothers, doctors, nurses, caregivers, aid workers, and teachers. They are often among the happiest people, because they exhaust themselves in giving. Lovers sense this as well. Love affords them glimpses of happiness. People employed in a job in which they feel productive appreciate this as well: they give themselves in their work, and this leads to "job satisfaction," which is also a glimmer of happiness. In fact, anyone who gives of themselves or their time in an unselfish way will experience some happiness. So, anyone interested in the "pursuit of Happiness" should take note: happiness is giving, not taking, having, or enjoying. Surely there is no more beautiful moral teaching than that. God says in the Qur'an (referring to good people):

> And they give food, they love it themselves, to the needy, and the orphan, and the prisoner, / [saying] "We feed you for the sake of God alone. We do not desire any reward from you, nor any thanks." (*Al-Insan* 76:8–9)

(II)(C) Why Is Happiness?

Why is happiness? Or rather, why is there happiness? There are two answers to this question: one theological, one ontological. In other words, "what is the purpose of happiness?" and "what is the origin of happiness?" The theological answer is very simple, and we alluded to it earlier. God created the world for His Mercy, and obviously happiness is part of that. What then is the origin of happiness?

Divine Bliss

Clearly God possesses all perfections. This is indicated in the Qur'an through His Most Beautiful Names in the Qur'an (*Al-Asma al-Husna*, as mentioned in *Al-A'raf* 7:180, *Al-Isra'* 17:110, *Ta Ha* 20:8, and *Al-Hashr* 59:24). Bliss as such—that is, perfect happiness, joy, and contentment—is clearly a perfection and therefore must be possessed by God. Indeed, the idea of Divine Bliss—that is, perfect infinite self-contained happiness, joy, and contentment—is specifically contained in the Divine Names that specifically indicate absolutely autonomous perfections, such as: *Al-Salaam* (the Flawless), *Al-Qayyum* (the Self-Subsistent), *Al-Quddus* (the Holy), *Al-Ghani* (the Rich), and *Al-Jamil* (the Beautiful). In short, Divine Bliss is inherent in Divine Perfection.

Divine Beatitude

The idea of a bliss superior even to paradise, which is granted by God to human beings, is mentioned both in the Qur'an and the *ahadith*. It is the supreme kind of happiness. It is a state of "being with God," and therefore of "divine beatitude" (*ridwan* in Arabic). The Prophet Muhammad ﷺ described it as follows:

> God will say to the people of paradise: "People of paradise!" They will say, "At Your service and Your pleasure, Lord; all goodness is in Your hands!" He will say: "Are you content?" They will say: "How could we not be content, Lord, when You have given us what You never gave any of Your creatures?" He will say: "Shall I not give you what is better?" They will say: "Lord, what could be better than that?" He will say: "I will enfold you in My beatitude, and will never be angry with you thereafter." (*Sahih Bukhari; Sahih Muslim*)

Consequently, God says in the Qur'an:

> God has promised the believers, both men and women, Gardens underneath which rivers flow, to abide therein, and blessed dwellings in the Gardens of Eden, and beatitude from God is greater. That is the supreme triumph. (*Al-Tawbah* 9:72)

In other words, divine beatitude is the supreme form of paradise, and paradise is merely a "taste" of this beatitude. In short, beatitude is the root of paradise.

Paradise

Paradise is nevertheless also a "great triumph." God says in the Qur'an:

> Whoever obeys God and His Messenger, He will admit him to Gardens underneath which rivers flow, abiding therein; that is the great triumph. (*Al-Nisa'* 4:13)

Eternal paradise is associated with human happiness. We have already cited God's words in the Qur'an:

> And as for those who are happy they shall be in paradise, remaining there for as long as the heavens and the earth endure, unless your Lord wills—uninterrupted giving. (*Hud* 11:108)

Therefore, paradise is the root of happiness, and that is the function of paradise precisely. Paradise is human happiness after death. That is also why the soul at peace from its own ego (by uninterrupted giving, precisely) experiences paradise. We have also already cited God's words in the Qur'an:

> O soul at peace! / Return to your Lord, pleased, pleasing. / Then enter among My servants! / And enter My paradise! (*Al-Fajr* 89:27–30)

In summary then, *uninterrupted giving* leads to happiness; the root of happiness is paradise; the root of paradise is divine beatitude; the root of divine beatitude is divine bliss, and divine bliss is inherent in God's perfection. And God knows best.

(II)(D) When Is Happiness?

When is happiness? Or rather, when are human beings happy? This question deals with the circumstantial aspect of happiness. In a sense, the answer is already provided in our definition of happiness as resulting from *uninterrupted giving*: happiness is so when the giving is uninterrupted. But then we must ask, when is giving uninterrupted? The answer to this is that it can only be uninterrupted through proper time management.

Time management

"Time management" has in recent decades become a very common topic at the workplace, largely because employers see it as a way of maximizing their profits. However, for all the talk about time management at work, there is little talk about private time management. In fact, private time is all regarded as "leisure time," with the idea that the more people have of it, and the more they spend it entertaining themselves or in indulging their pleasures, the happier they will be. This is of course the opposite of the truth. Happiness requires that this leisure time is properly spent on giving, not on enjoying or taking. The Prophet Muhammad said:

Make use of five things before five things happen: your youth before old age, your health before illness, your money before poverty, your free time before you are occupied, and your life before you die. (*Mustadrak Hakim*)

Al-Ghazali elaborates:

The obligatory acts constitute the capital by which salvation is attained. The voluntary acts are the profit by which are reached the high levels of success . . . You will not be able to rise to carry out the commands of God Most High until you monitor your heart and limbs in every moment and every breath, from the time you wake up until the time you sleep . . . .

Your time should not be without any structure, such that you occupy yourself arbitrarily with whatever comes along . . . A person who leaves himself without a plan as animals do, not knowing what he is to do at any given moment, will spend most of his life fruitlessly. Your time is your life, and your life is your capital: through it you make your trade, and through it you can reach eternal bliss, and nearness to God, Most High. Every single breath of yours is a priceless jewel, as it is irreplaceable. Once it is gone, it will never come back. Don't be like the fools who rejoice because their money increases while their lives decrease. What good is money when your lifespan is running out? (Abu Hamid al-Ghazali, *The Beginning of Guidance*, 1, trans. Mangera)

In short, in order to be happy, people need to manage their time carefully and balance between the responsibilities of work, worship, family, friends, and neighbors with their "own time," taking as little "own time" as they possibly can.

Time wastage

The average person in many countries—and particularly the average student—now spends more time every day on self-entertainment than at any other period in the history of the world. That is to say, the average person expends up to six hours or more a day—a quarter of their time alive; a third of their time awake—every day on television or movies, online surfing and chatting, social media, video games, pornography and adult entertainment, and music videos or pop music or radio. That works out to more than forty hours a week—which is the length of a full-time working week. It means giving a lifetime's worth of work and consumption to films and television, media, and internet giants for free. It is a hidden addiction and a form of internal slavery to fantasy and triviality. It is worldly life that has gone beyond play and diversion to misplaced passion and pride—and perhaps sown the seeds of social violence. And it is worldly life of the most removed-from-reality kind. It necessarily means making entertainment a religion and religion entertainment.

Of course, everyone needs to relax and unwind for an hour or so every day. However, six hours a day, without physical exercise, intellectual growth, or meaningful human interaction—to say nothing of religious, family, charitable, and social duties and activities—is an unprecedented waste of human time and, indeed, life. It also has profound negative psychological, cultural, sociological, medical, economic, and even political consequences. And it will never lead to happiness.

(II)(E) Where Is Happiness?

Where is happiness? That is, where is it to be found? The answer is, obviously: wherever happy people are. But what are the *agential* requirements for people to be happy?

Earlier, we saw that Islam requires people to be patient and steadfast in the face of the trials and tribulations of life, as best they can. However, to facilitate this, society—and, a fortiori, Islamic society—must protect people through establishing certain basic rights. The most important of these is *justice*.

The importance of justice

All human beings have an instinctive yearning for justice. Children have it, older people have it, and most of all, young people have it. Even when people cannot put it into words, they can generally identify it when they see it. Justice is essential for the proper functioning of any society, because it is an innate conviction of the human soul. No government and no institution can last long without justice. Moreover, behind every sincere call for change and reform in society lies a desire for justice (real or imaginary), so that search for justice is arguably the main driver for change in human history.

Conversely, the lack of justice—*injustice*—inevitably leads to discontent-
ment, protests, rebellions, revolutions, and civil wars. This has been true
throughout history. Injustice makes people angry and creates hatred. "Angry
young men" (and women) are usually angry because of an injustice—real or
perceived. For example, a large proportion of Islamist radicals and terrorists
become radicalized after a perceived injustice (although of course this does
not excuse them): often cruel mistreatment in prison, or the death or mistreatment of one of their relatives or friends. Nothing is more dangerous and
destabilizing than injustice.

In Islamic theology, God Himself punishes injustice wherever it occurs,
even when inflicted on people who do not believe in Him. The Prophet
Muhammad 🕌 said, remarkably:

> Beware of the prayer of someone who has been wronged—even if
> he [or she] be a disbeliever—for there is no veil between it and God.
> (*Musnad Ahmad*)

This *hadith* is remarkable because it is as if to say that even a disbeliever
will pray—or at least curse—when wronged, and that God listens to this
prayer and answers it, because injustice is so inherently wrong. Indeed, God
Himself says (in a *hadith qudsi*—that is, a hadith reported by the Prophet
Muhammad 🕌, where the speaker is God Himself):

> My servants, I have made injustice forbidden to Myself, and I have
> forbidden it to you, so do not be unjust. (*Sahih Muslim*)

What is justice?

But what exactly is justice? Obviously, it is important to be able to express
it clearly in words, in order to clear up confusion and to avoid the exploitation of perceived injustices for creating greater injustices—as often happens
nowadays. So, in order to implement justice and convince people of it, it is
necessary to be able to say exactly what it is—that is, to *define* it.

There is generally no legal or philosophical agreement on what exactly
justice is. The *Oxford English Dictionary* defines justice as "behavior or
treatment that is morally right and fair." This of course begs the questions

"What is right?" "What is fair?" and "On what is morality based?" God says in the Qur'an:

> Verily, God commands you to restore trusts to their rightful owners. And when you judge between people, that you judge with justice. Excellent is the instruction God gives you. God is ever Hearer, Seer. (*Al-Nisa'* 4:58)

One of the truly astounding things about this verse is that before commanding, "And when you judge between people, that you judge with justice," "God commands you to restore trusts to their rightful owners." That is to say that God gives a *definition* of justice before commanding people to enact it. In other words, justice is: "to restore trusts to their rightful owners." Now a trust is something of intrinsic value and given by God, to be benefited from temporarily but not wholly owned. It cannot be disposed of at will; we do not have an absolute right to throw it away or waste it. It is something to which we have rights and responsibilities in equal part. Regarding everything as a "trust" leads to lending things dignity, inherent rights as well as a reminder of their fragility.

Moreover, the Qur'an shows "trusts" to include everything, even—or perhaps especially—things that are not a matter of law. The greatest of these is no doubt the Trust of the very human state and life itself, and indeed we have cited God's words in the Qur'an:

> Indeed We offered the Trust to the heavens and the earth and the mountains, but they refused to bear it and were wary of it; but man bore it. Truly he has proved himself an ignorant wrongdoer. (*Al-Ahzab* 33:72)

This then means that justice is the basis of not only every functioning society but also is necessary for maintaining an equilibrium in the human state itself. There must first be justice for people to have the opportunity to find happiness.

The five fundamental rights

The concept of justice implies also fundamental human rights, because these rights are necessary for human beings to continue to exist and flourish. Consequently, they are necessary for human happiness. Specifically, they are (according to Muslim jurists):

(1) the right to life;

(2) the right to religion (some scholars even put this right first);

(3) the right to family, procreation, and honor (this right is sometimes split into two: family and procreation, and dignity);

(4) the right to reason or mind (and so to think for oneself), and

(5) the right to property.

Obviously, each of these rights in turn also implies certain freedoms and protections. Islamic scholars like Al-Ghazali (in his *Mustasfa*) and Ibrahim al-Shatibi (d. 790 AH / 1388 CE) have gone through every single commandment in the Qur'an and traced them all back to these five fundamental rights. Consequently, they are sometimes called the "aims of Islamic law" (*maqasid al-shari'ah* in Arabic), for every Islamic law can be shown to have one (or more) of them as its goal. And they are what makes it possible in fact to work towards being happy through *uninterrupted giving*.

Other Trusts

We have seen earlier that the "Trust" includes the meaning of human vicegerency of the earth. This means that the earth, the environment, and all living creatures in and on the land, sea, and sky are part of the Trust. So, looking after these—and *giving* to—are both necessary for, and part of, happiness. The rights of the neighbor are also part of the Trust, and indeed, they are both necessary for, and part of, happiness. Moreover, the concept of Trust also means spending time with family or friends, relaxing, looking after one's body, and spending time with one's spouse. The Prophet Muhammad ﷺ said:

> Your family has a right over you; your guest has a right over you; your soul has a right over you. (*Sunan Abu Dawud*)

And also:

> Your eye [i.e., sleep] has a right over you; your body has a right over you; your spouse has a right over you. (Al-Khatib al-Baghdadi, *Al-Muttafiq wa 'l-Muftariq*)

Furthermore, this concept of Trust extends to every legitimate aspect of one's personal needs, to social interactions, to one's profession or vocation, to one's time itself (as we have seen), and to every other aspect of human life, including the mind and the body. Finally, and perhaps most obviously, wealth and money are a "trust" and not something which we have an absolute right to dispose of—or hoard—without moral responsibility. God makes this crystal clear in the Qur'an:

> Believe in God and His messenger and spend from that over which He has made you trustees. For those of you who believe and spend theirs shall be a great reward. (Al-Hadid 57:7)

All this is to say, then, that in order for people to be happy, society has to give people their fundamental human rights. They then, in turn, have to give back to God, to the environment and all living things, to their families, to their neighbors and to society, to their work, to their friends, and to their personal needs in a balanced way, including maintaining the mind through learning and reading and the body through exercise. And God knows best.

(II)(F) How Is Happiness?

To whom do we give?

We have touched on this at the end of the previous section (and earlier). We "give" first of all to God through worship (though evidently this is for our benefit, not His). We also "give" towards destiny and hence God's Will by being patient and steadfast (though, evidently, again this is for our benefit, not destiny's, which is immutable). Then, we "give" to our families, our friends, our neighbors, our societies (including perhaps our countries), our environment, and all living things. We "give" to our minds through learning and reading, and to our bodies through healthy lifestyles, exercise, hygiene, and maintenance. Finally, we "give" to ourselves through rest, relaxation, and enjoyment, all the while keeping a balance.

What do we give?

Obviously, we give our time, our energy, our acts, our care, our mercy and our love, our knowledge, our possessions and wealth, and even perhaps our health and our bodies. Sometimes we give our lives, and this is martyrdom, the ultimate gift, but which in fact leads to life rather than extinguishing it and about which God says:

> And say not of those slain in God's way: "They are dead"; rather they are living; but you are not aware. (*Al-Baqarah* 2:154)

In short then, we give—or may give (depending on the circumstance)—all of ourselves.

The etiquette of giving

It is not just *what* we give that is important for happiness, but *how* we give it. Happiness cannot be attained by philanthropy alone or by punching in hours doing social work. Indeed, in the Qur'an there is a passage that seems to be specifically about *how* to give. This passage is completely remarkable for its delicacy and subtlety of feeling:

> The likeness of those who spend their wealth in the way of God is as the likeness of a grain of corn that sprouts seven ears, in every ear a hundred grains; so God multiplies for whom He will; God is Embracing, Knowing. / Those who spend their wealth in the way of God then do not follow up their spending with reminders of their generosity and hurtful words, their wage is with their Lord, and no fear shall befall them, neither shall they grieve. / A kind word and forgiveness is better than a charitable deed followed by injury; and God is Independent, Forbearing. / O you who believe, do not cancel out your charitable deeds with reproach and injury, like someone who spends his wealth only to show off to men and does not believe in God and the Last Day. The likeness of him is as the likeness of a smooth rock on which is soil, and a torrent smites it, and leaves it barren. They have no power over anything that they have earned. God guides not the disbelieving folk. / But the likeness of those who spend their wealth, seeking God's good pleasure, and to affirm [their faith] is as the likeness of a garden upon a hill; a torrent smites it and it yields its produce twofold; if no torrent smites it, then dew, and God sees what you do. / Would any of you wish to have a garden of date palms and vines, with rivers flowing beneath it, for him there is in it all manner of fruit, then old age smites him, and he has offspring, but they are weak; then a whirlwind with fire smites it, and it is consumed. So, God makes clear the signs to you, so that you might reflect. / O you who believe, spend of the

good things you have earned, and of what We have produced for you from the earth, and do not give away the bad things that you would never take yourselves without closing your eyes to them; and know that God is Independent, Laudable. (*Al-Baqarah* 2:261–67)

This passage is too rich and too deep to discuss in depth here, but it makes clear that in giving one has to, at least:

(1) give without pride and, if possible, anonymously, like the grain of corn falling into the ground;

(2) first of all, give the recipient their dignity through "A kind word" (and if necessary) "forgiveness," so that he or she feels loved;

(3) then, never mention the charity again: there should be no "reminders of their generosity" and [consequently] "hurtful words," so that the recipient is never embarrassed;

(4) the giving should never come "with reproach and injury"—this effectively gives with one hand while taking with other—so that the recipient is never humiliated; and

(5) the gift itself should be what we ourselves greatly value and love, and not what we "would never take ourselves," "without closing" our "eyes to them." This ensures that our giving is sincere, and that it is worthwhile for the recipient. It also contains the additional gift of not putting the recipient in a position to be ungrateful.

All this is to say then that *how* one gives can make the act of giving involve at least five different gifts at once for both the giver and the recipient: the thing given and the sacrifice that involves, the love and dignity given with it, the humility and gratitude one has to practice whilst giving, the anger management one has to practice in forgiveness, and the self-censorship one has to practice afterwards in order to never bring it up again. No wonder then that "God multiplies for whom He will" and that "their wage is with their Lord, and no fear shall befall them, neither shall they grieve."

(II)(G) Who Is Happy?

Happiness in the world?

The Qur'an never actually mentions the existence of happiness in the world. As seen earlier, it refers to happiness twice, both times in the context of paradise.

However, we also noted the uninterrupted giving in heaven is the result, and the reflection of, people's uninterrupted giving in the world. This would seem to imply that happiness can exist in the world. Moreover, we noted that even when people are incapacitated, they can give merely by being patient, which seems to indicate giving is possible at all times.

But is it realistic to expect the soul to give constantly without interruption? Doesn't the soul need something to sustain it in its uninterrupted giving?

The vision of the inner heart (fu'ad)

Earlier we mentioned that the "spiritual heart" (qalb in Arabic) perceives spiritual realities and truths from God and that God says in the Qur'an:

> Have they not traveled through the land with hearts to comprehend, or ears to hear? Indeed it is not eyes that are blind, but the hearts within the breasts. (Al-Hajj 22:46)

But strictly speaking, it is the "spiritual heart" (qalb) that can go blind, and it is the "inner spiritual heart" (fu'ad) that sees. God says in the Qur'an, referring to the Prophet Muhammad ﷺ:

> The inner heart (fu'ad) did not deny what he saw. / Will you then dispute with him concerning what he saw? / And verily he saw him another time, / by the Lote-tree of the Ultimate Boundary, / near which is the Garden of the Retreat, / when there shrouded the Lotetree that which shrouded [it], / His sight never swerved, nor did it go wrong. / Verily he saw some of the greatest signs of his Lord. (Al-Najm 53:11-18)

This "inner heart" (fu'ad) is associated with the spirit, as mentioned, but it cannot be experienced through human endeavor, but only by God's command:

> Exalter of ranks, Lord of the Throne, He sends the Spirit by His command upon whomever He wishes of His servants, that he may warn them of the Day of Encounter. (Ghafir 40:15)

The spirit

It is not, however, only prophets whom God "reinforces" with the spirit, it is also certain (select) believers, as God makes clear in His words:

You will not find a people who believe in God and the Last Day loving
those who oppose God and His Messenger, even though they were
their fathers or their sons or their brothers or their clan. [For] those
He has inscribed faith upon their hearts and strengthened them with
a spirit from Him . . . (*Al-Mujadilah* 58:22)

People who are "strengthened" with spirit are called God's "friends"
(*awliya* in Arabic). Because of their spiritual vision, they love God constantly and so can *give* without interruption. These are the people who find
true happiness in this life and in the next, and God knows best. God says in
the Qur'an:

Assuredly God's friends, no fear shall befall them, neither shall they
grieve. / Those who believe and fear [God], / Theirs are good tidings
in the life of this world and in the Hereafter. There is no changing the
Words of God; that is the supreme triumph. (*Yunus* 10:62–64)

Who is happy?

In summary then, if it is the *soul at peace* that is truly alive, it is the soul at
peace that is "strengthened" with the spirit that is *truly* happy, both in this
life and the next. Everyone short of that is happy to the exact extent that they
engage in *uninterrupted giving*. The state of being "strengthened" with the
spirit cannot be attained without submission (*islam* in Arabic) to God, with
all that this entails. God says in the Qur'an:

Is he whose breast God has opened to Islam, so that he follows a
light from his Lord [like he who disbelieves]? So woe to those whose
hearts have been hardened against the remembrance of God . . . (*Al-
Zumar* 39:22)

That is why we have called this tract "On the Truly Happy Life."

Conclusion

Summary

We can summarize the qualities of life and happiness as follows:

Life	Happiness
What is life?	**What is happiness?**
Life can be defined as something that, as a mercy from God, is self-aware (at certain times, and in certain ways, at least).	Human happiness can be defined as the sentiment and quality that, as a mercy from God, comes from *uninterrupted giving* of something positive with a good intention.
What is not life?	**What is not happiness?**
True human life is not the life of the ego. Human beings have a choice between a negative, worldly life, which is futile and subhuman, and a positive, fully human life of enduring goodness and righteousness.	The sentiment of "pleasure" comes from *feeling*, the sentiment of "joy" comes from *getting*, and the sentiment of "contentment" comes from *having*. None of these are exactly the same thing as "happiness."
Why is life?	**Why is happiness?**
God created people to worship Him and to love Him, so that He could be merciful to them and love them. Human worship necessarily involves virtue and kindness towards others, all others.	*Uninterrupted giving* leads to happiness; the root of happiness is paradise, the root of paradise is divine beatitude, the root of divine beatitude is divine bliss, and divine bliss is inherent in God's perfection.

When is life?	When is happiness?
Adults are morally responsible for their own lives. There are, however, unbearable circumstances under which people are absolved of moral responsibility.	Happiness can only be achieved through proper time management.
Where is life?	**Where is happiness?**
Society is the basis of human life. It requires many complex activities in order to function successfully.	In order for there to be happiness, societies must establish justice and five fundamental human rights, these being the rights to (1) life, (2) religion, (3) family and dignity, (4) reason, and (5) property.
How is life?	**How is happiness?**
Life can feel tough for everyone. It is supposed to. It involves a constant and vigilant struggle, first with one's own ego and then with the trials of life.	We may *give* our time, energy, acts, care, mercy, love, knowledge, possessions, wealth, health, and even our lives.
Who is alive?	**Who is happy?**
True life is the life of the soul at peace.	True happiness is when the *soul at peace* is *strengthened* with the spirit. Everyone short of that is happy to the exact extent that they engage in *uninterrupted giving*.

CONCLUSION

It will be clear from all that has been discussed that there is a philosophy—and, in fact, an exact science—of life and of happiness. It will also be clear that both of these may be deduced with perfect coherence from the Qur'an. Finally, it is clear that understanding these two can help—like roadmaps to our own inner landscapes—enormously in achieving both true life and true happiness. Indeed, without them, it is difficult to imagine being able to live a *truly* happy life.

All Praise belongs to God, Lord of the Worlds.

***

Passages are reproduced from HRH Prince Ghazi bin Muhammad's other writings with the permission of The Prince Ghazi Trust for Qur'anic Thought.

7

A Utilitarian Vision

Katarzyna de Lazari-Radek and Peter Singer

INTRODUCTION

We begin with a preliminary word about the suggested common format for this volume. We have been asked to discuss the good life under three separate headings: agential (what you do), circumstantial (how the world is for you), and affective (how you feel). We follow this format below, but we have to point out that it is a division that does not come naturally to utilitarians. For a utilitarian, the good life is one that is full of a certain kind of good—for classical utilitarians, it is a life with the greatest possible surplus of happiness over misery. Nothing else is intrinsically good. Because utilitarianism aims at promoting this good *universally* and not only for oneself, what one ought to do, as an agent, is quite distinct, conceptually and often in practice, from what will lead to the best possible life for oneself. Utilitarianism may require agents to sacrifice their own prospects of a good life in order to improve the lives of others. Therefore, we need to be clear that in general in this chapter, by "the good life" we mean the life with the most intrinsic good, and not "the life that the utilitarian agent ought to lead," or "the morally good life." Agency is not, for utilitarians, an intrinsic good. Agency is an instrumental good—in other words, its goodness depends on whether it brings about more of what is intrinsically good.

***

Utilitarianism is an ethical theory according to which our ultimate goal should be to make the world the best possible place by maximizing the good or well-being of all creatures whose lives can go well or badly. As we have just mentioned, in the classical version of utilitarianism, developed by Jeremy Bentham in the late eighteenth and early nineteenth centuries, "maximizing the good" is understood to mean the greatest possible surplus of happiness over suffering. For the classical utilitarians, "happiness" referred to pleasure and the absence of pain. This form of utilitarianism is also known as "hedonistic utilitarianism," from the Greek word for pleasure. Not all utilitarians are hedonistic utilitarians. Some philosophers think that well-being should be understood as having one's preferences satisfied. They are preference utilitarians. We are advocates for classical, hedonistic utilitarianism.

Utilitarianism is a perspective that continues to guide many people both in their personal ethics and in their judgments of institutional arrangements and social policies. Like the other perspectives described in this volume, utilitarianism developed at a particular time and place, but it also represents a tendency in thinking that has existed in many different times and places. Arguably, the first utilitarian of whom we have any knowledge was Mozi, a Chinese philosopher who lived from 490 to 403 BC, in an era known as the Warring States Period. Mozi criticized the customs of his time and argued that the test of any custom ought to be whether it leads to more benefit than harm. Moreover, in referring to harm, Mozi rejected the idea that we should be concerned only with harm to those with whom we are in some kind of relationship. We should be concerned about harm wherever it occurs. There are also clear utilitarian tendencies in Buddhist thinking, which cultivates compassion for all sentient beings. In ancient Greece, Epicurus argued that pleasure and pain are the proper standard of what is good and bad.

In Europe, the rise of Christianity overshadowed such ways of thinking, at least insofar as they focused on pleasure and the avoidance of pain in this world, rather than the next. Only with the coming of the Enlightenment could a climate more favorable to utilitarian ways of thinking emerge. The Swiss-French philosopher Claude Helvétius, the Italian jurist Cesare Beccaria, and the Scottish philosopher David Hume can all be regarded as precursors of Bentham. Even the eighteenth-century Christian clergyman William Paley was a utilitarian, for he argued that we ought to obey God's will, and God wants us to promote the happiness of all. In nineteenth-century England, utilitarianism's three most prominent figures were Bentham, John Stuart Mill, and Henry Sidgwick. The last of these, in his masterpiece, *The Methods of Ethics*, developed utilitarianism into a philosophically sophisticated system capable of overcoming many common objections. (We have recently brought his work into discussion with contemporary philosophical work in ethics and argued that it remains defensible.)[1]

Because utilitarians are concerned with the consequences of their actions, they are not bound by absolute rules that must be adhered to no matter what. In outlining the utilitarian perspective on what it is to live a good life, therefore, we are presenting a view that combines a normative commitment to making life as good as it possibly can be for everyone, with flexibility and openness to evidence regarding the ways of living that are most likely to achieve that goal.

THE UTILITARIAN CONCEPTION OF THE GOOD LIFE

Utilitarians hold that the best possible life is the life in which one has the highest possible well-being. As this statement suggests, the concept of a good life is not restricted to beings who are moral agents, responsible for their actions. The concept of living a good life—and its converse, living a bad life—applies to anyone of whom it makes sense to speak about their well-being. Depending on how we define well-being, that may include adults and small children, cats and dogs, pigs and chickens, aliens we have yet to meet, and—possibly at some future date—some forms of artificial intelligence.

In this section, we will start by examining more closely the utilitarian view of the good life, and then we will ask how this fits into the larger utilitarian picture of how we ought to live.

Well-Being: Differing Views

As we saw in the introduction, the classical utilitarian view is hedonistic: the best life for any sentient being is that which has the greatest possible surplus of pleasure over pain. If we use the term "affective" to cover all conscious experiences, then we could say that the good life is one with positive affective experiences. Sidgwick defended the hedonistic view of well-being by distinguishing between goods that are good in themselves, that is, intrinsically good, and those that are good because of their effects, that is, instrumentally good. He then argued that if we carefully reflect on what is intrinsically good, it can only be some form of consciousness. Without beings capable of experiencing anything, there would be no intrinsic value at all. Other popular candidates for intrinsic value, such as knowledge, virtue, or beauty, can only exist in conscious beings. Moreover, Sidgwick claimed, if we imagine any of these goods in circumstances in which they contribute nothing at all towards producing desirable forms of consciousness, we can see that we do not really value them for their own sake. They are instrumentally good, but not intrinsically good.

In the twentieth century, an alternative conception of well-being led to preference utilitarianism, a view that is clearly utilitarian, but not hedonistic. Preference utilitarians hold that the right action is the one that does most to satisfy, on balance, the preferences of all those affected by our actions. This view is based on a definition of well-being, and of utility in general, in terms of the satisfaction of desires or preferences. Part of the impetus for this view came from economists seeking to establish their discipline as a science. Troubled by the fact that states of mind like pleasure and pain are not observable or measurable, they began to focus on behavior. Suppose that I have a dollar, which is enough to buy either an apple or an orange. I choose the orange. That indicates that, at the moment I made the choice, I prefer an orange to an apple. Economists regard this as revealing that the orange increases my utility more than the apple would. This is not a prediction that I will get more pleasure from the orange than I would from the apple. On the economic position we are considering, whether I do or do not get more pleasure from my choice is unknowable and therefore irrelevant. It is the choice itself that reveals my preference-ordering at the time of the choice, and getting what I prefer constitutes my utility.

This new understanding of utility not only made economics appear to be more scientific than was possible for those who took utility to consist of certain mental states, it also enabled economists to avoid appearing to be paternalistically telling people what is good for them. Relating utility to preferences was, or seemed to be, a more democratic conception of utility. Partly for this reason, preference utilitarianism became popular among philosophers with utilitarian inclinations, and for a time this position seemed to have replaced hedonistic utilitarianism as the dominant form of utilitarianism. It was advocated, for example, by R. M. Hare, who held the chair of moral philosophy at the University of Oxford, and by one of the coauthors of this essay. In recent years, however, hedonism has made something of a comeback. This is due, at least in part, to the development of positive psychology and its interest in happiness, as well as to neuroscience and its new techniques for imaging the brain. The use of functional Magnetic Resonance Imaging (fMRI) has enabled scientists to track both pleasure and pain signals, thus providing new data on which some philosophers have drawn in defending hedonism. The preference view of well-being remains implicit in much economic thinking but is less popular among philosophers.

Derek Parfit, the renowned Oxford philosopher who died in 2017, has suggested that our understanding of well-being need not be limited to conscious states like happiness or pleasure, or to the satisfaction of desires. It can, Parfit suggests, include our achievements and also our moral goodness or lack thereof. Suppose, for example, that A is a person of good moral character and B is a person of bad moral character. Suppose too that B, over her lifetime, has a larger surplus of pleasure over pain than A (or, for preference utilitarians, we can suppose that more of B's preferences are satisfied, and fewer are frustrated, than is the case with A). Nevertheless, Parfit maintains, we could hold that A's life has a higher level of well-being than B's, because moral character is an element of well-being.[2] Given that utilitarians hold that well-being is of intrinsic value, this suggestion would make moral character an element of intrinsic value.

We are not persuaded that moral goodness or moral character should be regarded as an element of well-being. We hold that for something to be an element in a person's well-being, it must, as Peter Railton puts it, have a connection with what that person finds "in some degree compelling or attractive." Or as Chris Heathwood has put it, "It is hard to believe that showering a person with goods which in no way resonate with him is of any benefit to him."[3] We agree that to regard something as, in itself, an element of well-being, it must resonate in some way with the being whose well-being it is supposed to enhance. Resonance is a constraint on what can count as part of someone's well-being. Moral goodness has this resonance for many people; yet there are, regrettably, people for whom the idea of moral goodness, or having a good moral character, is not at all compelling or attractive. For this reason, we do not consider it plausible to hold that moral goodness or moral character is an intrinsic component of well-being.

We do not mean to suggest that for utilitarians the character of an agent is irrelevant. A utilitarian can agree that it is good to have certain character traits, namely those that make a person more likely to act in the manner that will best promote utility. These virtues may have great instrumental value, and the fact that many find the virtuous life to be an attractive life is a significant part of that instrumental value. All we are saying is that this value is derivative—they do not have value in themselves, independently of the good consequences to which they normally lead. The same holds for possessing a virtuous character.

Against the view that only conscious states like happiness or pleasure have intrinsic value, Robert Nozick has presented an influential thought experiment:

> Suppose there were an experience machine that would give you any experience you desired. Superduper neuropsychologists could stimulate your brain so that you would think and feel you were writing a great novel, or making a friend, or reading an interesting book. All the time you would be floating in a tank, with electrodes attached to your brain. Should you plug into this machine for life, preprogramming your life's desires? . . .
> Of course, while in the tank you won't know that you're there; you'll think it's all actually happening. Others can also plug in to have the experiences they want, so there's no need to stay unplugged to serve them. (Ignore problems such as who will service the machines if everyone plugs in.) Would you plug in? What else can matter to us, other than how our lives feel from the inside?[4]

Nozick's argument relies on the assumption that we would not want to plug in to such a machine. This shows, he thinks, that it cannot be the case that all that matters to us is our experiences. We don't want to be just a body floating in a tank, we want to *do* things—in other words, to act in the real world and to be agents.

Before we consider whether the experience machine thought experiment really refutes the view that only states of consciousness have ultimate value, we should note that preference utilitarians have a straightforward response. They hold that the good consists in the satisfaction of desires, and we can have desires for things that are not states of consciousness. I may desire, for example, that my colleagues esteem my work. I believe that they do, because they are unanimous in praising it. Perhaps, though, their praise is insincere—they know all about my fragile ego and how shattered I would be if I knew how poorly they really think of everything I do, and, as they are kind people, they are careful not to let their true opinions show. They do this so well that my states of consciousness are identical to those I would have had if they truly had admired my work. I never discover the deception and die happy in the belief that I have always enjoyed the esteem of my colleagues. My desire, however, was that my work should be esteemed by my colleagues, not that I should believe it to be esteemed by them, nor that I should have the desirable states of consciousness resulting from that false belief. So, preference utilitarians can agree with Nozick that we would not want to plug into the machine, and they can explain this by saying we have preferences that relate to reality and not to states of consciousness. Another way of putting this would be to say that we want to be agents, acting in the real world. For preference utilitarians, therefore, in contrast to hedonistic utilitarians, agency is valuable, at least for those who want to be agents.

In any case, we would question whether our reluctance to enter the imagined experience machine shows that hedonism and hedonistic utilitarianism cannot be true. One reason for this view is that this reluctance may be due to irrelevant factors, such as a bias towards the status quo, or fears that the machine will not work as described, or an admirable commitment to making the world a better place, rather than just retreating into a vat and abandoning everything else. (Nozick tells us that everyone will be able to plug into the machine, but that makes it even harder to believe in the story we are being told.) Or perhaps we have watched too many bad science fiction movies.[5]

In addition to these grounds for not reading too much into a hypothetical refusal to enter an imagined machine, we would argue, following Sidgwick, that the conscious experiences we would have in the experience machine are, in themselves, desirable. Is there something about the circumstances in which the person is having those experiences? But what would that be? The conditions under which the person in the machine is having the experiences can only detract from its value, we would argue, if they lead to worse states of consciousness, either for ourselves in future or for others. We cannot prove this, but to us it seems plausible.[6]

Our response to the experience machine indicates why hedonistic utilitarians will not accept the Christian view of joy, mentioned in other sections of this volume. According to that account, joy is "a positive affective response to an objective external good construed rightly and about which one is rightly concerned." For utilitarians, joy, as a kind of pleasure, is part of the good life, for it is a highly desirable state of mind, or in other words a great pleasure. It may in turn lead to further pleasures. But as a state of consciousness, it is not dependent on being a response to an objective external good construed rightly. A person may experience joy from a false belief about an objective external good. Indeed, insofar as Christians experience joy based on their belief that they have been "saved" by Jesus, atheists must believe that this is not a response to any objective external good construed rightly. According to the description given above, that implies that the feeling Christians experience is not joy at all. Utilitarian atheists, on the other hand, will say that it is joy and that it is valuable in itself, despite the falsity of the beliefs on which it is based. (On the atheist view, these false beliefs will have other consequences that may not be good at all and may outweigh the good of the experience of joy.)

Utilitarianism as a Moral Theory

Whatever well-being is, utilitarianism tells us that a good life has as much of it as possible. But since utilitarianism is a moral theory, its principle tells us that we should maximize well-being, not only for ourselves but for everyone, impartially, in accordance with Bentham's supposed dictum: "everybody to count for one, nobody for more than one."[7] Strictly, utilitarianism does not allow for special obligations to ourselves or to those close to us, unless special treatment of a specific group will bring about better consequences overall. Arguably, special treatment for our children, or close family members, can fit under that last exception because of the importance of close family ties for bringing up well-adjusted children and hence for maximizing the welfare of all members of society. But even that exception has limits that appear to be exceeded by the widespread assumption that parents should seek to pass on most of their wealth to their adult children, rather than use it to help others in much greater need.

This requirement that we should maximize good impartially has troubling implications, for it is contrary to the choices that most people make, and which they do not ordinarily consider wrong. Commonsense morality usually prescribes rules that are not especially difficult to follow: "Do not kill innocent human beings," "Do not steal," "Do not lie," and so on. Common sense recognizes some exceptions to these rules—for example, we may steal a loaf of bread to feed our starving child or lie to prevent a would-be murderer carrying out his aim—but in most circumstances, the negative form of the rules makes them easy enough to obey. Accepting utilitarianism changes this completely, for it rejects the idea that there is intrinsic significance in the distinction between acts and omissions. Failing to save a life may have consequences just as bad as killing, even if the motivation is very different. So, utilitarianism is not satisfied with obedience to rules beginning with "Do not . . ." It places positive obligations on us, including obligations to reduce the suffering of strangers, even when we have not been responsible for their suffering, and to make others happy. The only constraint on such positive duties would seem to be that we should not reduce our own happiness, or that of others, by as much as we are improving the lives of others. For people living in affluent countries, and not among the very poorest in those countries, that leaves almost endless opportunities to help others. We can do it 24/7, and still there would be much more to do.

Utilitarianism, its critics say, is just too demanding. Suppose that we give 10 percent of our income to a charity that pays for cataract operations for people in developing countries who cannot see because they have cataracts and cannot afford the simple procedure that restores sight. Still, we retain enough money to take the family on a winter holiday, flying to a beach resort where it is sunny and warm. We know that if we gave the money we will spend on the family holiday to the charity, that would be enough to restore the sight of several additional people. We also know that the difference between being blind and seeing is much more significant, in terms of well-being, than the difference between having a winter holiday at a sunny beach resort or staying at home. If we decide to take the holiday nonetheless, are we doing something wrong? The critics will say that this cannot be true and that such examples show that utilitarianism is not a plausible ethical theory.

Utilitarians may respond that the problem of demandingness does not come from their theory itself but rather from the state of the world in which we live. There are over a billion people living at a level of affluence that in previous eras was limited to a tiny elite, while almost a billion more are in extreme poverty, struggling to feed themselves and their family, to educate their children, and to obtain even the most basic health care. This discrepancy causes a vast amount of suffering that could easily be reduced if people acted even a little less selfishly. The world in which we all aim almost entirely at improving our own well-being and that of a few people close to us is a worse world than one in which we act more altruistically. Indeed, if all of the affluent people in the world were to be even a little more altruistic and to give, say, 5 percent of their income to charities that are effectively helping people in extreme poverty, the problem of extreme poverty could be overcome, or at least reduced to a small fraction of what it is today.[8] For the affluent, that would not be a great sacrifice. From this perspective, the problem of demandingness does not point to a flaw in utilitarianism: it points to a flaw in the world as it is today and to our failure to change that.

Although the above response may show that utilitarianism remains a plausible ethical theory, it is undeniable that in some circumstances utilitarianism requires us to make the lives of others better while making our own lives worse. This characteristic is not distinctive of utilitarianism. Many moral theories demand personal sacrifices. The terms "obligation" and "duty" suggest that we may be morally required to do what we do not want to do or what will not be in our own interests. Kant, for example, denied that an action done from liking or inclination has genuine moral worth; that comes only when one acts "not from preference but from duty."[9]

The only moral theory that can guarantee no clash between what we ought to do and our own interests is egoism, which tells us that we ought always to do what is in our best interests. Many philosophers deny that egoism is a moral theory at all. Egoism lacks, they say, the impartial perspective that is an essential component of morality, whether it is understood as acting only on maxims one is prepared to will to be a universal law, or as taking the perspective of an impartial spectator, or as choosing behind a veil of ignorance. We don't believe that this exclusion of egoism from the category "moral theory" achieves anything. To answer the egoist, it still needs to be shown that it is not rational to do what is in one's own interests, rather than what is right. Whether or not we regard egoism as a moral theory, a rational agent can still ask, "Why should I be moral?" and the question still needs an answer.

Secular utilitarianism cannot answer this question by saying that morality and self-interest always coincide, but utilitarians can find some degree of compatibility between the two and can do so on a solid basis of empirical research showing that those who concern themselves with the well-being of others are more likely to find happiness than those who live more self-centered lives. There is experimental evidence that happy people give more to charity and that those who give to others are happier and healthier. Moreover, the evidence indicates that this is not mere correlation. Doing good to others makes people happier than acting only for themselves.[10]

An analysis of Gallup Poll data from 136 countries showed that, in 122 of them, there was a positive correlation between subjective well-being and giving an affirmative answer to the question: "Have you donated money to charity in the last month?" The results were controlled for household income, so this was not simply a case of wealthier people being both happier and more likely to donate. In fact, donating to charity had the same positive impact on subjective well-being as a doubling of household income.[11] Researchers have also looked at what happens in people's brains when they do good things. They gave $100 to nineteen female students who, while undergoing magnetic resonance imaging, were given the option of donating some of the money to a local food bank for the poor. To ensure that any effects observed came entirely from making the donation, and not from knowing that others would think well of them, the students were informed that no one, not even the experimenters, would know which students made a donation. The research found that when students donated, the brain's "reward centers"—the parts of the brain that respond when you eat something sweet or see attractive faces—became active.[12]

Elizabeth Dunn and Ashley Whillans have found that altruistic behavior can lower blood pressure. They write: "We discovered that the more money people had reported spending on others, the lower their blood pressure was two years later. We thought this effect might be accounted for by variables such as income, physical activity or marital status, but no matter how we looked at the data, financial generosity was linked to lower blood pressure."[13] There are other studies with similar results, such as a study by Inagaki and Eisenberger that shows that "in humans, giving to others can reduce stressor-evoked sympathetic nervous system responding, which has implications for health outcomes."[14] These and other studies demonstrate that helping others is strongly, and causally, connected with personal happiness, and even with both mental and physical health.[15]

This may be the first time in human history that it has been possible to prove that the way we treat others has a direct and positive effect on our own well-being. Admittedly, this connection is contingent. It depends on human psychology, and it is worth noting that the subjects of the research were in secure circumstances and not competing with others to meet their basic physical needs. Moreover, even if it is true that for most people, treating others well improves our own well-being, it will still sometimes be true that following a utilitarian moral theory leads to a net sacrifice of one's own well-being. The conflict between following utilitarian morality and leading the good life oneself seems, at least from time to time, inevitable.

Life Going Well

In what kind of world is it best to live? In the previous sections we focused on what a good life is for the individual living it and on a utilitarian view of how individuals ought to act. In contrast, in this section we shift our focus from the individual to the world as a whole and ask: "What kind of world is good (or best) for everyone?"

At first glance, utilitarianism gives a clear answer to this question, describing in broad terms the conditions we should strive to achieve for all. A good world is one in which everyone's well-being is highly positive, and in the best world, everyone's well-being is as high as it can possibly be. Therefore, the circumstances that utilitarians will seek to bring about will be those that lead to the best, or at least a good, world. Like no other moral theory, utilitarianism has always given supreme priority to the practical outcome of its principle, which is to make the lives of all affected by our actions as good as possible.

Utilitarianism's Scope: Possible People

Nevertheless, this answer is not as clear as one might think. In the previous paragraph, we have used the term "everyone"—but that obscures a question first raised by Sidgwick, who noticed that it is within our power to influence the number of people who will exist. Assuming that people experience more happiness than misery, it will be possible to increase the total amount of happiness by bringing more people into existence, even though this means that the average level of happiness falls (because of, for example, reduced resources per person). So, the question arises, whether utilitarians should aim at the highest average level of happiness, or the greatest total. Sidgwick thought that they should aim at the greatest total. If we accept his view, then we may want to increase the number of people who exist, even if this reduces the average level of well-being, as long as it does not increase it so much that the total quantity of happiness is less. Others take a different view, saying that utilitarianism is about making people happy, not about making happy people. Derek Parfit has shown that resolving this debate is much more difficult than it appears, and we will not try to resolve it here.[16]

Utilitarianism's Scope: Animals

The term "everyone" is imprecise in another way. In most human ethical systems, the scope of ethical concern is limited to human beings, and in some cases, only to humans of one's own tribe, nation, religion, or race. Utilitarianism has always been consistent and emphatic in its concern for the well-being of all conscious beings. As we have seen, Bentham was an early advocate of extending legal protection to animals. Mill and Sidgwick agreed with Bentham that the pains and pleasures of all sentient beings, human or nonhuman, must be taken into account in calculating whether an action is right or wrong. Against the background of the Christian tradition, this was a radical innovation. The Roman Catholic Church, following Augustine and Aquinas, denied that we have any duties towards animals. Kant wrote something similar.

Today, the utilitarian position on animals is still a call for radical change, although it is gaining wider public support. Nevertheless, we use animals in many ways without taking their suffering seriously. Factory farming confines around sixty-five billion vertebrate land animals, mostly chickens and pigs, in conditions that are designed only to reduce costs to the producer, not to provide animals with what they need to live contented lives. Moreover, factory farming is completely unnecessary, because when we confine animals indoors, we have to grow grains and soybeans to feed to them. We get back only a small fraction of the food value of what we feed to them. Nor should we forget fish. We may not empathize with them as we do with warm-blooded animals, but estimates of the number killed start at a trillion per year, and virtually none of them experience a humane death.[17]

Utilitarian objections to the way we treat animals are based on reducing suffering and increasing happiness. Utilitarianism, as such, takes no stand on whether it is wrong to kill animals painlessly. What utilitarians think about that question will depend on how they answer the question we raised earlier when discussing the risk of extinction: should we limit our efforts to making people, or rather, sentient beings, happy, or is it also good to make happy people, or sentient beings? If we are concerned only with existing sentient beings, we will think it wrong to kill an animal if that animal could have continued to live and would, in the future, have experienced more pleasure than pain. On this view, it seems impossible to justify killing and eating animals, no matter how good their lives are. If, however, we are concerned with increasing happiness in general, that opens the door to an argument for continuing to kill and eat animals who live happy lives. For if no one is going to purchase meat from farmers who treat their animals well, the farmers will cease to raise animals at all. Suppose you are eating one of the rare chickens that did not spend its entire life in a crowded, ammonia-filled shed, but was raised outdoors, free to roam in a field. If that chicken had not been killed when still young, he or she could have continued to live a happy life. Yet if no one were to buy that chicken, or any other similarly raised chickens, there would soon be no more chickens living happy lives on that farm. So, one can argue, it is in the interests of chickens in general (though not of the particular chicken you are eating, once it was alive) that they are raised in good conditions *and* that there is a demand for their flesh.

As we have said, utilitarians are concerned about sentient beings. They therefore do not find intrinsic value in nonsentient nature—that is, in scenic peaks and rushing rivers, nor in verdant forests, or in the preservation of nonsentient species such as plants. Nevertheless, they may esteem these things as having great instrumental value—for example, for the recreational opportunities and aesthetic experiences they bring to human beings, and the habitats they provide to sentient animals.

Perhaps the most recent development in the area of creating circumstances that bring closer the achievement of utilitarian objectives is the search for ways of measuring happiness or well-being, and the increased interest in using these measures as a basis for national policy. The annual publication of the *World Happiness Report*, which began in 2012 under the auspices of the Sustainable Development Solutions Network, brings together some of the research in this area and also ranks many of the world's countries by their happiness levels.[18]

Institutions

Because utilitarians are concerned about consequences, they are not tied to any particular set of institutions. From Bentham onwards, most utilitarians have been democrats, and utilitarians have played important roles in extending the vote to those who had previously been excluded. Whether it was people who did not own property, or women, or people of a minority race, the utilitarian argument for universal suffrage was clear: if governments are to govern in the interests of all, then they need incentives for doing so, and the best incentive is that if they favor an elite, they will be voted out of office. Universal suffrage makes this outcome more likely. This is not to say that utilitarians have illusions about the wisdom of the majority. They may well agree with Winston Churchill that "democracy is the worst form of Government except for all those other forms that have been tried from time to time."[19] Nevertheless, if there were new and very strong evidence that a form of government other than democracy would, for the foreseeable future, lead to higher well-being than democracy, utilitarians could no longer defend democracy.

Making the World a Better Place

Although utilitarian support for any institutions is in this way dependent on the evidence that they lead to higher aggregate well-being, if we look at the historical record, we can glean what most utilitarians think about the circumstances most favorable for bringing about a good world. As we have already noted, the most prominent utilitarians have advocated far-reaching social and political reforms. The pattern starts with Jeremy Bentham, who wrote voluminously on a wide range of social issues. In his own time, he was famous for his proposals for electoral reform, prison reform, assistance for the poor, and new constitutional and legal codes. Today he is also well-known as a pioneering advocate of granting legal protection to animals. His essays opposing the criminalization of homosexual acts are less familiar, because they were not published until the twentieth, and in some cases the twenty-first, centuries. John Stuart Mill was a pioneering advocate of equality for women, arguing in *The Subjection of Women* that the inferior position given to women in his own time was contrary to the best interests of men and women alike. Mill was the first member of the British parliament to present a bill that would allow married women to own property. It was defeated, and the reform Mill was seeking had to wait another twenty-six years. Henry Sidgwick, together with his wife, Eleanor, were early supporters of admitting women to university and founded the first college for women in Cambridge.

Utilitarians have also generally been strong supporters of freedom of speech. John Stuart Mill's essay *On Liberty* is still often cited as the classic defense of freedom of thought and expression, which Mill expressly defended on utilitarian grounds. In the long run, he argued, freedom of expression best advances social and moral progress. Mill also contended that the state is not justified in interfering with individuals for their own good, whether that be their own physical good or their own moral good. The only proper reason for interference with individual liberty, in Mill's view, is to prevent harm to others. Today, in different circumstances and on the basis of compelling evidence of benefits, utilitarians are more likely to accept some paternalistic measures aimed at protecting individuals from physical harm—for example, laws requiring motorcyclists to wear helmets and people in cars to wear seatbelts.

In the twentieth century, utilitarians supported social reforms in developed countries, especially the development of a welfare state to protect people against poverty, unemployment, and illness. The introduction of a universal, free National Health Service in the United Kingdom in 1948 was very much in accord with utilitarian thinking, and the United Kingdom was soon followed by the Scandinavian nations, where utilitarian ideas are also prominent. Today, among affluent developed nations, only the United States, with its political tradition strongly based on individual rights, does not provide free health care for all. (We are not claiming that utilitarians are the only ones working for these reforms—their supporters had, as one would expect, a mix of philosophical and political motivations of varying kinds.)

In the last quarter of the twentieth century and down to our own times, utilitarians have continued the reforming tradition set by the founders of the theory, extending it to new fields in which suffering can be reduced and happiness increased. This period saw renewed interest in practical ethics, and utilitarians played important roles in discussions about new ethical and legal questions in medicine and the biological sciences, about the proper response of affluent people and their governments to the needs of people in extreme poverty, and—as we have already seen—about ending the ruthless exploitation of nonhuman animals.

Social changes and new biomedical technologies led to the development of bioethics, a field concerned with ethical, social, and legal issues raised by medicine and the biological sciences. In discussions of abortion, in vitro fertilization, experiments on embryos, genetic selection, and end-of-life decisions, utilitarians challenged taboos and questioned shibboleths. They denied the importance commonly attributed by medical practitioners and religious thinkers to the distinction between bringing about a death by the deliberate withholding or withdrawal of lifesaving measures and producing the same outcome by actively ending a life. Concern to reduce pointless suffering leads utilitarians to support legislation allowing physicians to respond positively, under specified conditions, to a patient's request for assistance in dying. For a life to go well, from a utilitarian perspective, it should also end well. Similarly, in vitro fertilization was at first widely condemned by religious leaders. Some said it was unnatural, while others objected to the fact that it severs the union between the marital and the reproductive acts. Utilitarians, on the other hand, looked to the consequences of the new technique, finding that they benefited infertile couples and did not harm the child who would not otherwise have existed, nor society as a whole.

Utilitarianism and Effective Altruism

For utilitarians, the well-being of people on the other side of the world has the same intrinsic significance as that of our neighbors. The only ethical justifications for doing more for our neighbors are practical: we may have greater knowledge of their needs, be able to help them more effectively, or have greater certainty that our assistance is reaching them and benefiting them. Modern methods of transport and communications, however, have narrowed the gap between what we can know about distant strangers and about our neighbors, and reduced the discrepancy in cost between providing assistance. Meanwhile the existence of effective aid organizations, whose work is rigorously assessed by independent agencies, has enabled us to have greater confidence in the positive impact of our assistance. Despite these changes in our circumstances, we still live in a world in which seven hundred million people are living in extreme poverty and nearly six million children die each year from causes that arise from poverty, and in many cases, this could be prevented at far less cost than is required to raise someone out of poverty in a developed country. At the same time, there are more than a billion people living at a level of affluence that enables them to spend money on many things that are clearly luxuries rather than necessities. Given that extreme poverty and preventable poverty-related premature death continue to cause a vast amount of human suffering, utilitarians regard these circumstances as in need of change.

The twenty-first-century movement known as effective altruism is one response to this situation, and utilitarians have played a prominent role in it—in fact, a 2015 survey of nearly three thousand effective altruists found that 56 percent described themselves as utilitarians. Peter Singer's essay "Famine, Affluence and Morality" influenced the thinking of younger philosophers such as Toby Ord and Will MacAskill, who set up an organization called Giving What We Can, soon followed by other organizations such as GiveWell, The Life You Can Save, and the Centre for Effective Altruism. The emphasis on effectiveness, rather than simply on being virtuous by thinking of others rather than oneself, is clearly consonant with utilitarianism. So is the impartial perspective that characterizes the effective altruism movement. If, with a given quantity of resources, we can do more good by helping people in a developing country than in our own community, effective altruists say, that is what we should do. Effective altruists also object, as utilitarians do, to discounting the future: the well-being of people a century hence is no less important than our own well-being. We may justifiably discount for uncertainty about the future, but not because we care more about the present and near future than we do about the more distant future. That judgment is highly relevant to discussions of what we should do about climate change.

Effective altruists are, once again, like utilitarians in that they are concerned about outcomes rather than about character or virtue. They are not much troubled, therefore, about whether people are acting in a purely altruistic way, or because they are aware that, as we mentioned above, helping others is likely to enhance their own happiness. What matters is that others are helped.

Effective altruists, like utilitarians, have generally focused on reducing suffering rather than on increasing happiness. That may be because it is often clearer how we can go about doing the former than the latter: if people are hungry, cold, or in pain, it is obvious how to alleviate their misery; if people are not particularly happy, it isn't at all obvious how to make them happy. It could also be that we perceive an asymmetry between happiness and suffering. Would you be prepared to experience another hour as bad as the worst suffering you have ever experienced, in order to have another hour as good as the greatest happiness you have ever experienced? If you answer that question with a firm "no," then you also think there is an asymmetry that justifies a greater focus on reducing suffering. Nevertheless, when effective altruists and utilitarians have the opportunity to increase happiness, they agree that this is a good thing to do. The Himalayan kingdom of Bhutan has been a forerunner in making happiness the primary goal of national policy. Already in 1979 when the king of Bhutan, Jigme Singye Wangchuck, was asked by journalists about Bhutan's Gross National Product, he said, "We do not believe in Gross National Product. Gross National Happiness is more important."[20] When Bhutan became a democracy in 2008, the goal of Gross National Happiness was written into its constitution. Government initiatives are screened for their impact on this goal by the Gross National Happiness Commission, and if the Commission assesses that impact as negative, the initiative will not be implemented.

At Bhutan's initiative, in 2011 the UN General Assembly unanimously adopted a resolution in recognizing happiness as a "fundamental human goal" and inviting member nations to measure the happiness of their people and take the results into account in setting policy. Other international bodies, including the Organization for Economic Co-operation and Development as well as the United Nations Development Programme, are taking steps to measure subjective well-being. Several national governments, including France, the United Kingdom, and Australia, have established commissions or government offices inquiring into national happiness. Nongovernment organizations, such as Action for Happiness, which has the Dalai Lama as its patron, are promoting happiness and encouraging both individuals and governments to take steps to achieve it.

Bhutan is a Buddhist nation, and the Dalai Lama is the world's best-known Buddhist leader. On the goal of promoting happiness in the world, there is clearly common ground between Buddhist and utilitarian perspectives.

The Risk of Extinction

Reducing global poverty and increasing happiness is one way of doing a great deal of good, but some effective altruists argue that we should give more thought to reducing the danger of our own extinction from causes such as nuclear war, a pandemic (either natural or deliberately started by terrorists), or a collision between our planet and a large asteroid. Nick Bostrom has argued that progress in artificial intelligence could lead to the creation of superintelligent computers and warned that to create something more intelligent than we are is "a basic Darwinian error." These risks may be very small, but utilitarians are concerned about "expected value," a concept that takes into account both the value, or disvalue, of an outcome and the probability of achieving or preventing it. On this view, eliminating a one-in-a-billion risk of an event that would cause ten billion deaths should be given ten times as much weight than the certainty of preventing one death.

Asking how bad the extinction of intelligent life on earth would be raises another, philosophically more difficult question. Should we, in making such calculations, take into account only the lives that will be lost if an extinction event occurs—for example, the more than seven billion lives that would be lost if a pandemic were to kill everyone on the planet this year—or should we also include the loss of the untold number of people who would have existed if the extinction event had not occurred? This raises the issue mentioned earlier in this section, about whether we should be concerned only to make people happy, or whether we should also see value in making happy people. In the case of human extinction, no one is made worse off by not coming into existence, because there is then no being at all. We agree with Sidgwick that it is good to maximize the total quantity of happiness. We also consider that human life in the future is likely to have a positive balance of happiness over misery. Hence we recognize that a world without human beings would, to that extent, have less value than a world with human beings.

FEELING GOOD

From what has been said so far, it is easy to see that utilitarianism closely connects a good life with positive feelings; hedonists especially associate a good life with a feeling of pleasure, but preference utilitarians will also think of satisfaction as one of the basic feelings that arises from fulfilling desires. Therefore we may say that "human flourishing" feels really pleasant to utilitarians! On the other hand, it is not so easy to say what exactly the positive feeling is, nor what its opposite is.

The classical utilitarians defined a good life in terms of happiness. By "happiness" they meant pleasure and the absence of pain. To modern hedonists and critics of utilitarianism alike, however, this has seemed to be too narrow a view of happiness. We believe it is better to differentiate these two aspects of life. Let us define happiness as a positive emotional evaluation, whether of a moment, a day, or the whole of your life. It can be understood as a kind of disposition, to be in a good mood, to be joyful and have a positive outlook on life. If it is a disposition, it can be valuable, however, only because of what it is a disposition towards. The disposition to be a good doctor is a good one because it leads to sick people being treated well. But there are, obviously, dispositions that may bring about bad effects—a disposition to be easily frustrated or angry, for example. If therefore we take happiness to mean a disposition, it is not happiness itself that is an intrinsic value but rather the feeling or feelings that it is a disposition to have.

Hedonists, of course, will take this feeling to be pleasure. But what is pleasure? We are all lucky enough to have experienced it, yet it is surprisingly

difficult to define. We feel pleasure when tasting delicious food, feeling
the warmth of the sun on our skin on a cool day, meeting friends, having
an engaging conversation, successfully completing an important piece of
work, jogging, or stroking a cat. But how do we know that all these experiences are pleasure? Do they have something in common that allows us
to call them pleasure?

Some philosophers believe that all pleasurable experiences share a common
characteristic. Pleasure is simply a distinct feeling and can be differentiated
from many other experiences by an intrinsic quality. This is sometimes called
the "feeling tone" understanding of pleasure, for it assumes that whatever the
source of the pleasure, whether we get it from exciting sex or from discussing
philosophy, it is the same kind of feeling. Other philosophers find that hard to
believe. They think that the different feelings we call pleasure have nothing in
common, apart from the fact that we have a positive attitude towards each of
them. This is an attitudinal understanding of pleasure.

Each of these ways to define pleasure has its pros and cons. The attitudinal view is closer to the commonsense view that physical pleasures are distinct from intellectual pleasures because they "just feel different." It also fits
with the idea that when I feel pleasure, it is the kind of experience that I want
to continue having, and not for any instrumental reason (as I may want the
feeling of muscle soreness after a good workout in the gym) but for its own
sake. This in turn makes a nice connection with an idea that for something
to enhance our well-being it must be the kind of thing that we want and are
motivated to have.

On the other hand, "the feeling tone view" is more in accordance with
current neuroscientific research. Some scientists believe now that wanting
something and finding it pleasurable are two distinct processes. In 1954, J.
Olds and P. Milner implanted electrodes into rats' brains and allowed the
rats to press a lever that sent an electric current to the parts of their brains
believed responsible for pleasure. The rats did that thousands of times, in
some cases to the point of starving themselves to death. Olds and Milner
believed that the rats got so much pleasure that they did not want anything else. But further research on animals and humans seems to undermine this thesis, for it suggests that the stimulation created a desire rather
than a pleasurable experience. If this is true, then we should not base our

definition of pleasure on something—wanting—that may occur without an experience of pleasure.[21]

Independently of the neuroscience on this issue, Alex Voorhoeve has questioned whether trying to have, or to sustain, a feeling is either a sufficient or a necessary condition of something being pleasure. To show that it is not sufficient, he uses the example of grief. When someone very close to us has died, we may want to sustain our grief. We may spend time looking at pictures of the person we loved, not because that gives us pleasure, but because we feel it is the proper feeling for us at that time. To show that trying to sustain a feeling is not a necessary condition of pleasure, Voorhoeve invites us to consider the phenomenon of schadenfreude. When we hear that a rival has suffered a misfortune, we may feel pleasure and yet at the same time be ashamed of ourselves for feeling it. We may try to cease feeling it, perhaps by telling ourselves that this person, though a rival, is nevertheless a good person who does not deserve the misfortune. Yet the feeling we experienced was definitely pleasure.[22]

Voorhoeve is right about the way many people will react in these examples, yet we do not think that they show that pleasure, considered purely as a state of consciousness, is not a feeling we try to have or to sustain. When someone we are close to has died, we may try to feel grief because we think that it is respectful to the deceased person, and hence right, for us to feel it. Perhaps we think it will, in the long run, help us to cope with our loss. We do not desire to have the feeling for its own sake. Something similar can be said about the case of schadenfreude. We try not to feel pleasure at a rival's misfortune only because we hold other views that make us think that we should not feel it. Otherwise, considered only as a feeling and independently of its object, the pleasure we got from the news is a feeling we would like to have.

CONCLUSION

Utilitarianism offers a clear answer to the question "What is a good life?" It locates intrinsic value in the conscious experiences of sentient beings and therefore holds that the ultimate goal is to maximize the well-being of all those who can have a good life. We hedonistic utilitarians hold that to have a good life is to have more pleasure than pain, overall, and the greater the surplus of pleasure over pain, the better the life is. At the same time, we encourage everyone to do the most good that he or she can do. By that we mean, to use your time and resources to do the most possible to increase well-being for all sentient beings. Acting in accordance with this utilitarian moral view will not always coincide with making your own life as good for you as it can possibly be, but we believe that, on the whole, people who strive to live an ethical life are more likely to find happiness than those who focus only on promoting their own interests.

Notes

1   See Katarzyna de Lazari-Radek and Peter Singer, *The Point of View of the Universe: Sidgwick and Contemporary Ethics* (Oxford: Oxford University Press, 2014).

2   Derek Parfit, *On What Matters* (Oxford: Oxford University Press, 2016), 3:401.

3   Peter Railton, *Facts and Values* (Cambridge: Cambridge University Press, 2003), 47; Christopher Heathwood, "Subjective Desire Satisfactionism," unpublished manuscript.

4   Robert Nozick, *Anarchy, State and Utopia* (New York: Basic Books, 1974), 43.

5   For a more detailed discussion of the role of all these factors, see de Lazari-Radek and Singer, *Point of View of the Universe*, 255–61.

6   On this point, see Mariko Nakano-Okuno, *Sidgwick and Contemporary Utilitarianism* (Hampshire: Palgrave Macmillan, 2011), 252–53, n. 10.

7   John Stuart Mill attributes this "dictum" to Bentham, but the closest variant to be found in his works is: "Every individual in the country tells for one; no individual for more than one," which occurs in Bentham's *Rationale of Judicial Evidence, specially applied to English practice*, edited by J. S. Mill, 5 vols. (London, 1827), iv. 475 (book VIII, ch. XXIX) (reprinted in *The Works of Jeremy Bentham*, edited by J. Bowring [Edinburgh, 1838–1843], vii. 334). The inclusion of the words "in this country" appear to reflect the focus of the work in which the passage appears, which is how to make a country's legal system work for the benefit of all who come under it, rather than of judges and lawyers. It is clearly not Bentham's view that utilitarians in general should only count the well-being of their compatriots. (We are grateful to Philip Schofield, Director of the Bentham Project at University College London, for this reference. Mill's version is to be found in ch. 5 of his *Utilitarianism*.)

8 Peter Singer, *The Life You Can Save: How to Do Your Part to End World Poverty* (New York: Random House, 2009; 2019 rev. online ed., www.thelifeyoucansave.org).

9 Immanuel Kant, *Groundwork for the Metaphysic of Morals*, trans. Jonathan Bennett (Cambridge: Cambridge University Press, 2008), 9, http://www.earlymoderntexts.com/assets/pdfs/kant1785.pdf.

10 Elizabeth W. Dunn, Lara B. Aknin, and Michael I. Norton, "Spending Money on Others Promotes Happiness," *Science* 319, no. 5870 (2008): 1687–88; Lalin Anik et al., "Feeling Good about Giving: The Benefits (and Costs) of Self-Interested Charitable Behavior," *Harvard Business School Marketing Unit Working Paper* 10–12 (2009): 1–23.

11 Lara B. Aknin et al., "Prosocial Spending and Well-Being: Cross-Cultural Evidence for a Psychological Universal," *Journal of Personality and Social Psychology* 104, no. 4 (2013): 635–52.

12 William T. Harbaugh, Ulrich Mayr, and Daniel R. Burghart, "Neural Responses to Taxation and Voluntary Giving Reveal Motives for Charitable Donations," *Science* 316, no. 5831 (2007): 1622–25.

13 Elizabeth W. Dunn and Ashley Whillans, "Give, if You Know What's Good for You," *New York Times*, December 25, 2015.

14 Tristen K. Inagaki and Naomi I. Eisenberger, "Giving Support to Others Reduces Sympathetic Nervous System–Related Responses to Stress," *Psychophysiology* 53, no. 4 (2015): 427–35.

15 For a wider perspective, see also Stephen Post, ed., *Altruism and Health* (Oxford: Oxford University Press, 2007).

16 Derek Parfit, *Reasons and Persons* (Oxford: Oxford University Press, 1984), pt. 4.

17 www.fishcount.org.uk.

18 World Happiness Report, http://worldhappiness.report.

19 Spoken in the House of Commons, November 11, 1947, and included in *Churchill by Himself*, ed. Richard Langworth (New York: Public Affairs, 2008), 547.

20 Tashi Dorji, "The Story of a King, a Poor Country, and a Rich Idea," *Business Bhutan*, 2012, http://earthjournalism.net/stories/6468.

21 Kent C. Berridge and Morten L. Kringelbach, "Affective Neuroscience of Pleasure: Reward in Humans and Animals," *Psychopharmacology*

199 (2008): 470–72. For the original research, see J. Olds and P. Milner, "Positive Reinforcement Produced by Electrical Stimulation of Septal Area and Other Regions of Rat Brain," *Journal of Comparative and Physiological Psychology* 47 (1954): 419–27.

22 A. Voorhoeve, "Discussion of 'A Defense of Hedonism' by Katarzyna de Lazari-Radek and Peter Singer" (Fellow's Seminar, University Center for Human Values, Princeton University, 2013). The example of schadenfreude is our own.

8

A Positive Psychology Vision

Robert A. Emmons and Roxanne N. Rashedi

Positive psychology (PP) aims to help people live and flourish rather than to simply exist.[1] It articulates a vision of the good life that is empirically testable. Since its introduction twenty-five years ago, positive psychologists have articulated the constitutive elements of the good life and empirically tested the viability of this framework. In that PP values cross-disciplinary exchange and the process of applying empirical evidence to historically significant theories of flourishing, it is ideally situated to dialogue with religious and philosophical perspectives.

In this chapter, we examine the vision of the flourishing life as delineated in the PP movement, particularly the ways in which it shares and overlaps visions of the tripartite model of the good life espoused by Volf[2] and by Croasmun and Volf in this volume. We contend that positive psychology provides a credible, complementary, and empirically supported scientific framework that answers the questions of what makes life worth living, how such a life can be achieved, and how it can be sustained. With gratitude as an illustration, we examine how a constructive engagement between PP and the humanities can produce significant theoretical, empirical, and practical advances into understanding the nature of a life well lived.

Since its launch in 1999, PP has initiated and established new and vital empirical research and practice in the fields of growth, virtues, strengths, and different ways or routes for how to live a good life. In the initial description of the field of PP, Martin Seligman connected positive psychology to the rich philosophical tradition of the investigation and cultivation of the "good life." He claimed that positive psychology could

> articulate a vision of the good life that is empirically sound and, at the same time, understandable and attractive. We can show the world what actions lead to well-being, to positive individuals, to flourishing communities, and to a just society.[3]

Understanding the factors that move a person closer to flourishing is a vital step in helping people live good lives.

At the outset, we wish to point out that the vision of human flourishing that positive psychology advocates is compatible with a number of philosophical and religious traditions, including those represented in this volume, as well as those that are not depicted here (e.g., Native American traditions, Sikhism). For example, Christian thought has promoted human flourishing throughout its history, with its focus on both individual and communal virtues. The former include faith, hope, self-control, righteousness, wisdom, and humility, and the latter compassion, generosity, gratitude, love, and forgiveness. Religious views, such as those offered by Christian theology, have, at least implicitly, contributed substantially to positive psychology. Conversely, positive psychology can, and has begun to, identify the psychological mechanisms responsible for how and why these virtues enable flourishing. Clearly, the teleology between positive psychology and Christian theology approaches differs in major ways. The telos for positive psychology might be defined as optimal functioning, in the form of maturity or flourishing of individuals and society. In the Christian narrative, the telos is a right relationship with God through identification with the finished work of Jesus Christ. One of positive psychology's distinctive contributions is an empirical test of the elements of flourishing espoused by Christianity or various other traditions advocated in this volume. For example, there is Buddhist positive psychology, Hindu positive psychology, and Muslim positive psychology. Toward that end, positive psychology is primarily, though not exclusively, concerned with the concept of mechanism: What are the processes by which practices and beliefs contribute to and promote flourishing?

INTRODUCTION

From its early days, the aim of PP has been to catalyze a change in the focus of psychology from an exclusive preoccupation with remediating weakness and distress to amplifying human flourishing by building strengths and virtues. Historically, psychologists have known much more about problems and how to mitigate them than how to move people beyond the zero point of distress and pathology to a life that is not simply better but actually good. A positive psychological perspective advocates for a focus of scientific theory and research on understanding the entire breadth of human experience, from loss, suffering, illness, and distress to connection, fulfillment, health, flourishing, and well-being. The foundational assumption of PP is that the good life is not the troubled life reversed, avoided, or undone. PP has grown by leaps and bounds over the past two decades. It constitutes a vital, active, and influential field of research within psychology. Evidence shows that positive emotional states and traits, strengths of character, and other positive psychological constructs have numerous positive effects on health, success, education, and other indicators of flourishing.[4] A key focus for the field is continuing to define, understand, and support human flourishing.

This being the case, there may be no scientific discipline better suited to articulating and examining the core elements of a good life than PP. Since its emergence two decades ago, PP's mission has been to provide scientifically based answers to the big questions of what is meaningful and valuable in life. Significant monographs describing and prescribing the landscape of positive psychology had titles such as *A Life Worth Living, Flourishing: Positive Psychology and the Life Well Lived*, and *Flourish: A Visionary New Understanding of Happiness and Well-Being*. Highly cited journal articles include those with the titles "Achieving and Sustaining a Good Life," "Formal Criteria for the Concept of Human Flourishing," "Foundations of Flourishing," and "What Makes Life Good?" Almost every philosophical and religious tradition over the millennia has described the meaning and purpose of life in terms of the pursuit of goodness—living well. We endeavor to illustrate in this chapter that by virtue of its being an empirical science, PP has a unique role to play in the examination of the good life.

The good life concerns a vitally important area of human experience that until recently was considered to be unreachable, if not unimportant in scientific psychology. For sure, there was a smattering of nonmainstream writings on the topic of flourishing, but it was not a vibrant focus of theoretical or empirical examination. That all changed with PP. The science of PP has provided a set of ideas and findings that adds to our understanding of how human life unfolds, what makes it worth living, and how such a life might be achieved. Smith and Davidson assert that all responsible science comes back to basic human questions about what is good and valuable in life.[5] That is not only true about the science of PP, it is in fact its hallmark. At the same time, addressing the deep question of what kind of life is worth living and how one might go about it is a task that should be approached with humility and in recognition of the limitations of the scientific method. Mihalyi Csikszentmihalyi, one of the founders of PP and editor of *A Life Worth Living*, said:

> Will these chapters add up to a complete and convincing argument about what kind of life is worth living and how one might go about it? Certainly not. The question is likely to remain open for as long as humans continue to reflect on their existence. But it is a question that needs to be asked again and again during each generation to prevent our understanding of life from becoming outdated.[6]

We believe that a major factor in the growth and popularity of the field is precisely its willingness to embrace the big, meaning-filled questions. The public has been eager to receive insights and recommendations from PP researchers and practitioners, so the quest has had a practical bent from the start. Even prior to the inception of PP as a distinct discipline, psychologists have long advised people on what pathways best led to a flourishing life, and they have tried, though not always successfully, to base their recommendations on research findings.

A POSITIVE PSYCHOLOGY OF THE GOOD LIFE

What is the concern of PP proper? Two decades ago, PP was founded by Martin Seligman in the course of his tenure as president of the American Psychological Association (1999). In the beginning, it was characterized as the study of the conditions and processes that contribute to the flourishing or optimal functioning of people, groups, and institutions. Seligman challenged his fellow psychologists to research "positive" human attributes and processes, to examine the sources of psychological health and wellness as thoroughly as the field had investigated pathology and dysfunction. Positive psychology was initially seen as the science of positive subjective experience, positive individual traits, and positive institutions. In this sense, the field provided new topics of investigation as well as new ways of thinking about existing constructs within the scientific study of psychological processes and human behavior. A core foundational belief shared among most positive psychologists is that humans strive to lead meaningful, happy, and good lives. The good life as a key object of study and cultivation within the field—especially the factors contributing to the best routes for obtaining it, how to build a good life—became the primary focus of theory, research, and practice in PP. In so doing, attention was turned to identifying and investigating those aspects of human condition widely accepted to be at the center of human flourishing (happiness, well-being, purpose, meaning). Marked by innovative approaches, interdisciplinary collaboration, and empirical investigations, positive psychologists moved their agenda forward.

Taking a broad approach, the founders of the field connected PP to the rich philosophical traditions of the investigation and cultivation of the good life. Seligman claimed that positive psychology could "articulate a vision of the good life that is empirically sound and, at the same time, understandable and attractive. We can show the world what actions lead to well-being, to positive individuals, to flourishing communities, and to a just society." PP does not identify itself as a religion. However, it shares concerns with those of religious philosophies, such as describing virtuous approaches to living and at times advocating the contributions of religious communities to the development and promotion of virtues and strengths. Many of the activities and explorations of PP are fundamentally concerned with what factors are conducive to the flourishing life and, by extension, what factors lead to its opposite state, languishing.

Positive Psychology's Aristotelian Heritage

Positive psychology articulates the presumptions of the Aristotelian approach to human nature and development, and this includes the view of the good person—the idea of the individual with positive character, strengths, and virtues. The most fundamental assumption about human nature and functioning from the Aristotelian perspective is the teleological idea that human life and human well-being consist in nature-fulfillment and that people are inwardly driven by a dynamic of ever more optimal functioning. Positive psychology is inspired by the Aristotelian model of human nature: to grow, improve, and function optimally is for positive psychology a fundamental or core concept. Positive psychology also powerfully draws on the concept of exercise and practice. It adopts and revitalizes an Aristotelian frame of reference and asserts that the science of psychology should once again include assumptions about the essence-driven motivation toward something better—that is, more optimal functioning. The Aristotelian model—an essentialist theory—holds that the development of any organism, including human beings, is the unfolding of natural, fixed, or innate potentialities. Within the Aristotelian model of development, therefore, there is a right, optimal, or perfect functioning that is teleologically fixed as the realization of innate patterns of growth. The Aristotelian model, moreover, clearly underlines how the developmental process of fulfilling human nature results in well-being. Or as Haybron points out, "In broad terms, Aristotelian theories identify well-being with 'well-functioning,' which is to say functioning or living well as a human being: the fulfillment of nature."[7] Aristotle also claims that "none of these of characteristics arise in us naturally. . . . Rather we are by nature able to acquire them, and we are completed through habit."[8] Thus, it is up to the individual to realize his or her full potential. Positive psychology stresses that the concept of good character constitutes one of the conceptual cornerstones of positive psychology. Virtue is a character trait a human being needs to flourish or to live well. In Hursthouse's account, virtues benefit their possessor and make the possessor a good human being. Human beings "need the virtues in order to live well, to flourish as human beings, to live a characteristically good human life."[9] Similarly, "the virtues are at once conducive to and constitutive of eudaimonia; each true virtue represents a stable character state . . . that is intrinsically related to flourishing as a human being."[10]

In the course of past decades, ethical theory in philosophy has focused increasingly on the assumption of the individual as having virtuous motives,[11] and positive psychology tries to revitalize this idea of human nature. Parts of psychology and other social sciences have always taken as a starting point that people in the past, present, and future have some common capacities or characteristics. Aristotle argues that when we travel and meet people in different cultures, we nevertheless "can see how *every human being* is akin and beloved to a human being."[12] Aristotle thus argues the position of common human features in different cultural groups.

One of PP's most notable contributions was the development of the Values in Action taxonomy of human strengths and virtues.[13] It was designed to "reclaim the study of character as a legitimate topic of psychological inquiry and informed societal discourse."[14] A systematic study of various writings of philosophers and spiritual leaders in China, South Asia, and the West led to the postulation of six ubiquitous core virtues, namely courage, justice, humanity, temperance, wisdom, and transcendence.[15] Peterson and Seligman argued that these virtues are universal, perhaps grounded in biology through an evolutionary process that selected for these aspects of excellence as means of solving the important tasks necessary for survival of the species. Character strengths are the psychological ingredients—processes or mechanisms—that define the virtues. Said another way, they are distinguishable routes to displaying one or another of the virtues. For example, the virtue of wisdom can be achieved through such strengths as curiosity, love of learning, judgment, creativity, and personal intelligence. The virtue of transcendence can be displayed through an appreciation of beauty, awe and wonder, gratitude, hope, and spirituality.

Positive psychology also argues that these strengths and virtues can be successfully and sustainably cultivated, and that their development and realization is conducive to human flourishing. As a consequence, a most particular aim for positive psychology is to develop and test interventions to build these strengths. These ideas of a common core nature for all human beings and of the continuous development and realization of these human potentials as the source of well-being and happiness constitute the central agenda for positive psychology. For positive psychology, in congruence with the Aristotelian model, goodness and morality, to sum up, do not come from outside the person. They do not arise from cultural sources or from the moral rules of society, but from the potentials of the human being him- or herself. It is up to the individual to realize his or her full potential. People have an inherent capacity for constructive growth, for kindness, generosity, and so on. But it needs to be continuously exercised. Fostering these virtues is a central aim for positive psychology, because measuring and building human flourishing is the mission of positive psychology.

PERMA: The Elements of Flourishing

The questions addressed in this volume are: What does it mean for us to lead our lives well? Under what circumstances should we hope to live? What does the good life feel like? The field of positive psychology is well positioned to answer these sorts of questions. If these questions are to be pursued productively by PP, "living well" in psychological terms needs to be defined. There are multiple definitions and theories surrounding human flourishing, but it can generally be defined as feeling good and functioning well in life.[16] Yet psychology has not spoken with a single voice. There is no single, coherent, or unchanging account of the good life. Nor has there been consensus on whether the good life should be defined prudentially or morally. Rather, a number of thought leaders, both classic and contemporary, have contributed insightful thoughts concerning core components of a life well lived:

- Maslow (1954: satisfying basic needs and then achieving self-actualization)[17]
- Freud (1909/1960: "love and work . . . work and love . . . that's all there is.")[18]
- Erikson (1963: developing psychosocial virtues such as trust, autonomy, initiative, competence, identity, intimacy, generativity, and wisdom)[19]
- Jahoda (1958: displaying self-acceptance, growth, personality integration, autonomy, accurate perception of reality, and environmental mastery)[20]
- Ryff and Singer (1998: self-acceptance, positive relations with others, environmental mastery, purpose in life, personal growth)[21]
- Deci and Ryan (2000: experiencing autonomy, competence, and connectedness)[22]

- Seligman (2002: attaining pleasure, engagement, and meaning)[23]
- Seligman (2011: positive emotions, engagement, relationships, meaning, and accomplishments)[24]

Of these formulations, we focus next on the most recent and comprehensive of these frameworks, Seligman's theory of flourishing. Flourishing is a dynamic psychological state of psychosocial functioning that arises from operating well across multiple psychosocial domains. Seligman identified five measurable components or elements of well-being: positive emotions, engagement, relationships, meaning, and achievement—hence the PERMA acronym. The PERMA model of well-being meets the following criteria: each element is pursued for its own sake and not just to serve another element (intrinsicness); each element can be defined and measured independently of each other (exclusiveness); and the elements lead to specific interventions to produce sustainable change in that element (modifiability). The list of elements is exclusive, but it is not exhaustive. For example, health, vitality, and responsibility are additional candidate elements. Together, these five elements constitute the "building blocks of well-being." The five elements are posited as universally shared means by which all individuals seek to flourish. The PERMA theory has quickly risen in the psychological discourse, and empirical analyses to ratify its viability have begun to appear with some regularity.[25] Seligman asserts that his model is descriptive rather than prescriptive and is prospectively directed: the goal of PP is to increase the amount of flourishing in individual persons and on the planet; the PERMA model aims to describe the means by which individuals and societies can flourish. Together, these five elements comprise well-being, but well-being cannot be reduced to any one of them. As Forgeard, Jayawickreme, Kern, and Seligman note, "Just as we do not have a single indicator telling us how our car is performing (instead, we have an odometer, a speedometer, a gas gauge, etc.), we suggest that we do not want just one indicator of how well people are doing."[26] People flourish when they experience a balance of positive emotions, engagement with the world, good relationships with others, a sense of meaning, and the accomplishment of valued goals. Although there is some debate over whether the elements of PERMA are causally conducive to, or merely constitutive of, well-being, there is considerable agreement that any comprehensive account of well-being must include these five components.

Positive Emotion

The first component of well-being centers on the maximization of positive emotions. Positive emotion encompasses hedonic feelings such as happiness, pleasure, and comfort as well as the discrete emotions of joy, gratitude, compassion, awe, hope, love, and other pleasant feeling states. This element of the PERMA model engenders conditions conducive to emotional well-being. The ability to cultivate and focus on positive emotions extends beyond outward expressions such as smiling behavior. Rather, this element requires the ability to optimistically view the past, present, and future from a positive vantage point. Adopting a positive perspective in life can enhance relationships, inspire occupational endeavors, and promote creativity. Positive emotions and experiences can function as markers of flourishing and are thus notably worthy of cultivating. Experiencing positive emotions is a primary goal of individuals around the world, and research suggests positive emotions are a key indicator of well-being; they are positively related to life satisfaction, resilience, mindfulness, social rewards, work outcomes, and physical health.

Empirical evidence demonstrates the value of positive emotions in human flourishing. Positive emotions result in numerous, interrelated benefits. First, positive emotions shift people's mindsets for the better. Research has documented that positive emotion expands the scope of attention, enhances intuition, and increases creativity. In addition, positive emotions change people's bodily systems. For example, one study showed that induced positive emotion resulted in a speedier healing process from cardiovascular challenges. Further, positive emotions are robust contributors to establishing and maintaining optimal mental and physical health outcomes. Prospective studies have found that frequent positive emotions predict the following: (a) greater happiness, (b) increased resilience, and (c) reductions in cortisol levels and stroke.[27] Lastly, and perhaps most fundamental to human flourishing, positive emotions predict people's longevity. Longitudinal studies have demonstrated a strong correlation between frequent positive emotions and longevity.

Engagement

The second facet, engagement, refers to psychological connection to activities or organizations that inspire people to learn, grow, and feel absorbed in activities and projects that facilitate flourishing. Engagement refers to a deep psychological connection to a particular activity, organization, or cause (e.g., being interested, engaged, and absorbed). When engagement is maintained over time, individuals are rewarded with a state of flow, characterized by anticipation, intense and focused concentration, control, a loss of self-consciousness, time distortion, and the experience being rewarding. A flow experience must provide sufficient challenge to stimulate the person but not be so challenging that feelings of anxiety, frustration, or stress arise within the context of the activity itself. When a person is utterly absorbed into the present and immersed in a given activity, such as dancing, playing an instrument or sport, or practicing yoga, feelings of exhilaration and happiness are engendered, particularly since flow experiences strike the balance between challenges and skills.

Engagement also hinges upon the identification and use of character strengths, the positive traits reflected in behaviors, thoughts, and feelings. Not talents or skills, strengths reflect one's character and personality. Examples of strengths include love (valuing relationships, caring, sharing), kindness (being generous, nurturing, and altruistic), citizenship (social responsibility, group loyalty), and integrity (taking responsibility for one's feelings and actions). Activities that provide rules, goals, feedback, and the use of effort and skills against challenge carry the potential for flow.[28] Intrinsically motivated individuals experience greater states of flow and, over time, become self-motivated to perfect skills and elevate themselves beyond the ordinary.

A growing body of literature suggests that engaging in flow experiences is strongly correlated with positive psychological functioning. A study involving American teenagers investigated the relationship between environmental factors, happiness, and flow. The results suggested that social, active, and passive leisure activities (e.g., sports in comparison to watching TV) were rated as above average in happiness, whereas school activities were rated as below average. The researchers found that relationships correlated to varying levels of happiness, in that being alone resulted in the lowest rate of happiness and being with friends corresponded to the highest rate of happiness. Of most relevance to engagement in the PERMA model, feeling active and engaging in flow experiences were the strongest predictors of long-term happiness. Engagement in flow experiences has also been examined in the workplace. Ceja and Navarro reported that balancing enjoyment, interest, and absorption at work can enhance flow and yield greater employee flourishing.[29] Additionally, engaging in flow experiences has been examined in secondary education. In fact, one study demonstrated that secondary teachers who experience greater flow are better equipped at utilizing personal strengths and resources. Engagement increases academic commitment and achievement in high school students[30] and end-of-semester academic performance in college students.

Relationships

Social relationships are fundamental and foundational to life. Humans are social beings and thrive on intimate connection, love, and a meaningful emotional and physical interaction with others. Close relationships represent a fundamental human need.[31] Relationships, the third element in PERMA, include both objective indicators (e.g., number of persons in one's social sphere, number of close social ties) as well as subjective satisfaction with one's relationships. The latter includes the perception of being socially integrated, supported by others, and satisfied with one's social connections. Establishing and maintaining positive relationships with family members, peers, and friends provides people with support and can serve as a buffer against the automatic responses that often accompany hardship and adversity. Feeling valued by others and having close, mutually satisfying relationships is a key indicator of well-being. Research has shown that relationships with friends are positively associated with self-esteem and that perceived increases in friendship quality are related to increases in well-being. Furthermore, college students who socialize more frequently and who have stronger romantic and social relationships tend to be happier than students without these relationships. Moreover, a study that included a sample representative of three-fourths of the world's population across fifty-five nations found that a good relationship was the only common predictor of happiness.[32]

Additional scientific evidence substantiates the roles that positive relationships play in human flourishing. Research has demonstrated that people who have greater social integration and experience more support and fulfilling relationships have better mental health, higher levels of subjective well-being, and lower rates of mortality. Moreover, being more socially integrated in a network of deep relationships predicted mortality more robustly than a host of other behaviors, including physical activity, smoking, healthy diet, and drug use.[33] Thus, relationships are critical for positive physical health, or what has been dubbed physical flourishing.

Meaning

The fourth element in the PERMA model is meaning—having a sense of purpose derived from something viewed as larger than the self. A sense of meaning has been defined in terms of having direction in life, connecting to something larger than the self, and feeling that there is a purpose to what one does. Meaning infuses purpose in human lives, and pursuing meaning through purposes outside the self makes life worth living and provides a sense of fulfillment. Meaning involves the use of strengths for causes beyond the self, such as belonging to a community, civic, political, or religious group.[34] It involves the sense made of experiences that combine the self, the world, and one's relationships with others,[35] and includes judgments about the value and purpose of life as well.[36] Meaning is associated with other indicators of well-being throughout the adult lifespan and relates to greater life satisfaction, higher rates of happiness, and fewer psychological problems.

Psychological research on meaning in life has recently gained traction, perhaps in conjunction with the emphasis on positive traits and psychological strengths as well as the availability of measurement instruments. Meaning in life has been regarded as an indicator of competent adaptive coping and therapeutic growth. Having meaning in life is regarded to provide the conditions from which happiness can flourish. Meaning is not merely a Western invention. Cross-culturally, meaning in life is an important component of well-being. Steger found that Japanese young adults reported a greater sense of search for meaning compared to same-aged adults in the United States. However, the relationships between the presence of meaning and well-being were similar in the United States and Japan.

Meaning in life is also fundamental to optimal psychological functioning among adults. One study examined four hundred young adults and found that participants with higher life meaning had less depression, whereas participants with higher depression scores had a lower sense of meaning in life. Further, participants with higher meaning of life presented better psychological health.

Accomplishment

Striving for accomplishment is the fifth and final element of PERMA. Accomplishment is a persistent or determined drive to master or achieve something for its own sake. Accomplishment involves setting personal goals, feeling capable to do daily activities, and having a sense of achievement. Across many cultures, making progress towards one's goals and achieving superior results can lead to both external recognition and a personal sense of accomplishment. Although accomplishment can be defined in objective terms, it is also subject to personal ambition, drive, personality differences, and societal norms. For example, a mother who raises a beautiful, compassionate family might see her life as extremely successful, whereas her husband may define success as achieving a promotion at work. Additionally, accomplishment is often pursued for its own sake. For example, research shows that expert bridge players are driven to play to the best of their ability; even if they lose, they feel a sense of accomplishment in the knowledge that they played well.

Accomplishment involves making progress toward internally motivated goals, rather than striving to reach an externally imposed standard. For example, accomplished people may draw daily because they enjoy thinking and expressing themselves visually. That is, they do not draw to win an award for being the best artist, or to earn a high grade in art class. Rather, people may draw (or play a musical instrument, dance, read, etc.) because the process itself is fulfilling. Identifying realistic goals and ambition in life can help provide people a sense of satisfaction. When people achieve the goals they set, a sense of personal pride and fulfillment may result. Accomplishments in life are essential to inspiring people to thrive and flourish. The pathway of achievement involves the successes attained by using one's skills and efforts towards specific and fixed goals. Like other elements or pathways to well-being, accomplishment is pursued for its own sake, even when it brings no positive emotion and no meaning or contributes nothing to positive relationships.

Empirical evidence has demonstrated how accomplishments are associated with human flourishing. A review of twelve school-based positive psychology interventions conducted across junior high and high schools found that students who received these interventions had significant gains in academic performance. The benefits of accomplishment and PERMA-oriented interventions at large may be attributed to how accomplishment can correspond to the process of identifying one's goals, along with the motivation to progress toward those goals and learn the ways to achieve those goals. The process of thinking about one's goals, along with the motivation to move toward those goals (agency) and the ways to achieve those goals (pathways), is intrinsically rewarding and contributes to overall well-being.

Similar to accomplishment, the theory of hope puts forth that goals anchor purposive, meaningful behavior. One study, for instance, found that children's hopeful thinking was positively associated with mental health and with perceived competence. Likewise, in another study examined the effectiveness of a five-week, hope-based intervention with middle-school students, findings showed that the intervention group had significant improvements in levels of hope, life satisfaction, and self-worth. Furthermore, these benefits were maintained at the eighteen-month follow-up assessment.

To summarize, the PERMA model proposes five pillars or elements that are constitutive of well-being, or flourishing. Flourishing is a dynamic state of psychosocial functioning that arises from well-tuned and harmonious functioning across multiple spheres of living. Each domain is pursued for its own sake, and each can be defined and measured independently. Different people will derive well-being from each of these five elements to varying degrees. The beauty of the PERMA model is that it takes the abstract concept of flourishing and articulates five constituent domains that can be measured, developed, and sustained.

POSITIVE PSYCHOLOGY AND THE TRIPARTITE FORMAL STRUCTURE OF THE GOOD LIFE

What are the points of connection between the PERMA model and the tripartite model of flourishing proposed by Volf and colleagues?[37] Volf and

Croasmun articulate a tripartite structure for the good life: life going well, life led well, and life feeling well. The good life, then, has three basic dimensions or aspects: agential (what you do), circumstantial (how the world is for you), and affective (how you feel). Each of the three components has its origins in the broad tradition of reflection of human nature and destiny, as well as the configuration of the formal features to which the term refers in a given philosophical or religious tradition.[38]

Each aspect—agency, circumstance, and affect—is a significant part of flourishing, though, as in the PERMA model, there is no requirement that all three aspects equally contribute to flourishing for a given person. The agential aspect encompasses deeds, character or virtue, and goals or projects. Volf and Croasmun do not assume that flourishing can be reduced to what is right or good to do; rather, what one does is one aspect of human flourishing. It would seem that life going well—circumstantial well-being—is a function of objective circumstances in one's life: for example, having sufficient resources to meet basic needs, opportunities for education, access to health care, residential safety, and the like. While there would be a subjective aspect of each of these (perceptions of feeling safe and secure in one's neighborhood), each could be identified objectively as well (e.g., unemployment rate, neighborhood crime, zip code life expectancy). Life led well refers to the "agential" dimension of the flourishing life, to the good conduct of life—from right "thoughts of the heart" and right acts to right habits and virtues. This would seem to most closely mirror the Meaning component of PERMA. Life feeling well refers to the "affective" dimension of the flourishing life, to states of happiness, fun, contentment, or joy, and this clearly corresponds to the Positive Emotions element of PERMA. The circumstantial aspect encompasses relationships that, in part, result from the exercise of agency and require the continual exercise of agency if they are to flourish. Lastly, Engagement, as involving emotional, cognitive, and behavioral dimensions, likely connects to all three dimensions of the good life.

Having sketched these preliminary connections, it is likely that there are no simple or straightforward correspondences between the tripartite model and PERMA, but the fact that there are logical points of connection between these models from different traditions (theological and scientific psychology) leads us to conclude that their similarities may be greater than their differences. To that end, positive psychology agrees with theology that a truly flourishing life is the most important concern in life.[39] These perspectives will inevitably take different pathways in articulating this vision. For example, psychology will tend to privilege descriptive approaches—describing the building blocks or elements of flourishing—over prescriptive accounts of flourishing, whereas theology will be more comfortable in boldly declaring that the flourishing life defines the good toward which humans are meant to strive.[40]

GRATITUDE AND THE LIFE WORTH LIVING

Recall that the first element in the PERMA model is positive emotions. One of the most commonly felt emotions is gratitude. Gratitude is a human quality with unusual power, an essential element of human flourishing, critical to harmonious functioning. As the positive emotional response to benevolence, gratitude is perhaps the quintessential positive trait, an amplifier of goodness in oneself, the world, and others. As the "moral memory of mankind," gratitude makes life better for oneself and others. Awareness of its importance raises inescapable big questions: How gratefully or ungratefully will each of us live our own lives? Why will we choose to do so, and with what effects on ourselves and those around us? Writing in the *Notre Dame Journal of Law, Ethics, and Public Policy*, Elizabeth Loder noted, "Gratitude affects how a person conceives the world and expects others to behave. It increases interpersonal receptivity. It seeps into one's being and affects all dispositions pervasively." Throughout history, the concept of gratitude has been seen as central to the smooth running of society, a mainstay of philosophical and religious accounts of living, leading it to be deemed "not only the greatest of the virtues, but the parent of all others."

Gratitude provides a window into the ways that PP helps us see the unity and interrelations between the three aspects of the tripartite structure: life going well, life feeling well, and life led well. French philosopher Comte-Sponville wrote, "gratitude is the most pleasant of the virtues, and the most virtuous of the pleasures." It is virtuously pleasant because experiencing it not only uplifts the person who experiences it, but it elevates the person to whom it is directed as well.

Gratitude is a positive, moral emotion that people experience when they receive direct benefits or gestures of caring support from others. As a morally compelling emotion, it motivates recipients of aid to express appreciation toward benefactors and reciprocate in some normatively appropriate way. We can see here that the affective component of gratitude contributes to agential flourishing. Gratitude goes beyond mere reciprocity, because it also motivates people to help others beyond their immediate benefactors, a phenomenon known as upstream reciprocity. A declaration of appreciation for some act of kindness received may thus function as a reliable signal of a person's inclination to cooperate with others in everyday exchanges. The function of gratitude is to motivate the formation and strengthening of mutually beneficial relationships by signaling to another that he or she is valued. Thus, communities that hope to maintain cooperative relations are likely to institute clear prescriptive norms for expressing gratitude. Individuals who express gratitude when they receive benefits are rewarded in various ways. By eliciting positive circumstances, the expression of this positive state impacts circumstantial well-being. In turn, those who fail to express gratitude may suffer reputational penalties. Ungrateful people are likely to be perceived as both low in competence, because they required assistance, and low in warmth, because their ingratitude violates cooperative norms, and these perceptions arouse intense feelings of contempt. Gratitude may indeed be the parent of the virtues, but ingratitude is a universally powerful accusation.

Psychological research into gratitude over the last two decades has overwhelmingly focused on the benefits of experienced and expressed gratitude. Study after study declares its benefits for psychological, physical, relational, and spiritual well-being. Once again, the associations between gratitude and affective, agential, and circumstantial well-being are manifold. People who live gratefully are more generally appreciative of the positive in themselves, others, and the world. Research and practice suggest that setting aside time on a daily basis to recall moments of gratitude associated with even mundane or ordinary events, personal attributes one has, or valued people one encounters has the potential to interweave and thread together a sustainable life theme of highly cherished personal meaning just as it nourishes a fundamental life stance whose thrust is decidedly positive. As an integral element of moral character, gratitude is an open and receptive stance toward the world that energizes a person to return the goodness they have received. Gratitude's intrinsic function is to affirm the good in life, embrace that good, and then transform the good in purposeful actions to accomplish something that is at once meaningful to the self and of consequence to the world beyond the self.

Gratitude is also central to life feeling well, because conceptually and causally, gratitude is foundational for another positive emotion, joy. Grateful people appreciate the good in their lives and view life through a lens of giftedness. This way of thinking and seeing enhances joy, because one has to first be able to find and recognize the good and then incorporate and absorb this good before they can experience joy.[41] Moreover, seeing the good as gifts that are neither deserved nor earned based on personal efforts will amplify the experience of joy. Both gratitude and joy reflect a fully alive, alert, and awake state of attunement between the self and the world, necessary for any account of human flourishing. The joyful act of praising God is a thankfulness flowing nearly automatically from a recognition of divine gifts, and cosmic gratitude is foundational to human flourishing.

The link between gratitude and joy is strengthened on account of the amplification or magnification theory of gratitude developed by Philip Watkins in 2014.[42] The term magnification in relation to affect was first used by Silvan Tomkins in his script theory of emotions, with joy being one of the central affects Tomkins viewed as a building block of personality.[43] Two dynamic principles were postulated by Tomkins: affective amplification and psychological magnification. For any experience to become important in the first place, it must trigger one or more in an innately given set of affects: the intrinsically rewarding affects of joy or excitement; the intrinsically punishing affects of anger, contempt, disgust, distress, fear, and shame; or the "resetting" affect of surprise.

As we are using the term *amplification* here, this theory specifically seeks to explain how gratitude enhances joy. The theory leads to the prediction that gratitude enhances joy by psychologically amplifying the good in one's life. Stated differently, gratitude increases the signal strength of what and who is good in one's life. Perceiving a positive experience as a gift may be a form of cognitive amplification that enhances a positive affect such as joy.

Thus, expressing gratitude may provide direct emotional and social benefits for those who express their thanks. In suggesting that expressions of gratitude complete the enjoyment of a blessing, it follows that gratitude might be beneficial insofar as it amplifies the good in one's life. Just as an amplifier increases the volume of sound coming out of a microphone, so gratitude "turns up the volume" of the good in one's life. With gratitude there is amplification, strengthening, and deepening of the entire awareness of life. Our amplification theory implies that it is the grateful processing of positive memories that should be important. If gratitude amplifies the good in cognition, when one recalls a positive event and then processes it in a grateful fashion, this should enhance the event in memory. Amplification theory suggested that it was the grateful processing of positive memories that is of prime importance. Affective amplification, as first articulated by Tomkins,[44] accounts for only the short-term importance of any experience. Its long-term significance depends on the process of psychological magnification: cognitive-affective processes in which scenes become interconnected and then expanded by recruiting ever more thought, action, and feeling.

From a psychological perspective, this fullest sense of gratitude represents a substantial altering in a person's outlook. To elaborate, to experience this degree of gratitude brings about an expansive enlargement of a perceptual hermeneutic. In short, this degree of gratitude nourishes a more or less all-encompassing hermeneutics of appreciation. This appreciative lens fosters within individuals a radical openness to and receptivity of the world. This openness and receptivity allow for an altruistic acuity that enhances the giving away of goodness. Stated succinctly, as one experiences life, gratitude's intrinsic function allows one to approach the world by embracing it, nourishing it, and transforming it. Authentic gratitude leads people to experience life situations in ways that call forth from them an openness to engage with the world and to share and increase the very goodness they have received. It is the feeling of connection with humanity emerging from a sense of wonder and joy that participating in an intricate network of existence brings. When embraced, gratitude's essence can be construed not only from behaviors that are measurable, but from ways of living that are both pathways for aspiring to the good life and passages for attaining it, thereby illustrating in a profound way the interrelations between the three aspects of tripartite flourishing. Through a weaving together of contemporary research with historical reflection, the case can be made for gratitude as a prominent touchstone of the good life.

Conclusions

In closing, we would like to invoke a metaphor introduced by Pawelski in his two-part manifesto on the meanings of the "positive" in positive psychology:

> Positive psychology research and practice has flourished in the years since its founding. If positive psychology were a tree, we could point to a trunk that has reached impressive heights already and that supports healthy and growing branches of research. Maturing from these branches are practical fruits that are of great use in areas as disparate as education, medicine, clinical psychology, and business. To support its continued growth, however, this tree must have deep conceptual roots. Although roots are rarely visible and thus easy to ignore, it is crucial that they never be taken for granted, since they are essential for the life and stability of the tree they support. The rapid growth of positive psychology in the last two decades requires a commensurate deepening of its roots, and much more attention needs to be paid to the basic concepts and theoretical grounding of this domain.[45]

The present essay is intended to underscore this need to deepen the roots of positive psychology. Our strong belief is that engagement with philosophical and religious reflection can serve as a sort of fertilizer for deepening and strengthening the root structure of PP. While it is certainly not incumbent upon psychologists to ground their studies in religious or philosophical discussions concerning the nature of a good life, they ignore this work at their own peril. It is undeniable that PP has made great strides through the work of investigators who have not sought inspiration in philosophy or theology. But it is time to move forward. We believe there is merit to a religiously engaged positive psychology. But this engagement needs to be more than mere window dressing or simply a nod in the direction of interdisciplinary complementarity. Those positive psychologists who bring the tools of science to the study of constructs and questions should provide more than just citations of the philosophical and theological origins to their research questions. They should provide a careful delineation of the contentions under investigation and the implications that would follow from findings of empirical support, or the lack thereof. Most importantly, positive psychology and theologies of flourishing share the goal of improving our understanding of what makes for a life well lived. They can, and should, serve as complementary endeavors capable of enhancing and strengthening each other's efforts at theory building, research, and ultimately increasing the proportion of flourishing people on this planet.

Notes

1   We are grateful to Matt Croasmun and Sarah Farmer for their insightful comments on an earlier version of this chapter and to the Yale Center for Faith & Culture for financial support of our project, "A Positive Psychology of the Good Life."

2   Miroslav Volf, "The Crown of the Good Life: A Hypothesis," in *Joy and Human Flourishing: Essays on Theology, Culture, and the Good Life,* ed. Miroslav Volf and Justin E. Crisp (Minneapolis: Fortress, 2015), 127–35.

3   Martin Seligman and Mihalyi Csikszentmihalyi, "Positive Psychology: An Introduction," *American Psychologist* 55 (2000): 5–14.

4   See Mihalyi Csikszentmihalyi and Isabella Csikszentmihalyi, *A Life Worth Living: Contributions to Positive Psychology* (New York: Oxford University Press, 2006); E. Diener and M. Y. Chan, "Happy People Live Longer: Subjective Well-Being Contributes to Health and Longevity," *Applied Psychology: Health and Well-Being* 3, no. 1 (2011): 1–43; E. Diener and L. Tay, "A Scientific Review of the Remarkable Benefits of Happiness for Successful and Healthy Living," in *Happiness: Transforming the Development Landscape* ([Thimphu, Bhutan?]: Centre for Bhutan & GNH Studies, 2017), 90–117; S. D. Pressman and S. Cohen, "Does Positive Affect Influence Health?" *Psychological Bulletin* 131, no. 6 (2005): 925.

5   Christian Smith and Hilary Davidson, *The Paradox of Generosity: Giving We Receive, Grasping We Lose* (New York: Oxford University Press, 2014.)

6   Mihaly Csikszentmihalyi, *Flow: The Psychology of Optimal Experience* (New York: Harper & Row, 1990), 7–8.

7   Daniel Haybron, *The Pursuit of Unhappiness: The Elusive Psychology of Well-Being* (New York: Oxford University Press, 2010), 35.

8   Daniel Haybron, *The Pursuit of Happiness: The Elusive Psychology of Well-Being* (Oxford: Oxford University Press, 2008).

9   Rosalind Hursthouse, *On Virtue Ethics* (New York: Oxford University Press, 2002), 29, n. 11.

10   Hursthouse, *On Virtue Ethics*, 29, n. 11.

11   Marcia W. Baron, Philip Pettit, and Michael A. Slote, *Three Methods of Ethics: A Debate* (Hoboken, N.J.: Wiley, 1997).

12   Michael L. Morgan, *Classics of Moral and Political Theory*, 3rd rev. ed. (Indianapolis: Hackett, 2001), 268 (emphasis added).

13   Christopher Peterson and Martin E. P. Seligman, *Character Strengths and Virtues: A Handbook and Classification*, vol. 1 (Oxford: Oxford University Press, 2004).

14   Peterson and Seligman, *Character Strengths and Virtues*, 3.

15   K. Dahlsgaard, C. Peterson, and M. E. P. Seligman, "Shared Virtue: The Convergence of Valued Human Strengths across Culture and History," *Review of General Psychology*, no. 9 (2005): 203–13.

16   F. A. Huppert and T. T. So, "Flourishing across Europe: Application of a New Conceptual Framework for Defining Well-being," *Social Indicators Research* 110, no. 3 (2013): 837–61.

17   Abraham H. Maslow, "The Instinctoid Nature of Basic Needs," *Journal of Personality* 22, no. 3 (1954): 326–47.

18   Sigmund Freud, "Analysis of a Phobia in a Five-Year-Old Boy," *Standard Edition* 10, no. 3 (1909); and *The Ego and the Id*, ed. James Strachey, trans. Joan Riviere (New York: Norton, 1960).

19   Erik Erikson, *Children and Society* (New York: Norton, 1963).

20   Marie Jahoda, *Current Concepts of Positive Mental Health* (New York: Basic Books, 1958).

21   Carol D. Ryff and Burton Singer, "The Contours of Positive Human Health," *Psychological Inquiry* 9, no. 1 (1998): 1–28.

22   Edward L. Deci and Richard M. Ryan, "Intrinsic and Extrinsic Motivations: Classic Definitions and New Directions," *Contemporary Educational Psychology* 25, no. 1 (2000): 54–67.

23   Martin E. P. Seligman, *Authentic Happiness* (New York: Simon & Schuster, 2002).

24   Martin E. P. Seligman, *Flourish* (New York: Free Press, 2011).

25 J. D. Bartholomaeus et al., "Evaluating the Psychometric Properties of the PERMA Profiler," *Journal of Well-Being Assessment* 4, no. 2 (2020): 163–80.

26 Marie J. Forgeard et al., "Doing the Right Thing: Measuring Wellbeing for Public Policy," *International Journal of Wellbeing* 1, no. 1 (2011).

27 A. Steptoe, J. Wardle, and M. Marmot, "Positive Affect and Health-Related Neuroendocrine, Cardiovascular, and Inflammatory Processes," *Proceedings of the National Academy of Sciences* 102, no. 18 (2005): 6508–12.

28 M. Csikszentmihalyi, "Happiness, Flow, and Economic Equality," *American Psychologist* 55, no. 10 (2000): 1163–64.

29 Lucia Ceja and Jose Navarro, "'Suddenly I get into the zone': Examining Discontinuities and Nonlinear Changes in Flow Experiences at Work," *Human Relations* 65, no. 9 (2012): 1101–27.

30 M. Carli, A. Delle Fave, and F. Massimini, "The Quality of Experience in the Flow Channels: Comparison of Italian and U.S. Students," in *Optimal Experience: Psychological Studies of Flow in Consciousness*, ed. Mihaly Csikszentmihalyi and Isabella Selega Csikszentmihalyi, 288–306 (Cambridge: Cambridge University Press, 1988), 288.

31 E.g., Christopher Peterson, *A Primer in Positive Psychology* (New York: Oxford University Press, 2006).

32 E. Diener et al., "Similarity of the Relations between Marital Status and Subjective Well-Being across Cultures," *Journal of Cross-cultural Psychology* 31, no. 4 (2000): 419–36.

33 J. Holt-Lunstad and T. B. Smith, "Social Relationships and Mortality," *Social and Personality Psychology Compass* 6, no. 1 (2012): 41–53.

34 T. G. Plante, "What Do the Spiritual and Religious Traditions Offer the Practicing Psychologist?" *Pastoral Psychology* 56, no. 4 (2008): 429–44; M. E. Seligman, T. Rashid, and A. C. Parks, "Positive Psychotherapy," *American Psychologist* 61, no. 8 (2006): 774; M. F. Steger, "Making Meaning in Life," *Psychological Inquiry* 23, no. 4 (2012): 381–83.

35 Steger, "Making Meaning in Life."

36 J. A. Hicks and L. A. King, "Meaning in Life as a Subjective Judgment and a Lived Experience," *Social and Personality Psychology Compass* 3, no. 4 (2009): 638–53.

37 Miroslav Volf and J. E. Crisp, eds., *Joy and Human Flourishing: Essays on Theology, Culture, and the Good Life* (Minneapolis: Fortress, 2015); Miroslav Volf and Matthew Croasmun, *For the Life of the World: Theology That Makes a Difference* (Grand Rapids: Brazos, 2019).

38 See Volf and Croasmun, this volume.

39 Volf and Croasmun, *For the Life of the World*.

40 Volf and Croasmun, *For the Life of the World*.

41 Philip C. Watkins et al., "Joy Is a Distinct Positive Emotion: Assessment of Joy and Relationship to Gratitude and Well-Being," *Journal of Positive Psychology* 13, no. 5 (2018): 522–39.

42 Philip Watkins, *Gratitude and the Good Life: Toward a Psychology of Appreciation* (New York: Springer, 2014).

43 S. S. Tomkins, "Script Theory: Differential Magnification of Affects," *Nebraska Symposium on Motivation* 26 (1978): 201–36.

44 Tomkins, "Script Theory."

45 James O. Pawelski, "Defining the 'Positive' in Positive Psychology: Part II. A Normative Analysis," *Journal of Positive Psychology* 11 (2016): 357–65, 363.

Contributors

ISMAIL FAJRIE ALATAS is Associate Professor of Middle Eastern and Islamic Studies, New York University.

STEPHEN C. ANGLE is Professor of Philosophy and East Asian Studies, Wesleyan University.

YONATAN Y. BRAFMAN is Assistant Professor of Modern Judaism, Tufts University.

DREW COLLINS is Associate Research Scholar, Lecturer, Yale Divinity School; Associate Director, Christ & Flourishing Program, Yale Center for Faith & Culture.

MATTHEW CROASMUN is Associate Research Scholar, Lecturer, Yale Divinity School; Director, Life Worth Living Program, Yale Center for Faith & Culture.

ROBERT A. EMMONS is Professor Emeritus, Department of Psychology, University of California, Davis.

PAUL JEFFREY HOPKINS is Founder and President, UMA Institute for Tibetan Studies; Emeritus Professor of Tibetan Buddhist Studies, University of Virginia.

KATARZYNA DE LAZARI-RADEK is Assistant Professor, Institute of Philosophy, University of Łódź.

RYAN McANNALLY-LINZ is Associate Director, Yale Center for Faith & Culture.

ALAN MITTLEMAN is Aaron Rabinowitz and Simon H. Rifkind Professor of Jewish Philosophy, The Jewish Theological Seminary.

HRH PRINCE GHAZI BIN MUHAMMAD is Chief Advisor for Religious and Cultural Affairs, Personal Envoy, and Special Advisor of H.M. King Abdullah II; Professor of Islamic Philosophy, Jordan University.

ANANTANAND RAMBACHAN is Professor of Religion, St. Olaf College.

ROXANNE N. RASHEDI is Lecturer, Human Development and Women's Studies, California State University, East Bay.

PETER SINGER is Ira W. DeCamp Professor of Bioethics in the University Center for Human Values, Princeton University.

BIN SONG is Assistant Professor of Philosophy and Religion, Washington College.

MIROSLAV VOLF is Henry B. Wright Professor of Systematic Theology, Yale Divinity School; Founding Director, Yale Center for Faith & Culture.

JONGBOK YI is Associate Professor of Asian Philosophy, Stockton University.